SOVIET

RUSSIA

IN

CHINA

SOVIET

RUSSIA

IN

CHINA

A SUMMING-UP AT SEVENTY

BY

CHIANG CHUNG-CHENG
(CHIANG KAI-SHEK)

FARRAR, STRAUS AND CUDAHY

NEW YORK

The translation of *Soviet Russia In China* was made under
the direction of Madame Chiang Kai-shek.

AUTHOR'S NOTE

Time speeds by like an arrow and with it are borne away first the months, then the years. In this very year, 1956, I passed the milestone of the seventieth birthday in my life's journey; on this very day, December 1, 1956, my wife and I are quietly celebrating our thirtieth wedding anniversary. But the National Revolution still remains, alas, an unaccomplished task! In reviewing our past, my wife and I share an acute consciousness of failure in not living up to the lofty ideals instilled in us by our mothers through our childhood training. It was their constant and cherished expectation that we "return thanks to the state by delivering our people from evil and suffering." We share this consciousness in fear lest we should fail in the task of bringing the Revolution to a successful conclusion in our race against time. The double challenge of the mainland remaining unrecovered and our people therein crying out in vain for deliverance aggravates our sense of regret. As a solemn token of our determination not to fail in the end, I hereby dedicate today the manuscript of my book *Soviet Russia in China* to the sacred memory of our dearly beloved mothers, the late Madame Chiang, née Wang, and the late Madame Soong, née Nie. By this token my wife and I dedicate ourselves once more, as it were, to the supreme task to which we are called and thus strive to be not unworthy of our upbringing.

Chiang Chung-cheng
(*Chiang Kai-shek*)

Sun Moon Lake
Taiwan
Republic of China
December 1, 1956

CONTENTS

SOVIET

RUSSIA

IN

CHINA

INTRODUCTION

From the American Declaration of Independence of 1776 to the emergence of a number of former European colonies and protectorates in Asia and Africa as independent states in the years following the end of World War II, there had been two major revolutionary trends of far-reaching importance. One was marked by a steadily growing demand of the individual for greater freedom and equality. The other was a gradual awakening of national consciousness culminating in the surge of nationalism, particularly in Asian countries.

The ideas and emotions fostered by the French Revolution of 1789 were in themselves mainly concerned with the assertions and claims of the individual in his relationship to the state, though their influence on contemporary and subsequent events was by no means confined to the struggle for personal rights and liberties alone. It was the success of the American Revolution, however, which set a forceful precedent for subject peoples to aspire to self-government and political independence.

In 1885, one hundred and ten years after the American Declaration of Independence, a young Chinese medical doctor named Sun Yat-sen began preaching his revolutionary principles. Ten years later, in 1895, he founded in Honolulu the first Chinese revolutionary party with what then must have seemed an unbelievably ambitious aim of overthrowing the monarchical system of government which had been in continuous existence in China for forty centuries. Although his immediate target was to bring about the downfall of the Man-

3

chu dynasty, his ultimate objective was to free China from foreign domination and to set the country on the road to political and social democracy.

Dr. Sun had received a Western education which enabled him to reappraise the cultural assets of his own people in the light of modern political thinking. He found in China's traditional institutions of government such useful features as those of the civil service examinations and of the independent power of impeachment, which he later incorporated in his theory of Five-Power Constitution. But his basic political philosophy undoubtedly came from the ideals of the American and French Revolutions. In fact, his Three People's Principles* could be best paraphrased in Abraham Lincoln's famous saying: ". . . government of the people, by the people, for the people."

It was in 1911 that Dr. Sun and his followers finally succeeded in establishing a republican form of government for the Chinese people. But before the gains of the Revolution could be consolidated, Yuan Shih-kai, a remnant of the Manchu dynasty who was then in control of the armed forces in the North, conspired with the Imperialists. He overthrew the young republic and restored the monarchy with himself as the founder of what he had hoped to be a new dynasty. This was the Republic of China's first setback. Although the new monarchy was a short-lived one, the government subsequently fell into the hands of war lords who set up regional regimes and fought among themselves. Finally the country was plunged into chaos. Dr. Sun and his followers had to continue their work in their original base of Canton where in 1917 a revolutionary government was founded. His plan was to rally all revolutionary elements and to make preparations for a punitive expedition against the war lords in the North. In the ensuing years he repeatedly sought external aid but all

---

* The Three Principles are Nationalism, Political Democracy and People's Livelihood.

his efforts were in vain. Not only did the Western Powers turn a deaf ear to his appeals, some of them were actually in collusion with the war lords for selfish ends. Japanese militarists were particularly active in scheming with one war lord after another, seeking all the time to further their own aggressive designs. As conditions throughout the country worsened, the Republic, founded by Dr. Sun and his followers, for all practical intents and purposes ceased to exist.

The successful *coup d'état* led by Lenin in 1917 not only ushered in a new regime in Russia but was destined to become the most powerful challenge to humanistic civilization in Asia as well as in Europe.

The most appealing argument of Russian Communism was its promise of a short cut to Utopia by a world revolution of the masses. This revolution was to justify all means of violence and subversion on the assumption that, once realized, it would lead to the creation of a permanent ideal state for all mankind. The appeal had an electrifying effect on progressive elements in all Asian countries where a century of Western colonial rule had already sown deep-seated resentment and accumulated discontent. Thus, the Russian Communists were able to capitalize on this state of mind to launch the initial phase in their program of World Revolution in Asia.

In China, where a subcolonial state had resulted from a series of unequal treaties imposed upon her, the Russian Communists found fertile soil for the reception of their ideas, and thus prepared the way for their subversive infiltration. The Chicherin Statement of 1918 and the Karakhan Declaration of 1919, announcing Russia's readiness to relinquish her special rights in China, immediately captured the imagination and unprecedentedly won the good will of the Chinese people. While initiating steps for negotiations with the government at Peking on this subject on the one hand, Russian emissaries approached Dr. Sun with offers of military and technical assistance on the other. At the same time, be it noted carefully, they proceeded to organize the Chinese Communist Party, and provided it with financial help as well as political directives.

In January 1923 Dr. Sun and Adolf Joffe reached an agreement by which the Russian Communists were to extend to Dr. Sun's political party (Kuomintang, literally the National People's Party) all the necessary assistance to achieve national unification in accordance with the revolutionary programs Dr. Sun had laid down. The Russian Communists were also to instruct Chinese Communists to join Kuomintang and follow Dr. Sun's leadership in China's National Revolution. This marked the beginning of a period of cooperation and "peaceful coexistence" between Kuomintang and the Chinese Communist Party as well as between China and Russia. It soon proved itself a failure.

In spite of the failure of the first trial run of "peaceful coexistence," Kuomintang, and later the Chinese Government under my leadership, went through two more periods of "peaceful coexistence," resulting in the total loss of the Chinese mainland. Under Russian Communists' instigation, the Chinese Communists tried to sabotage the National Revolution and overthrow the Republic of China by resort to violence. Since they seized the mainland, they have imposed on the Chinese people there a totalitarian dictatorship. This is tantamount to a repetition of what Yuan Shih-kai did to the National Revolution early in the Republic. The methods used by the Chinese Communists in betraying the country and oppressing the people, however, are far more shameless and vicious than those of the northern war lords. This is an important reason for the Republic's second setback. I feel that I owe it to my own people and to the world at large to give a truthful account of the circumstances in which my party and my government were compelled to give "peaceful coexistence" two more trials even though the first had ended in failure. In all three instances, it will become clear in the following pages, prior consideration had to be given to certain overriding factors of national or international importance.

In presenting this record to the world, I am filled with mixed feelings. On the one hand, I am fully aware that my country has been a victim of circumstances which drove her to temporary alignment with Soviet Russia on more than one occasion in spite of the known treacherous character and the aggressive aim of international Communism; on the other, I can lay claim to the proud fact that I have incessantly fought Communist aggression and Communist ideas for the last thirty-odd years. Like Dr. Sun himself, who on signing the agreement with Joffe declared that Communism was totally unsuitable to the needs of the Chinese people and, therefore, could not be endorsed by Kuomintang, I remain firmly convinced that the only road open to the Chinese people is that marked out by Dr. Sun's Three People's Principles. It must be noted that throughout the book I have used the word "revolution" consistently in the sense of China's National Revolution. The Communists are opposed to our National Revolution. Their aim is to practice Communism in China. Therefore, I regard Communism as a counterrevolutionary movement. It will help my readers if they will bear in mind that I shall continue to view world events in the light of this distinction.

It is my earnest hope that the bitter lessons China has learned may prove instructive to countries and governments, and especially those in Asia which now face the same threat of Communism. Often it is not easy for most people to realize the presence of this threat in their midst, and by the time they do, it may already be too late to prevent its thrusting them behind the Iron Curtain at least for a time. If this book can in any way help enhance the vigilance and determination of those who are defending the cause of freedom and democracy and to bring home to the avowed neutralists the realization that they are unwittingly serving the Communist purpose, my labor will have been rewarded and the great sacrifices that the Chinese people have made will not have been in vain.

PART
ONE

"Peaceful Coexistence" Between China and Russia

PART
ONE

BEGINNINGS

The First Period (1924-1927)

The Chinese Communist Party is not indigenous to China. It is an outgrowth of Soviet Russia and the Communist empire. Because of its incompatibility with tolerable human existence and still less with the structure of Chinese society, this offshoot of Soviet Communism in its early formative stage had to hide in and to live as a parasite on Kuomintang so that it could grow and organize workers, farmers and the masses through Kuomintang organs and to stir up class struggle under their cover. Its aim was to set up in the course of China's wars of unification and independence a Soviet puppet regime and to create the first satellite in Asia.

Had it not been for the suppression of the Canton revolt on March 20, 1926, and the all-out purge which rid Kuomintang of Communists on April 12, 1927, and which enabled China to achieve unification and independence under the leadership of the National Government, the Republic of China would have become a Bolshevik laboratory and satellite during that early period, and Soviet Russia would not have had to wait till ten years after World War II before she turned a nation with a territory of 12,000,000 square kilometers and a population of more than 450,000,000 into an incomparably strong base for World Revolution, seriously to threaten the peace and security in Asia and other parts of the world.

Today it should be evident that the world crisis stems directly from the encroachments of Russia on China. Only an independent and sovereign China can stand between Soviet

Russian aggression on the one side and Asian security and world peace on the other. I am of the belief that the history of China's National Revolution under the leadership of Kuomintang should be reappraised in the context of Asia's struggle against Communism.

China's Revolutionary and National Reconstruction Movement

In the middle of the 19th century when Western European powers were knocking at China's front door along her eastern seaboard, Czarist Russia was making inroads into China's Sinkiang, Mongolia and Manchuria. These powers acquired leased territories and concessions, and then under the protection of consular jurisdiction and controlled tariff rates, proceeded to extend their economic and political tentacles into the interior of the country by virtue of their concessions to build and administer railways and to operate shipping both along the coast and on China's inland rivers. Had China been partitioned in the years immediately following 1895,* Czarist Russia would have obtained an area north of the Yellow River which constitutes nearly 40 per cent of the entire Chinese territory. But from 1900,** the United States stood opposed to the partition of China by advocating the Open Door Policy. This made it possible for China to retain a nominal independence. Czarist Russia and Japan, however, did not relax in their territorial encroachments in the vast region stretching from Manchuria to Sinkiang. After her defeat in the Russo-Japanese War of 1904, Czarist Russia reached an understanding with Japan whereby their respective spheres of influence in this region were delineated.

It was for the purpose of saving China from being partitioned that Dr. Sun Yat-sen began to work for a national revolution. He sought to free China from the oppression of

* The Sino-Japanese War of 1895.
** The Boxer Rebellion.

colonial powers, to abolish the unequal treaties and to build up China as a free and independent nation. Though the Revolution of 1911 resulted in the overthrow of the Manchu dynasty and the establishment of the Republic, the creative task of revolution and national reconstruction remained to be achieved. Remnants of the Manchu regime and northern war lords led by Yuan Shih-kai persisted in their attempts to restore the monarchy and to overthrow the new Republic. In this they were able to secure help from some foreign powers which enjoyed special political and economic rights in China. The Japanese militarists were particularly active in inciting the Chinese war lords to set up regional regimes to pave the way for their interference in China's domestic affairs for the eventual carving up of the country. The young Republic found it impossible to develop her national industries because both her sovereign rights and administrative authority had been impaired. Even her agriculture and handicraft industry were on the decline. Democracy, so-called, became a mere excuse for unscrupulous politicians and ambitious gentry to scramble for selfish gains. The people at large, with their rights and liberties unprotected, sank deeper in poverty.

Soviet Russia's First Profession of Friendship Toward China

Toward the end of World War I, revolution broke out in Russia. The world was soon to be startled by the successful Bolshevik *coup d'état* led by Lenin, by the formation of a government of workers, farmers and soldiers and by the sudden powerful response to the call of Marxist Communism.

After the war, various Western colonial powers again turned their eyes toward China in the hope of restoring their special rights, which had suffered a temporary recession during the period of fighting. Soviet Russia alone expressed friendliness for China. In his report to the Fifth Soviet Congress on July 4, 1918, G. V. Chicherin, Soviet Russia's commissar of foreign affairs, stated that the Soviet Government would discontinue the Czarist regime's various forms of aggression in Manchuria, relinquish Russia's extraterritorial rights in China and Mongolia, renounce Russia's financial impositions on the Chinese people under various pretexts, withdraw troops formerly stationed in Russian consulates in China and return to China the Russian portions of the various Indemnity Funds. Leo Karakhan's declaration of July 15, 1919, was based on Chicherin's report. It said among other things: "The Soviet Government returns to the Chinese people without demanding any kind of compensation, the Chinese Eastern Railway, as well as all the mining concessions, forestry, gold mines, and all the other things which were seized from them by the government of Czars, that of Kerensky, and the brigands Horvat, Semenoff, Kolchak, the Russian ex-generals, merchants and capitalists."

This was the first instance of Soviet Russia's "smiling diplomacy" in the Far East as a stratagem in her scheme of World Revolution. This declaration, when there appeared no reason to doubt its validity, struck us in the Orient as the noblest declaration in the annals of international relationship in our dealings with the West. It naturally led the Chinese people to believe that the Russian Revolution had marked the end of an old rapacious imperialist regime characterized by aggression and totalitarianism and the establishment of a new regime of equality and good will. Soviet Russia was, in fact, the first foreign power to renounce voluntarily her unequal treaties with China which had bound our country for almost a century. This declaration had an immediate effect on China, and Soviet Russia was able to gain widespread Chinese good will from this timely move. It should be recalled, however, that the Chinese (Peiyang) Government in Peking* did not receive the Karakhan Declaration until March 1920 and it was not until the autumn of 1922 that Moscow sent Adolf

* Peking was then the capital.

Joffe to China to conduct negotiations for implementing the declaration. In September 1923 Karakhan was sent to China to resume negotiations in which the Russian delegates repeatedly went back on their promises. The most conspicuous instance was their denial that there had been any mention in the Karakhan Declaration of an intention to return the Chinese Eastern Railway to China without compensation. The Sino-Soviet agreement for the settlement of disputes then pending was not signed until May 31, 1924, after protracted negotiations. This agreement provided the first pattern of "peaceful coexistence" between China and Soviet Russia which was to be repeated in subsequent years.

The Creation of a China Branch of the Communist International

Moscow's China policy was a double-faced one. On the one hand, the Soviet Foreign Office carried on diplomatic negotiations with the Chinese Government. On the other, the Communist International proceeded to set up a Chinese Communist Party.

Earlier, in the spring of 1920, Gregori Voitinsky, chief of the Eastern division of the Communist International, arrived in China to arrange with Li Ta-chao and Chen Tu-hsiu for the formation of the Chinese Communist Party. In 1921 Moscow sent a Dutchman named G. Maring, also known as Sneevliet, to take charge of the organization of the Chinese Communist Party. At the time the Chinese Communist Party was little more than an association of intellectuals who had accepted Karl Marx's dogmas, who felt friendly toward Soviet Russia and who sought to develop their party organization by means of labor movement.

The Chinese Communist "United Front"

As early as 1912, while Lenin was in exile in Brussels, the Socialist *People's Daily* published an article by Dr. Sun Yat-sen entitled "China's Second Step," setting forth the goal of China's revolution and reconstruction. Thereupon Lenin published his "Democracy and Narodism in China."* He compared China's National Revolution to Russia's Narodic movement and said that "in Asia there still exists a bourgeoisie capable of representing sincere, militant, consistent democracy." The Second Congress of the Communist International, held in July 1920, formulated the twenty-one articles governing the adherence of national Communist parties to the Communist International. Article 8 directed the Communists in various countries "to expel Imperialism from the colonies" and to "carry on agitations among the armed forces of the Imperialist countries to oppose oppressions of the colonies." At the same Congress Lenin came up with his "Outline of the Colonial Problem," which laid down the Communist basic stratagem in all national revolutionary movements. This mandate was largely responsible for their choosing China's National Revolution as a target for the Chinese Communist Party.

At their Second National Congress, held in August 1922, the Chinese Communists decided to form a United Front with Kuomintang. They issued a manifesto which said in part as follows:

> Out of consideration for the immediate benefit of workers and poor farmers, the Chinese Communist Party is to lead the workers and have them help the democratic revolutionary movement so as to form a democratic United Front with the poor farmers and the petty bourgeoisie.
>
> The workers in this democratic United Front, however, must not become an appendage to the petty bourgeoisie. . . . Therefore, the workers should constantly bear in mind that they constitute an independent class, should develop their own organization and combat capabilities, and together with poor farmers prepare to establish a Soviet form of government for the purpose of achieving complete liberation.

* Lenin's *Selected Works,* vol. IV, p. 307.

Once democracy succeeds, the now immature bourgeois class will grow rapidly and assume a position in opposition to the proletariat. For this reason, the proletariat must work against the bourgeoisie and join with the poor farmers in setting up a dictatorship of the proletariat.

This was to say that the Chinese Communist Party, though cooperating with Kuomintang as a United Front, and directing its members to join Kuomintang for participation in the revolution, was to retain its independent identity secretly to prevent China's National Revolution from becoming a success by taking advantage of a farmers' revolution to seize power and establish a "dictatorship of the proletariat."

Dr. Sun's Aim In Alignment With Russia

To carry out this sinister plot Moscow sent Maring on a special trip to see Dr. Sun in Kweilin in 1921 with a proposal for cooperation between Kuomintang and the Russian Communist Party.

For the sake of winning Dr. Sun's consent, Maring assured him that instead of practicing Communism Soviet Russia had adopted the New Economic Policy. Dr. Sun in his telegram to Liao Chung-kai* said: "Russia's economic conditions as yet do not provide the necessary conditions for Communism. That is why I was quite surprised when I first heard of Communism being practiced in Russia. I have since learned with gratification from Maring that there is not much difference between Russia's New Economic Policy and our Program of Industrialization."

Owing to Chen Chiun-ming's** revolt, Dr. Sun left Canton for Shanghai on June 16, 1922. In December Joffe arrived in Shanghai to see him. The question of cooperation between the Russian Communist Party and Kuomintang was discussed. On January 26, 1923, they issued a joint statement, and the basis

* A member of Kuomintang.
** A war lord in Kwangtung province.

of Dr. Sun's policy of alignment with Russia was given in the very first paragraph as follows:

"Dr. Sun holds that the Communistic order or even the Soviet system cannot actually be introduced into China, because there do not exist here the conditions for the successful establishment of either Communism or Sovietism. This view is entirely shared by Mr. Joffe, who is further of the opinion that China's paramount and most pressing problem is to achieve national unification and to attain full national independence, and regarding this task, he has assured Dr. Sun that China has the warmest sympathy of the Russian people and can count on the support of Russia."

Dr. Sun's telegram to Liao Chung-kai following his talks with Maring and his joint statement with Joffe clearly represented his considered views on the questions of cooperation between Kuomintang and the Russian Communist Party. First, Dr. Sun regarded Communism as something which could not be carried out in China. Secondly, China's pressing need was to achieve national unification and to attain full independence. Soviet Russia's aid to Kuomintang was meant to help it in its tackling this stupendous task. And Kuomintang's cooperation with the Russian Communist Party was precisely for the same purpose of ensuring successful completion of this task.

The Sun-Joffe joint statement was the basis of the first phase of Sino-Russian "peaceful coexistence," and of the peaceful cooperation of Kuomintang with the Chinese Communist Party. Dr. Sun followed it up with a manifesto of Kuomintang and went ahead with plans for its reorganization. As a result of revolts by Chen Chiun-ming and Shen Hung-ying,* the Kuomintang Party fell into a state of disorganization and its members, though totaling some 300,000, were inadequately trained.

For this reason, Dr. Sun asked me to go to Moscow to study

* A regional war lord in Kwangtung.

its postrevolution party system, and its political and military organizations for our reference.

My Observations on the Russian Trip

Upon Dr. Sun's instructions I arranged a meeting in Shanghai on August 5, 1923, with Maring to discuss the composition, etc. of the mission to Russia. Accompanied by Shen Ting-yi, Wang Teng-yun and Chang Tai-lei, I left Shanghai on August 16, crossed the border at Manchuli on August 25 and reached Moscow on September 2. I began my return trip on November 29 and arrived in Shanghai on December 15, where I prepared and dispatched a report to Dr. Sun with such data and impressions as I had gathered through investigation and conversations during my three-month trip. Later, in compliance with his desire that I should in addition report to him at greater length in person, I went to Canton on January 16, 1924, to do so.

During the three months in Russia we studied its party, the military and political organizations, inspected various installations and listened to briefings by responsible officials. In party affairs we inspected the Central Party Headquarters of the Russian Communist Party where Rudzutak, secretary of the Political Bureau, gave us an account of the Russian Revolution and of the circumstances in which the Russian Communist Party was formed. At meetings of the Communist International's Executive Committee, which I was invited to attend, I expressed my confidence that our National Revolution, having as its highest aim the fulfillment of the Three People's Principles, would succeed in two or three years' time. I also pointed out that the Communist International did not fully understand the actual conditions of our revolutionary movement and the work we were doing, and hoped that the Communist International would send more men to China to see things for themselves. Later on I saw a resolution of the

Communist International vis-à-vis Kuomintang. By its tenor I could tell that the Communist International did not fully understand the real nature of China's National Revolution and arbitrarily divided Chinese society into classes and advocated struggles between them. In fact, they paid more attention to the task of devising ways against their friends than their foes. I was profoundly disappointed.

In military affairs we inspected the Red Army, military schools of various services at different levels and army party organizations in Moscow. In Petrograd we inspected the Naval Academy and other service schools as well as the Kronstadt naval base and the Russian fleet there. My impression was that the Military Academy and the troops in Moscow were well organized and looked neat and trim, but the Naval Academy at Petrograd and the Russian fleet appeared to be depressed in spirit. Two years previously, the Kronstadt naval base was the scene of a revolt against the Bolshevik dictatorship and the Communist oppression and cruelty perpetrated during the civil war. The revolt was soon put down. When we were in Petrograd, the local authorities and naval officers were cautiously silent over the incident. Judging by the attitude of the local population and naval personnel, however, one could see that the revolt had left deep scars.

In political affairs we visited various ministries and commissions of the Russian Government, inspected village and city Soviets and observed proceedings at the Moscow Soviet Congress. From my observation of the ways whereby discussions were held and resolutions were passed in the Soviets at various levels and from my conversations with important party and political leaders, I easily perceived that fierce struggles, both open and secret, were going on among various sections of the Russian society and among the Russian Communists themselves. I became more convinced then ever that Soviet political institutions were instruments of tyranny and terror and basically incompatible with Kuomintang's political system which is based on the Three People's Principles. This was something that I had to go to Russia to find out; I could never have imagined it if I had remained in China.

Russian Communist leaders, party, political and military, warmly welcomed our delegation wherever we went. But whenever I discussed Sino-Russian problems and touched on Soviet Russia's interests, their attitude immediately changed. My visit to Soviet Russia coincided with Karakhan's negotiations in Peking for the conclusion of a new treaty after his declaration on the abrogation of unequal treaties with China. In the joint statement of January 26, 1923, Joffe had declared that Soviet Russia "has no intention of practicing Imperialist policies in Outer Mongolia or causing its separation from China." But whenever I mentioned the Outer Mongolia problem in my talks with responsible Russian party and political leaders, I discovered that they had not given up their aggressive designs on it. This came not only as a great disappointment to me, but also enabled me to assess the degree of Soviet Russia's sincerity in her offer to assist China to achieve independence and freedom.

When I arrived in Moscow, Lenin was already seriously ill. In fact he was in coma. A talk with him was out of the question. Responsible Soviet party, political and military leaders told me that in all her state policies and revolutionary strategy Soviet Russia would adhere strictly to the lines laid down by Lenin. I had more talks with Trotsky than with other Soviet leaders. I found him to be the most forthright of them all both in speech and in conduct. In my last interview with him before leaving Moscow, we discussed the problem of revolutions in Asian countries and touched on the situation in Japan, Indo-China, India and Turkey. He mentioned in particular the failure of revolutionary movements in Germany and Poland and gave me his analysis of the matter. Finally, returning to the subject of Russian assistance to China's National Revolution, he asked me to take back a verbal message to Dr.

Sun, saying that after the war with Poland in 1920 Lenin had issued a new directive regarding the policy of World Revolution. It ruled that Soviet Russia should give the utmost moral and material assistance to colonies and subcolonies in their revolutionary wars against capitalist imperialism, but should never again employ Soviet troops in direct participation so as to avoid complications for Soviet Russia during revolutions in various countries arising from questions of nationality. He said to me in all seriousness: "Except direct participation by Soviet troops, Soviet Russia will do her best to help China in her National Revolution by giving her positive assistance in the form of weapons and economic aid." He also asked me to convey Lenin's respects to Dr. Sun. I was particularly interested in this part of the conversation.

Most of the Russian leaders holding responsible party and government positions who expressed regard for Dr. Sun and sincere desire to cooperate with China in her National Revolution were Jews, the only exceptions being Kamenev and Chicherin who were Russians. These Jews, long in exile in other European countries during the Czarist days, had returned to Russia only after the Revolution of 1917. This aroused my special interest. I found that men like Trotsky, Zinoviev, Radek and Joffe were, comparatively speaking, more concerned with the question of cooperation between Kuomintang and the Russian Communist Party. Joffe, however, lost his influence shortly after his return to Russia from China.

I also noticed that the feud between the internationalist clique headed by Trotsky and the domestic organizational clique headed by Stalin continued to rage furiously within the Russian Communist Party even as Lenin lay seriously ill. I was extremely worried lest this conflict should seriously affect Sino-Russian cooperation after Lenin's death. Out of the impressions received during my visit in Russia, there crept into my mind the notion that once the Russian Communists consolidated their regime, the possibility of a revival of the political ambitions entertained by the Czarist regime certainly could not be ruled out, and that, in that eventuality, the consequences would be unthinkable for our country and our National Revolution.

In my written report to Dr. Sun, I put down all my impressions of Russia formed during the trip. I expressed my personal views on the question of cooperation between Kuomintang and the Chinese Communist Party in my subsequent report to Dr. Sun. In my letter to Liao Chung-kai, dispatched from Fenghua on March 14, 1924, and copies of which were circulated among members of Kuomintang's Standing Committee, I frankly stated my views on the same subject as follows:

There is another thing I wish to say to you frankly. It is the question of the Russian Communist Party. A line of distinction should be drawn between facts and principles. We must not ignore facts because of our faith in the principles. According to my observation, the Russian Communist Party is not to be trusted. I told you before that only 30 per cent of what the Russians say may be believed. That was really an understatement because in view of the excessive trust you seem to repose in the Russians I did not want to upset you too much. As to those who expressed respectfulness for Dr. Sun, they are not Russian Communists but members of the Communist International. Chinese Communists in Russia always speak of Dr. Sun slanderously and with suspicion.

The Russian Communist Party, in its dealings with China, has only one aim, namely, to make the Chinese Communist Party its chosen instrument. It does not believe that our Party can really cooperate with it for long for the sake of ensuring success for both parties. It is the policy of the Russian Communist Party to turn the lands inhabited by the Manchus, Mongols, Moslems and Tibetans into parts of the Soviet domain; it may harbor sinister designs even on China proper.

Success in anything is absolutely impossible if one has to depend entirely on the help of others. It would be the height of folly if our people, surrendering all self-respect, should so idolize others with the expectation that they would make righteousness prevail for its own sake. Their so-called internationalism and World Revolution are nothing but Caesarism in another name, the better to hoodwink the outside world.

The Russian Communists, in the first flush of victory following upon their capture of political power, offered to join hands with all the proletariat in the Western countries in revolutions and promised to help Oriental nations achieve independence. On hearing of this news, those working for our National Revolution welcomed it as a godsend and regarded its authors as saviors of mankind. That was why Russia's assistance was accepted without any reservations. This was no doubt an important factor in Dr. Sun's decision to align Kuomintang with Russia.

Before I went to Russia I, too, had believed that the offer of the Russian Communist Party to help our National Revolution was motivated by a sincere desire to treat us as an equal and not with ulterior motives. As a result of my visit to Russia, however, I was completely disillusioned. I came to the conclusion that our policy of aligning with Russia and admitting Chinese Communists into our ranks, though it might prove to be useful in fighting Western colonialism for the time being, could not in the long run bring us to our goal of national independence and freedom. Furthermore, I felt that Soviet Russia's stratagem and the objective of her World Revolution program were even more dangerous to national independence movements in the Orient than the old colonialism.

After listening to my report Dr. Sun considered my views on the future of Sino-Russian relations overcautious and unsuitable particularly in view of the revolutionary realities of the moment. He was of the firm belief that in the circumstances the only way to deter the Chinese Communists from inciting class conflicts and sabotaging our National Revolution was to place them under the leadership of Kuomintang and to subject them to our Party's unified direction. He thought that the moment the Northward Expedition* came to its successful conclusion the Three People's Principles could be implemented according to schedule, and that by that time it would be too late for the Chinese Communists to disrupt our National Revolution even if they should so try. Besides, was it not a fact that Soviet Russia recognized our Party as the only political party to lead China in her National Revolution, and was it also not a fact that Soviet Russia had asked members of the Chinese Communist Party to join our Party, and to obey its leadership and in the meantime had admitted the impracticability of Communism for China? For these reasons Dr. Sun stuck to his policy of alignment with Soviet Russia and the admission of Chinese Communists into Kuomintang.

During the First National Congress** of our Party, I discovered how the Chinese Communists both in words and in actions tried to increase their own importance by playing up Soviet Russia, and how some of our own Party members had been swayed by Communist doctrines. I was full of misgivings regarding our Party's ability to carry out the task entrusted to it by Dr. Sun. In consequence at the end of the Congress I declined my appointment as commandant of the Military Academy and turned over the preparatory work to Liao Chung-kai and left Canton for my native place in Chekiang. It was not until April of that year and only after having been repeatedly urged by Dr. Sun through letters and telegrams to obey orders as a member of a revolutionary party, that I returned once more to Canton, this time as commandant of the Whampoa Military Academy.

Li Ta-chao's Memorandum

Li Ta-chao was the first Chinese Communist to join Kuomintang following the Sun-Joffe statement of January 26,

* Military campaign planned for the specific purpose of overthrowing the northern war lords and unifying the country.
** Held in Canton in January 1924.

1923. Many others followed shortly afterward. Kuomintang's First National Congress, convened on January 20, 1924, adopted a new constitution and elected members of the Central Executive and Supervisory Committees. Among those so elected were Tan Ping-shan, Li Ta-chao, Lin Tsu-han, Han Lin-fu, Mao Tse-tung, Chang Kuo-tao, Yu Fang-chow and Chu Chiu-pai, all of them Communists. During the Congress, Fang Jui-lin, Chiang Wei-fan, and Huang Chi-lu proposed that members of Kuomintang must not join other parties. On behalf of the Communists, Li Ta-chao submitted a memorandum in which he gave reasons for their joining Kuomintang. He said, in part:

We believe that China today is a "semicolony" of the Western powers, or a "subcolony" as Dr. Sun has well called it. It will be impossible for China to remove the double oppression imposed by foreign Imperialism and our own war lords who curry favor with foreign powers, unless we throw the strength of the entire nation into the National Revolution. In order to bring the revolution to a successful conclusion, it is essential to have a national revolutionary party that is united and comprehensive in scope. We feel that at this moment, we should not allow the forces of revolution to be dissipated through disunity because this would result in weakening them and hindering their progress. It is absolutely necessary to put the nation's heart and strength together in a single party.

Looking around the country, we find that Kuomintang is the only revolutionary party which has history, principles and leadership. It is also the only one that can be developed into a great and comprehensive national revolutionary party to assume the responsibility of liberating the people, restoring to them their rights and assuring them a secure livelihood. For this reason, we have decided to join this Party.

We feel that the strength resulting from uniting the various revolutionary groups into a common front is not enough. Therefore, it is necessary that we join this Party and allow ourselves to be organized into one team so that in coordinated steps we can take part in our National Revolution under Dr. Sun's leadership and the unified discipline of our Party.

We have joined this Party because we have something to contribute to it and to the cause of China's National Revolution, and certainly not because of any intention to take advantage of the situation to propagate Communism in the name of Kuomintang.

We join this Party as individuals, not as a body. We may be said to have dual party membership. But it may not be said of Kuomintang that there is a party within a party.

Before joining it, we have made a detailed study both of the theories and of facts. Dr. Sun has given us permission to retain our relationship with the China branch of the Third International. Consequently, our joining this Party and at the same time keeping our membership in the Communist Party is an open and honorable action, not a surreptitious move. On the contrary, since we have joined the Party and so long as we remain its members, we shall carry out its political program and abide by its constitution and bylaws. We shall obey the disciplinary measures or punishment imposed by this Party in case we fail to do so.

Li Ta-chao's memorandum sounded as if he were being perfectly frank. This was because the Communists, in wishing to join our Party, had no alternative but to accept the conditions laid down by Dr. Sun following serious and detailed discussions with Moscow's emissaries, including Voitinsky, Maring, Joffe and Borodin.* All Li Ta-chao did was to reiterate them openly. Nevertheless, toward the end of his statement he could not help revealing that the Chinese Communist Party's action was designed to facilitate those with dual membership in their plot ultimately to undermine our Party. For he said:

"It is my hope that since we have already been permitted to join this Party, our senior comrades will not entertain suspicions about us or take precautionary measures against us. If it is felt that our joining this Party is improper, there is room for discussion. So long as it is good for the Party, such considerations as have prompted us to join can also prompt us to leave. Suspicions and precautionary measures will be obstacles in the Party's further progress and it is essential that

* Michael Borodin was a Russian political adviser to Kuomintang.

they be recognized as such and removed at the outset of the Party's reorganization."

This appeal had its desired effect: our Party failed to take the necessary precautions. The Communists were allowed to work through their secret cells and they met with no opposition whatever as they moved to seize control and to manipulate our Party by plotting internal dissension and disruption.

The Three People's Principles and the General Outline of National Reconstruction

After the First National Congress Dr. Sun gave three series of lectures on the Three People's Principles. From March 30 to August 24, 1924, he gave a weekly talk at National Chungshan University. Altogether he devoted six talks each to the first two principles on Nationalism and Democracy. On the third principle of People's Livelihood, he had had time only to give four talks as he had to proceed to Shaokwan in northern Kwangtung to supervise the launching of the Northward Expedition. Therefore, the third series was not completed. After the withdrawal of the expeditionary forces from Kian, he left for Peking where he died shortly afterward.

In his lectures Dr. Sun called for special vigilance in view of the Communist elements' deliberate misrepresentation of the Principle of People's Livelihood. He devoted the first talk of the series on this Principle to a refutation of Karl Marx's materialistic conception of history and his theories of surplus value and class struggle. Dr. Sun said the motive force in history is not that of materialism but a struggle for existence. He rejected the theory about the value of labor in commodity as at variance with facts, for the entire process from invention through manufacturing to exchange and consumption contributes toward production. He maintained that human progress is made possible only through the cooperation of the majority of the people and not as a result of class struggle.

He emphasized that economic and social problems should be solved by peaceful means instead of by class struggle and mass violence.

In order to forestall any Communist attempt at sabotaging China's National Revolution, Dr. Sun caused the promulgation, on April 12, 1924, of the General Outline of National Reconstruction which he had himself prepared. In the manifesto Dr. Sun reiterated the purpose in stipulating the methods and measures for the realization of the Three People's Principles as follows:

The objective of the Revolution is the realization of the Three People's Principles which, in turn, must proceed by certain prescribed methods and measures. Whether or not the influence of the Three People's Principles can reach and benefit the people depends on the methods and measures of implementation. . . . Henceforth in our revolutionary effort we should not only strive hard to destroy but strive harder to build, and certain procedures should be set which must be followed. It is for this purpose that the General Outline of National Reconstruction is hereby formulated. It begins with the removal of obstacles and ends with the completion of reconstruction work. This is what is meant by arranging what is basic and what is not in a proper order of priority.

The General Outline of National Reconstruction may be said to be the Magna Carta of our National Revolution. In accordance with the procedure stipulated therein, we used force to remove obstacles in the way and used peaceful methods to solve social and economic problems and to prevent the occurrence of class struggle and social unrest. The General Outline of National Reconstruction as a practical program of revolution not only has nothing in common with Communism, what is more, it is the only way to forestall the spread of Communism in the course of our National Revolution.

Dr. Sun's dicta on the National Revolution based on the Three People's Principles could brook no misrepresentation or distortion whatever. This also showed that he had not

failed to take into consideration what the Communists might
do to obstruct our National Revolution. In fact, he had taken
preventive measures accordingly. Consequently I have reposed
an abiding faith in Dr. Sun's teachings and have always believed that there are no Communist or Russian Bolshevik
elements in the ideological structure of the Three People's
Principles and the practical program of National Revolution
as laid down by Dr. Sun.

Commencement of Communist Subversion in the Party

Our Party's First Central Executive Committee had under
it eight departments in charge of organization, publicity,
youth, workers, farmers, military affairs, women, and overseas activities. Later, two more departments were added,
namely, the departments of commerce and industry. When
candidates were being considered for the various departmental
posts, the Communists paid particular attention to those of
organization, workers and farmers. In order not to arouse the
suspicion of our Party members, however, they did their best
to conceal their real intentions. At first, they nominated Tan
Ping-shan as secretary of the Department of Organization and
Feng Chiu-po as secretary of the Department of Workers and
Lin Tsu-han as secretary of the Department of Farmers.

At the time it was Dr. Sun's intention to make Lin Tsu-han,
one of the Communist elements, head of the Department of
Farmers and to have old Kuomintang members in charge of
the seven other departments with Liao Chung-kai in charge
of organization. Later, it was felt that in view of the importance of organizing Cantonese workers, a Cantonese Party
member should be made the leader. Consequently, Liao offered to serve as the head of the Department of Workers, and
let Tan Ping-shan become the head of the Department of
Organization. Tan was originally a member of Kuomintang
and was asked by Liao to join the Communist organization at

its inception in 1920. Liao thought that Tan would be loyal to the Party and work for the realization of the Three People's Principles. Once Tan became the head of the Department of Organization he recommended one Yang Pao-an as secretary of the department. Now Yang was a Marxist. He was put in the department to use it as a channel for Communist infiltration.

After Lin Tsu-han became the head of the Department of Farmers, he recommended one Peng Pai, a Communist, as secretary. Later he himself resigned in order not to attract the attention of the Party members. Peng Pai stayed on as secretary despite repeated changes at the top. All training classes set up for farmers were controlled by Communist elements, and the students admitted were also either Communists or members of their front organizations. Similarly, the farmers' unions and "farmers' volunteer corps" were manipulated by the Communists.

The Communists used their weekly magazine *Hsiang Tao* (Guide) as an official organ. They also published books and periodicals to propagate Marxism. At the same time they infiltrated the propaganda and educational agencies of our Party. Communists and fellow travelers used ideas of dialectical materialism and class struggle to misinterpret the Three People's Principles. The latter became acceptable "revolutionary ideology" only when they were interpreted in terms of Marxism, whereas the sound orthodox interpretation by members of Kuomintang was branded as "nonrevolutionary" or "reactionary." Meanwhile in the schools the Communists manipulated student organizations, stirred up troubles and harassed teachers who were unwilling to follow Marxism. The most glaring case was provided by the persecutions of Tai Chi-tao, head of the Department of Publicity, and Tsou Tu, head of the Department of Youth, by the Communists in Canton's Chungshan University. Finally, the two became so disgusted that they quit.

At the time Dr. Sun endeavored to attract youths into Kuomintang and also encouraged them to take part in activities at lower levels. For instance, the Party office in Canton was composed of elements loyal to the Party. The Canton Machine Workers' Union steadily remained under our Party's direction, and did not give the Communists any chance to infiltrate into it. The same thing was true of party organizations comprising educated youths who had come under the banner of the National Revolution, and of a number of popular organizations.

The Communist elements at first did not seek to control our Party organization as a whole. Their first step was infiltration. Then it was followed by division. They applied themselves to labeling our members leftists, rightists and centrists. The slogan used by the Communists was, "Let those who are revolutionary turn left." Soon opportunistic and wavering elements in our Party began to go over to the Communists' side and emulate their ways of doing things in order to appear "progressive" or "revolutionary." Soon a chain reaction was started within the Party. Wavering led to dissension, which in turn aroused mutual suspicions and recriminations. Within one year of the Party's reorganization, Communist flames were already spreading far and wide causing grave apprehensions among the farsighted members of the Party.

Impeachment of the Chinese Communists and Dr. Sun's Directives

In March 1924 the Chinese Socialist Youth Corps published in its official organ the resolution adopted by the Chinese Communist Party at its Enlarged Executive Committee meeting. It asked its members to accept the Chinese Communist Party's directives and educate its members in Kuomintang in methods of organization and operation. It also stipulated that "while expanding the Kuomintang organization, naturally they must not cease in the expansion of the Chinese Communist Party's own organization." Earlier, members of the Chinese Communist Party were directed "to join Kuomintang but retain our own organization, to attract revolutionary elements from among various labor bodies and leftist groups in Kuomintang and to abide strictly by our discipline in order to establish a strong Communist base among the masses."

On June 1, 1924, the Canton City Kuomintang Headquarters brought an impeachment against dual-party members for disrupting the party.

On June 18 members of the Central Supervisory Committee of our Party impeached dual-party elements for conspiracy against the Party before the Central Executive Committee on the basis of Communist documents. They pointed out that their impeachment was not against individual members of the Chinese Communist Party or of the Chinese Socialist Youth Corps who had joined Kuomintang. It was entirely for the sake of the Party's existence and growth that they opposed the state of a party within a party, and that since the dual-party members concerned had secret cells of their own, they could not be loyal to the Party. They also pointed out that the actions of these dual-party members were completely contradictory to their avowed purpose in joining Kuomintang as set forth in Li Ta-chao's memorandum. The Party's Central Executive Committee was, therefore, asked to take sanctions without delay.

Dr. Sun gave specific instruction to Teng Tseh-ju and others. He said: "It was the belief of the Russian Communists themselves after the success of their revolution that their regime could be consolidated only after the successful completion of Socialist revolutions in the industrialized nations of Eastern Europe. Later they thought national revolutions in the Orient could hasten Socialist revolutions in the West. Therefore, they wanted to help us in our National Revolution and to cooperate with our Party." It was in view of this point and of the assurance by Maring and Joffe and other international Communists in 1921 and 1922 that Russia's offer of help was not for the purpose of propagating Communism that Dr. Sun decided in favor of alignment with Russia and the admission of Chinese Communists into our Party. The alignment was for mutual aid; it was not to be in any way a concession to the Chinese Communists. His final directive to Teng Tseh-ju and others was to the following effect: "If the Chinese Communists should use our Party to propagate Communism, to engage in class struggle and to sabotage our National Revolution, we could easily take sanctions against them. Even in the case of Chen Tu-hsiu, if he should try to destroy our Party organization, we should have no difficulty in checkmating him." This was the original purpose of Dr. Sun's policy.

Dr. Sun's policy of alignment with Russia was based on nationalism and not on the belief that Communism was applicable to China. Furthermore, this policy of alignment with Soviet Russia was no reason for allowing ourselves to be intimidated by the Communists or to appease them or to compromise with them.

The Central Executive Committee subsequently adopted the following resolution:

"Communists who have joined the Party and accepted its political programs are to be held accountable as members."

Dr. Sun's Trip to Peking and His Death

On November 10, 1924, Dr. Sun issued a statement on his proposed trip to Peking, in which he announced two things, namely, the "abolition of the unequal treaties" and "the convocation of a national people's conference." He reminded the nation that only a revolutionary force which was identified with the interests of the people could put an end to warlordism supported by the Imperialist powers, and bring about China's independence, freedom and unification. On account of his opposition to Imperialism and his avowed intention to exterminate warlordism, his impending trip to Peking, center of the northern war lords' sphere of influence, would naturally earn the support of the whole nation as well as the enmity of the war lords. Members of our Party all tried to persuade him not to undertake the trip in view of the attendant danger. Nevertheless he set out on his journey on November 12.

The next day, when his ship passed by Whampoa, he disembarked and stayed overnight. He inspected the Military Academy and saw cadets of the first class building defense works at the Yutsu Fort across the Pearl River. On the way back to the Academy he said to me: "I am going to Peking. Whether I can come back is not yet certain. Anyway, I am going there to carry on our struggle. Having seen the spirit of this Academy, I know it can carry on my revolutionary task. Even if I should die, my conscience will be at peace."

Before Dr. Sun's departure, Borodin forwarded to him Moscow's invitation for him to go to Russia. He asked me for my view and I told him I was against it. My main reason was that we were cooperating with Russia for the sake of achieving independence and freedom for our country. If he should visit Russia, the Communists could spread rumors to confuse the people and this would cause a serious obstacle to our National Revolution. He never again mentioned the subject to me.

Following Dr. Sun's departure for the North, the Communists stepped up their disruptive efforts within our Party. Their intention to create dissension among cadets in the Military Academy and eventually to seize control of the Academy itself became clearer than ever. On January 25, 1925, Michael Borodin and others sponsored a Young Servicemen's Club to draw into it dual-party elements in the Academy and in various armed units. They even spread a rumor that I, too, had

joined the Communist organization. Led by Chen Cheng,*
officers and cadets in the Academy and in the armed forces
who were loyal to the Three People's Principles and to our
Party found they could no longer endure such organized
oppression and formed a rival group named Society for the
Study of Sun Yat-senism.

At the time of Dr. Sun's death I was away leading our
Party's armed forces against Chen Chiun-ming's rebel troops
in Kwangtung's East River region where we had already
captured Chaochow and Meihsien. When I returned to Canton on April 5 I discovered that the Yunnanese and Kwangsi
troops were plotting a revolt against the Party because of its
policy of aligning with Russia and the admission of Chinese
Communists into our Party. I hurried to Chaochow and
Meihsien to bring my troops back to Canton, and on June 13
I succeeded in putting down the revolt of Yang Hsi-ming
and Liu Chen-kwan, and in recovering Canton itself. On June
15, the General Headquarters in Canton was expanded to
become the National Government, and the Party forces were
renamed the National Revolutionary Forces. Thenceforth
Canton and the unified province of Kwangtung became the
base of our National Revolution.

At the time some members of our Party who had made
known their opposition to the Communists met in Peking and
Shanghai. They constituted the so-called "Western Hills
Caucus Faction." Responsible leaders of our Party in Canton
were all united and showed no signs of any schism. But the
Communists countered with more intensive efforts to create
dissension in our Party by spreading suspicions and causing
provocations. They branded Hu Han-min, Tai Chi-tao and
other anti-Communist members as "rightists," and Wang
Ching-wei, Liao Chung-kai and pro-Communist members as
"leftists," thereby setting Hu Han-min and Wang Ching-wei
against each other. Soon afterward Liao Chung-kai was as-

* Chen Cheng is now China's vice-president.

sassinated in Canton on August 20, and there was fear of an imminent calamity at the center of our Party.

Continuing their struggle against the "rightists" in our Party, the Communists worked hard on Wang Ching-wei with a view to isolating him; the latter soon fell under their spell. On the strength of suspected complicity in Liao Chung-kai's assassination, he forced Hu Han-min to leave Canton for Russia on a special mission. Thus Wang became both chairman of the National Government and chairman of the National Military Council. Next the Communists turned around and used the same tactics to stir up misunderstandings between Wang Ching-wei and myself in an attempt to create a new contradiction in our Party.

The Chungshan Gunboat Incident

Chen Chiun-ming's remnants in the East River region revolted again on October 1, 1925, and once again I had to take an army eastward to put it down. The operation resulted in the recapture of Waichow, Haifeng and Lofeng, followed by the occupation of Chaochow and Meihsien. Next came the suppression of a second revolt in southern Kwangtung and of a third on Hainan Island. Kwangtung was thus reunited. The National Government's next task was to launch the Northward Expedition to unify the rest of the country.

Hostilities in the East River region were just over and I was still in the Chaochow-Swatow area when the Communists in Canton started a smearing campaign against me. In January 1926 I was in Canton again to attend the Second National Congress of the Party and to lay before it my proposal that the Northward Expedition be launched as planned. Both during and after the Congress, Wang Ching-wei was in favor of the proposed expedition. Even Borodin did not raise any objections. But after the Congress, Borodin was suddenly recalled to Moscow for consultation for unknown reasons.

Shortly after Borodin's return to Russia, Kissanka, head of the Russian military advisory mission, predicted in conferences at the Military Academy that the expedition would certainly result in failure. In conversations with me he also advised against it. In handbills against the expedition which appeared in Canton, I was described as a new war lord. Finally, Kissanka openly took steps to sabotage our plan for the expedition.

I had to decide whether to adopt a negative attitude and resign or to take positive measures to overcome the difficulties and to carry out Dr. Sun's plan to its successful conclusion as my contribution to the Party and to the nation. For a while I could not decide.

On February 8 I announced that I would not assume the post of inspector-general of the National Revolutionary Forces. The following day I tendered my resignation as member of the National Military Council and as Canton's defense commander. Wang Ching-wei neither accepted my resignation nor asked me to stay on. There was no action on my case for as long as a fortnight. I called on Wang on February 27 to inform him that if it was his wish not to accept my resignation then Kissanka should be asked to return to Russia. On March 8 I called on Wang again and said to him with a heavy heart: "The actual power of directing the revolution must not fall into Russian hands; even in the matter of liaison with the Third International, we must draw a line somewhere. In no circumstances should we forfeit the freedom of making our own decisions." Soon afterward Kissanka came to know of this confidential conversation and I realized that Wang and the Communists were already in collusion.

Subsequently the Communists and Kissanka became bolder than ever and overtly accused me of being a counterrevolutionary and a new war lord. Up to March 14 Wang Ching-wei had not accepted my resignation but had indirectly hinted for me to leave Kwangtung; further it was intimated that were I to remain in Kwangtung my life would be in danger. Yet, if

I should actually leave without my resignation having been accepted, I could be accused of desertion. I was indeed in a quandary.

On March 18 Li Chih-lung, a Communist, who was acting director of the Naval Forces Bureau, forged an order for the gunboat *Chungshan* to move down the river from Canton to Whampoa. He told the dean of the Military Academy that he had the commandant's orders to send the ship down to stand by. I was then in Canton and knew nothing about the move. Later Li Chih-lung telephoned me to ask whether I wanted the ship back in Canton. Whereupon I asked him by whose order had the ship been sent down to Whampoa in the first place. He had no answer. As a matter of fact, the ship was sent downriver to load up enough coal for a long voyage. On the evening of March 19 the ship returned to Canton. Through the night its engine was kept running and the lights were on, and precautions of the most rigid kind were enforced on board. I sensed a Communist plot. At the time, however, all that I suspected was that they intended to stage a revolt to harm me. I had no idea of the extent of their plans. Only after it was all over did I learn of their plan to seize me on board the *Chungshan* when I was to take it to go back to the Military Academy at Whampoa from Canton. They would then send me as a prisoner to Russia via Vladivostok, thereby removing the major obstacle to their scheme of using the National Revolution as a medium for setting up a "dictatorship of the proletariat."

That night I felt that at a critical moment like this what might happen to me personally was inconsequential, but for the sake of the Party and our revolutionary cause, I could no longer put off a decision. Early next morning, in my capacity as Canton's defense commander, I declared martial law and had Li Chih-lung and the other Communists arrested and members of the Communist-dominated Canton-Hongkong

Strike Committee* disarmed. Simultaneously I sent troops to regain control aboard the gunboat.

On March 22 a representative from the Soviet consulate in Canton came to see me about this incident. He asked me: "Was it directed against the persons concerned or against Russia?" I told him that the former was the case. I also expressed the hope that Borodin would soon come back. That being so, he said that there was no cause for anxiety and that Kissanka would be ordered to return to Russia. The same day the Central Political Committee decided to ask Kissanka and others to leave Canton. After the meeting Wang Ching-wei pleaded illness and moved to another address for medical treatment. He wrote to a Chang Jen-chieh, member of the Central Supervisory Committee, that he would no longer shoulder any political responsibility. On May 11 he secretly left Kwangtung for France ostensibly for reasons of health.

Borodin returned to Kwangtung from Russia on April 29. Several times he conferred with me on problems concerning Kuomintang and the Chinese Communists. Measures for the readjustment of Party affairs were later submitted to Kuomintang Central Executive Committee at its Second Plenary Session under the following eight points:

1. The Communist Party should order its members to modify their expressions and attitude toward Kuomintang. Particularly in relation to Dr. Sun Yat-sen and the Three People's Principles, no aspersions must be cast.
2. The Chinese Communist Party should give the chairman of Kuomintang's Central Executive Committee for safekeeping a complete list of its members in the Party.
3. Only those without dual-party membership would be eligible for appointments as heads of departments in the Central Headquarters of Kuomintang.

* The Canton-Hongkong Strike Committee formed in Canton following the Shameen Incident on June 22, 1925, to enforce a general strike against Hongkong, was controlled by Communist elements. Its pickets were armed.

4. Communists with Kuomintang membership must not call any party caucus in the name of the Party without the latter's specific permission.

5. Communists with Kuomintang membership must not have separate organizations or take separate actions without orders from the Party.

6. The Chinese Communist Party and the Third International should submit to a joint conference of Kuomintang and the Communists any instructions or directives on strategy for its approval before sending them to Communists in Kuomintang.

7. Without first obtaining permission to quit the Party, no Kuomintang member could acquire membership in any other party. Having left Kuomintang and joined the Communist Party none would be readmitted into Kuomintang.

8. Party members violating the foregoing stipulations would be deprived of their membership and subject to penalties commensurate with the seriousness of their offense.

During the discussions, Borodin's attitude toward me was extremely conciliatory, and at several points he made reasonable concessions to meet my views. Meanwhile, in accordance with Dr. Sun's teachings, I refused to appease or compromise with the Communists just because of our alignment with Russia. That was how we were able to reach this eight-point understanding with them.

The Communists' failure to seize Canton meant the removal of the last obstacle to the projected Northward Expedition. The Central Executive Committee of the Party, at a plenary session held on May 21, issued a manifesto on the national situation and announced its decision to launch the military campaign. This was a turning point in China's National Revolution. It marked the reversal of the trend of Communist ascendancy in its relative strength to that of Kuomintang.

Happenings During the Northward Expedition

In 1926 the military strength of the northern war lords was roughly as follows: Wu Pei-fu claimed to have 250,000 men in his forces in occupation of Honan and Hupeh provinces, with some in regions as far south as Hunan, Szechwan and Kweichow provinces. He also had connections with the remnants of former rebel troops in Kwangtung and Kwangsi provinces. Sun Chuan-fang had an army of about 200,000 men, entrenched in Kiangsu, Chekiang, Anhwei, Fukien and Kiangsi provinces. Chang Tso-lin had no fewer than 500,000 men under his command including his own troops as well as Chihli and Shantung forces which had attached themselves to him. They were in occupation of Manchuria, Jehol, Chahar, Hopoi and Shantung provinces.

After the National Government had unified Kwangtung and Kwangsi and set a date for its Northward Expedition, Wu Pei-fu and Chang Tso-lin, long at loggerheads with each other, reached a compromise to cope jointly with the military threat from the south. Though Sun Chuan-fang's declared intention was to maintain peace and order in areas under his control, he was, in fact, in league with the Chihli and Shantung forces and opposed to us. Our Revolutionary Forces had less than one-tenth of the northern war lords' strength both numerically and financially. From this one can imagine how difficult it was to launch the Northward Expedition.

On July 1, 1926, the Military Council of the National Government in Canton issued the necessary mobilization orders for the momentous campaign. The Revolutionary Forces were redeployed with the Third Army concentrated at Chalin, the Fourth Army at Yuhsien, the Fifth Army at Guayyang, the Sixth Army at Anjen, the Seventh Army at Yungfeng and the Eighth Army at Hengshan, with the First Army concentrated at Hengyang as a general reserve. The first task was to clear the Hunan province of all hostile forces so as to make it possible for the various armies to converge on Wuhan area, including Wuchang, Hankow and Hanyang on the Yangtze.

On July 9 the Revolutionary Forces held an oath-taking ceremony and issued a manifesto in which it was pointed out that "the purpose of the military campaign is to build an independent nation on the basis of the Three People's Principles and to protect the interests of the nation and of the people." It called on all troops in the country to join the fight for the National Revolution and asked the people to do their share for the cause. The Revolutionary Forces occupied Changsha* on July 10. Subsequently, they moved forward in three columns. In the center were the Fourth, the Seventh and the Eighth Armies with Wuhan and Wushengkwan to the north as their goal. On the right were the Second, the Third and the Fifth Armies, plus the Independent First Division, all under my personal command, with Nanchang** and Kiukiang as our targets. Meanwhile a part of the First Army was to advance toward Chekiang by way of Fukien and later to join with the right column in operations against Shanghai and Nanking. On the left were the Ninth and the Tenth Armies, moving toward Kinchow and Shasi above Hankow on the Yangtze. On October 10 our central column captured Wuchang. On November 9 the right column took Nanchang. The rapid advance of the Revolutionary Forces not only caused the northern war lords to lose heart but also came as a great surprise to the world at large.

In November the Seventh Enlarged Executive Committee of the Communist International, meeting in Moscow, adopted a resolution on the situation in China. It regarded the rapid progress of the Northward Expedition and the Chinese people's enthusiastic response as marking the third stage in the world-wide revolutionary movement. It said that during this

* Changsha is the capital of Hunan province.
** Nanchang is the capital of Kiangsi province.

stage "the national liberation movement should pass on to a new revolutionary situation." This was, in Communist jargon, another way of saying that "the national liberation movement and the farmers' revolution should be combined into one." More specifically, the idea was for the Chinese Communists to utilize the National Government's organs as a channel for contacts with the farmers in order to carry out their so-called Programs for Rural Areas and to create what they called a "Farmers' Revolution." Their aim was to organize a military force through uprisings in the rural areas and to establish a Communist regime for the purpose of directing the Chinese Communists in carrying out their "thoroughgoing rural policy." Moscow felt that Borodin was not aggressive enough and dispatched M. N. Roy and Tan Ping-shan to China.

To implement this resolution the Chinese Communists divided their operations into two parts. On the one hand, by taking advantage of the progress made by the Revolutionary Forces and working through the Party's mass movement activities, they sought to collect all the riffraff and vagabonds in the cities as well as rural areas in order to control labor unions and farmers' associations, and to create an army of their own. On the other hand, they sought to create disunity in the Party and to foster ill feelings and conflicts among our armed units in order to facilitate their infiltration, extend their influence and try to seize control.

I was at the front when our forces on the right flank captured Nanchang. Shortly afterward I arrived in that city. My next task was to plan operations against Sun Chuan-fang's troops in the East. In November members of the Party's Central Standing Committee and of the National Government reached Nanchang, and it was decided that all organs of the National Government should stay in Nanchang temporarily to take charge of military and administrative affairs in connection with the pacification of the southeast provinces.

On December 13, however, Borodin called a meeting of

some members of the Central Executive Committee and of the National Government in Wuhan at which it was decided to set up a "Joint Conference" with Hsu Chien as chairman to exercise what they called the "supreme power of the Party." This was obviously done upon Moscow's instructions to split our Party. In order to preserve solidarity in our Party and unity in our military command, I had to exercise the utmost restraint. On December 19 and 20 I sent two telegrams to Wuhan, voicing my concurrence with the resolutions of the Wuhan Joint Conference. I also urged members of the Central Executive Committee and of the National Government then in Nanchang to go to Wuhan so that the Third Plenary Session of the Central Executive Committee could be held there. Furthermore, to prove my sincere desire for internal solidarity, I tendered my resignation as chairman of the Central Standing Committee to the plenary session when it met in March, 1927.

After the Third Plenary Session of the Central Executive Committee the Communists became bolder than ever. The "Central Authorities" at Wuhan, under Communist manipulations, nullified the rulings of the Second Plenary Session against the appointment of dual-party members as heads of departments in Kuomintang. They also set at naught the decisions of the Second Plenary Session on the submission of a complete roster of dual-party members and on the formation of a two-party joint conference, as if these decisions had never existed. This deepened our belief that any agreement signed with either the Chinese Communists or the Russian Communists amounted merely to a scrap of paper, for they would never abide by it. As a result, all Party organs handling the labor unions and the farmers' movement remained in the hands of dual-party members. In fact, the situation became progressively worse.

The General Labor Union in Wuhan and the farmers' associations in various places all came into possession of arms and a Red reign of terror was created wherever these people were in operation. In the meantime commerce and industry in the cities and agriculture in the rural areas came to a standstill under the baleful influence of riffraff and vagabonds.

The Political Department of our armed forces became a principal object of Communist infiltration. Under the cloak of auxiliary political service, they did their best to strain relations between the various units. They even held up supplies and munitions from troops in southeast provinces and interfered with the movement of reinforcements from regions on the upper Yangtze to the Kiangsu and Chekiang fronts, their intention being to cut off our forces on the coast from the rear. Despite all these obstructions units forming the right wing of our Revolutionary Forces pushed forward and successfully effected the occupation of Shanghai and Nanking according to the original timetable.

On March 24, 1927, following the entry of Revolutionary Forces into Nanking some soldiers suddenly broke loose and began attacking European and American residences, including those of members of foreign consular staffs and missionaries. This resulted in the loss of several lives. I should mention that at the beginning of the Northward Expedition in my capacity as commander-in-chief of the Revolutionary Forces, I had issued a proclamation* in which I solemnly stated that, "In launching the Northward Expedition, my purpose is not only to unify China but also to promote world peace. I shall hold myself completely responsible for the protection of life and property of all aliens in China, irrespective of their nationalities, so long as they refrain from obstructing the movement and operations of our Revolutionary Forces." Earlier, when our forces entered such cities as Changsha, Hankow, Kiukiang and Hangchow, no harm was done to any foreigners. Now it happened in Nanking, of all places. Communists in the armed forces had created this incident in the hope of provok-

* On August 20, 1926.

ing a direct clash between the foreign powers and the Revolutionary Forces. I shall not enter into the details of their plot, the evidences of which were conclusive.

When our forces were moving toward Shanghai workers led by the Party declared a general strike to signify their support for the revolutionary cause. The Communists again tried to capitalize on the situation by organizing labor pickets and supplying them with arms. Their scheme was to start uprisings so that they could set up a labor government in the city or at least to cause conflicts between the Western powers and the Revolutionary Forces in Shanghai. It was in these chaotic circumstances that our forces occupied Shanghai. I hurried to Shanghai from Kiukiang on March 26 to take personal command of the situation in this international metropolis in the East and to forestall a repetition of what had happened in Wuhan. On April 12, to prevent Communist uprisings, the Revolutionary Forces, in cooperation with local labor unions and chambers of commerce, disarmed the Red labor pickets and kept Communist saboteurs under surveillance. Only then was the situation in Shanghai brought under control.

At an emergency meeting of Kuomintang's Central Supervisory Committee held in Shanghai on April 2, more evidences of Communist subversion and treason were submitted by Wu Ching-heng.* Other members made similar reports on happenings in Hunan, Hupeh, Kiangsi, Chekiang, Anhwei and Shanghai, where the Communists, upon orders from the Communist International, had tried to sabotage the revolution by engineering disturbances. It was unanimously resolved to ask the Central Executive Committee to take emergency measures and place all Communist ringleaders under the surveillance of local security organs. The Political Council of the Central Executive Committee further recommended that the Party take steps to rid itself of Communists. On May 5 principles

* A member of Kuomintang's Central Supervisory Committee

guiding the implementation of the decision were passed by the Central Standing Committee. A special committee was set up to be in charge of the purge, which was resolutely carried out in Nanking, Shanghai and Canton. In this way law and order was maintained and our southeastern provinces were spared the ordeal of serving as a proving ground for Communism and escaped the disastrous consequences resulting from intra-party disputes in Moscow.

On April 18 the Party's Central Standing Committee and the National Government's State Council, in accordance with Dr. Sun's bequeathed wishes, resolved to make Nanking the national capital, and numerous organs of the National Government were set up in Nanking soon afterward.

Tragedy of the Wuhan Leftists

The resolution on China adopted by the Communist International's Executive Committee at its seventh session was the handiwork of Stalin whose idea it was to turn the Wuhan administration into a "democratic dictatorship of the proletariat, farmers and other exploited classes." This later became part of Stalin's over-all blueprint after World War II for setting up a series of "people's democratic dictatorships," first in countries in Eastern Europe and then in China.

By March 1927 the Communist International in Moscow realized that in view of the totally unexpected progress made by our Revolutionary Forces, it would be difficult openly to defy the Central Authorities at Nanking, destroy our Party and sabotage our Northward Expedition by merely relying on the Joint Conference* and the leftist organizations at Wuhan. Consequently it asked Wang Ching-wei, then in France, to return to China by way of Moscow. Shortly after his arrival in Shanghai, Wang issued a joint statement with Chen Tu-hsiu, advocating the establishment of a "democratic

---

* Set up in Wuhan in December 1926 to exercise the "supreme power of the Party."

dictatorship of all oppressed classes in order to suppress the counterrevolution." This was actually a reiteration of Stalin's policy. Whereupon Kuomintang and the National Government in Nanking decided to purge the Party of Communists.

Meanwhile in Moscow there was a serious difference of opinion in the Communist International. Trotsky favored the withdrawal of the Chinese Communists from the Wuhan "leftist" organizations and the setting up of their own Soviet regime. Stalin disagreed. He maintained that the Chinese Communists should continue to cooperate with the "leftists" in Kuomintang. Saying that the time was not ripe for the establishment of a Soviet regime in China, he sought to change the Wuhan administration from a "democratic dictatorship of workers, farmers and petit bourgeoisie" into a "revolutionary democratic dictatorship of the proletariat and farmers." The resolution on China adopted by the Communist International's Executive Committee at its eighth session in May 1927 was forced through by Stalin's highhanded action in his struggle for power.

The "leftist" Central Party Headquarters and the government at Wuhan, headed by Wang Ching-wei, were dominated by Communists who, with their fellow travelers, had taken charge of all mass movement activities. For instance, the head of the Department of Farmers was Tan Ping-shan, a Communist who carried out Moscow's resolutions and directives to the dot. Units of the political departments of the Revolutionary Forces in Hunan and Hupeh were also mostly controlled by the Communists. Owing to the dissension caused by the Communists, it was impossible to harmonize views between these units. Meanwhile in the Communist camp itself there was considerable confusion arising from internal party strife in Moscow as well as from disputes within the Chinese Communist Party.

People in Hunan and Hupeh provinces had had enough of

the Communist reign of terror and class struggle, and especially the Communist policy for the concentration of cash and food supplies. In May 1927 the farmers of Changsha rose against the Communists. This was followed by farmers in other places. These were the same farmers who had previously welcomed the Communists and their "agrarian revolution." It was a great blow to the Communists in their farmers' movement.

Meanwhile at Wuhan the "leftists" and the Chinese Communists were sharply divided. There were two opposite views on military matters. One group, with which Borodin and the "leftists" were identified, was in favor of driving northward and eastward to break Wuhan's isolation and to expand their political and military influence. Another group, represented by Roy, advocated moving southward to promote a farmers' revolution in Hunan, Hupeh, Kwangtung and Kwangsi, to consolidate the social foundation of their regime and to encircle the southeastern provinces.

Regarding the farmers' movement there were also two views. One, held by Borodin, was that cooperation between Kuomintang and the Chinese Communists should be maintained, and excesses in the farmers' movement curbed. Another, advocated by Roy, was in favor of armed uprisings by the farmers.

At the time Stalin's instructions to the Chinese Communists were:

1. The confiscation of land was to be effected at the lower level and not to be done by orders of the "National Government."
2. The Party was to check excesses on the part of the farmers.
3. All unreliable military officers were to be removed, 20,000 Communist members were to be armed and a new army was to be formed to be composed of 50,000 workers and farmers to be selected in Hunan and Hupeh provinces.

4. New workers and farmers were to replace the old elements as members of the Party's Central Committee.
5. Revolutionary courts were to be set up with well-known Kuomintang members sitting in trial of reactionary officers.

Stalin's telegram to the above effect reached Wuhan on June 1. Borodin suggested that it be kept from Wang Ching-wei, but without Borodin's knowledge Roy showed it to Wang. Only then did the "leftists" at Wuhan realize that Moscow was taking advantage of our National Revolution to communize China. As a result, some of them, too, decided to break away from the Chinese Communists.

On June 30 the Chinese Communists at an enlarged meeting of their Central Committee passed an eleven-point resolution concerning relations between Kuomintang and the Chinese Communists. This was a deliberate "retreat" in order to preserve cooperation between the two parties. On July 3 it was decided to send Roy back to Russia. On July 15, however, the leftist government at Wuhan took definite steps to expel the Communists, whereupon Borodin had no choice but to leave. He returned to Russia by way of the Northwest which was then garrisoned by Feng Yu-hsiang's forces.

The head of the Russian military advisory mission in Hankow, General Bluecher, also known as Ga-lin, came to see me in Shanghai on his way back to Russia. Ga-lin first came to China in 1924. In my opinion he was an outstanding Russian general as well as a reasonable man and a good friend. What was most unusual about him was that he had none of the traits associated with Bolsheviks. I often thought of him in the intervening years. After his recall in 1925 he was succeeded by Kissanka who was later involved in the *Chungshan* gunboat incident referred to above.

Between the spring and summer of 1926 I asked Russia to send General Ga-lin to Canton again to head the military advisory mission. As before, he and I got along well. Every now and then he would show his disgust with what Borodin was trying to do. At the time of the split between Nanking and Wuhan he was summoned from Nanchang to Hankow, where he stayed until the Wuhan regime decided to expel the Communists. It was then that he came to bid me good-by. He felt greatly depressed. At parting I said to him: "We may have another opportunity to work together, so please do not feel so badly about your leaving." His reply was: "I hope, too, this is not the last time we shall see each other. So, till we meet again!" This was one of the most moving partings in my life. Later on, when diplomatic relations between China and Russia were resumed,* I asked Stalin several times to let General Ga-lin come back to China as military advisor. Stalin never replied. In 1939 when Sun Fo, president of our Legislative Yuan, went to Russia, I asked him to renew the request with Stalin in person. It was only then that Stalin disclosed that General Ga-lin had already been executed for succumbing to the charms of a Japanese woman spy!

Stalin's Need of Urban Uprisings By Chinese Reds

The Wuhan regime's rupture with the Communists forced Stalin to adopt Trotsky's views, i.e., the setting up of a Soviet regime in China. He dispatched Heinz Neumann and Besso Lominadse to China to carry out the plan. The Chinese Communists' August Seventh Meeting was held under Neumann's direction. In an open letter to party members the meeting tried to defend Stalin in connection with the resolution on China adopted by the Communist International at its Eighth Plenary Session. They blamed everything on Chen Tu-hsiu and Tan Ping-shan and condemned them as "opportunists." Whereupon Chen Tu-hsiu lost his position as secretary-general of the Chinese Communist Party and Chu Chiu-pai,

* In December 1932.

Hsiang Chung-fa and Li Li-san were elected members of the Standing Committee to lead the Communist Party in a new policy of violence.

In preparing his attacks against Trotsky at the Fifteenth National Congress of the Russian Communist Party Stalin needed some Chinese Communist uprisings in the cities so that he could capitalize on their importance to prove that he had been right and also to justify his ruthless liquidation of his opponents.

The Nanchang Uprising of July 31, 1927, was instigated by Besso Lominadse and carried out by Ho Lung and Yeh Ting. Ho Lung, who began his career as a local bandit, was commander of the 20th Army of the Revolutionary Forces. Upon Communist instigation, Ho planned to pillage Nanchang, seize more arms and then march southward to set up a "new government" in Canton. Yeh Ting was commander of the 24th Division of the 11th Army of the Revolutionary Forces. He was a Communist, and so were most of his cadres. He was ordered by the Chinese Communists to take his troops to Nanchang. The opportunity came when the Third and the Ninth Armies were away on garrison duty elsewhere, leaving only a small force in Nanchang itself. Taking advantage of this vacuum, the two Communist units mutinied on July 31. They struck in the middle of the night, breaking into the Central Bank, ransacking shops and homes and arresting Kuomintang members.

On August 1 a public notice was issued in the name of the "Revolutionary Committee of Kuomintang" which included among its presidium the name of Chang Fah-kwei, field commander of the Second Front Army of the Revolutionary Forces. But in less than four days' time forces under Chang Fah-kwei and Chu Pei-teh, another field commander, moved against the rebels. Members of the so-called Revolutionary Committee, including Tan Ping-shan and others, wanted the rebel forces to fall back on Canton, but Yeh Ting insisted on retreating toward Swatow. Finally they fled to Swatow where they raided and pillaged the city before moving to eastern Kwangtung to set up a Soviet regime in conjunction with men under Peng Pai, a local Communist brigand.

Following the August Seventh Meeting the Communist Party sent Mao Tse-tung to Changsha to organize uprisings. The purpose was to build on the ruins of their earlier "agrarian revolution" there an army of workers and farmers and to establish a Soviet regime. But he found it impossible to incite workers to rise up in the cities. Nor could he accomplish much in the rural areas besides sporadic burning, killing and looting. The so-called "Autumn Crop Uprising" was also a complete failure. Mao Tse-tung and a handful of followers had to seek refuge in the Chinkan Hills on the Hunan-Kiangsi border.

Despite the dismal failure of the Nanchang Uprising, Moscow instructed the Chinese Communists to stage similar revolts in Canton and other cities. The Canton Uprising of December 11 was organized and directed by Heinz Neumann and Gerhart Eisler* from the local Soviet consulate and carried out by the so-called Training Regiment of the Second Front Army. This regiment was composed of students from the Wuhan Military and Political Academy and the Farmers' Movement Training Institute. Among them were many Communists and members of the Communist Youth Corps. Their slogans calling for "bread for the workers" and "land for the peasants" were taken from Russia's October Revolution. They also organized a so-called Soviet of Workers, Farmers and Soldiers. On December 13 loyal troops under Li Fu-lin entered the city from Honam** and the Fourth Army under Hsueh Yueh also hurried back to Canton. Members of the

---

* Another agent sent to China by the Communist International to direct the Communist uprisings.
** Honam is separated from Canton by the Pearl River.

Machine Workers' Union rallied to us and formed dare-to-die corps to take part in the fighting, and the rebellion was speedily put down.

Severance of Diplomatic Relations with Russia— End of the First Period of Peaceful Coexistence

During the Canton uprising, a Russian vice-consul and his assistant were arrested on the scene. Subsequent investigations resulted in the discovery of secret documents which proved that the Russian consulate and Russian commercial establishments in Canton were really espionage and subversive organs where the insurrection had been planned. On December 14 the National Government issued an order closing all Russian consulates in the country and called on the Russian commercial establishments to cease their operations.

When a correspondent of the *Osaka Mainichi Shimbun* interviewed me one day about the termination of diplomatic relations with Russia, I said:

In terminating diplomatic relations with Russia we are merely breaking off relations with the Soviet Russian Government. There is no change in the Chinese people's feeling toward the Russian people.

Just look at the Russian consulates in various places in China. They are, in fact, branches of the Third International and, at the same time, hotbeds of Chinese Communist intrigues. For its own self-defense as well as for the sake of our National Revolution and peace in the Far East, Kuomintang has taken this resolute action. It is the logical thing to do.

Diplomatic relations between China and Soviet Russia thus came to an end. During these five years the Communist International had directed its China branch to join Kuomintang, to establish contact with the masses and to stir up troubles by using the National Revolution as a medium. Their final aim was to overthrow Kuomintang, to usurp revolutionary leadership and then, in the name of the Three People's Principles, to lead the Northward Expedition in order to occupy the whole of China. The failure of this ambitious scheme in 1927 had the effect of putting off the Communist control of the Chinese mainland for twenty-three years.

CHAPTER TWO

DEVELOPMENT

The Second Period (1932-1945)

The suppression of the Communist revolt in Canton on March 20, 1926, and the subsequent purge of Communists from the rank and file of Kuomintang dealt a severe blow to the Communists in their plot to communize China in the course of our National Revolution. The Chinese Communists' policy of sovietization reached a dead end in 1935. Abiding by the Communist International's directive on "United Front," they asked for "cooperation between Kuomintang and the Chinese Communist Party for united resistance against Japan." They sought to break their political isolation by resort to neutralism tactics, so that they would have a chance to expand their military strength for a comeback. Their fond hope was to overthrow the Government during the Sino-Japanese War, which then already seemed inevitable, and to put the country under Russian domination. Moscow's "Peaceful Coexistence" slogan and its political offensive and neutralism tactics against the free world today are mostly patterned after the stratagems which the Chinese Communists used against the Government between 1935 and 1945. Consequently, there is a need today for us to review the historical events during this period.

The Chinese Eastern Railway
Incident and the Li Li-san Line

The Communist International held its sixth plenary session in Moscow in July 1928 when Stalin, having defeated the

Trotskyites, turned against the "rightists" led by Bukharin. In order to attack the "rightists," he himself turned leftist. This switch caused the Chinese Communists to decide during their Sixth National Party Congress not only to continue but to intensify their earlier policy of uprisings although it had already failed to achieve its purpose. The Chinese Communist Party Congress announced "Ten Big Demands," of which the principal ones were the "overthrow of the National Government," "confiscation of all lands owned by landlords," and "establishment of a Soviet form of government." These demands formed the basis for the so-called Li Li-san Line.

On October 12, 1929, there occurred the Chinese Eastern Railway Incident. Russian troops invaded Manchuli and Hailar in Manchuria and forced our local authorities there to sign the Khabarovsk Protocol on December 22, another proof that Soviet Russia was continuing Czarist Russia's aggressive policy toward China. At the same time Moscow was driving the Chinese Communists harder than before and wanted them to recognize that "the high tide of revolution is here," and called on them to coordinate their activities in the cities with those in the villages, "to capture a few political and industrial centers," and "to strive for an initial victory in one or more provinces." In the areas under their control the Chinese Communists made Russia the model for everything and their political organization was called a Soviet, and their land policy began with the equal distribution of land among the farmers and ended with the establishment of collective farms and the reduction of farmers to the status of serfs.

On July 28, 1930, when the Government forces were busy putting down a revolt in the Northwest, Communist troops broke into Changsha and even tried to attack Wuhan. The Communist International in Moscow was jubilant and bragged about "the victory of workers, farmers and soldiers acting together." This enthusiasm, however, was short-lived, for soon afterward Government troops drove the Communists out of Changsha and removed the threat to Wuhan.

If Li Li-san had succeeded in carrying out Moscow's orders, that would be to Stalin's credit. Since he had failed, he had to bear the blame. In September 1930 control of the Chinese Communist Party passed into the hands of Russian-returned internationalists led by Pavel Mif.

From Urban to Rural Uprisings

Heinz Neumann, alias A. Neuberg, who was present at the Chinese Communists' August Seventh Meeting in 1927 was a Soviet Russian expert in uprisings. The series of uprisings which the Chinese Communists staged at Nanchang, Swatow and Canton, had all been carried out according to the theory and practice of the Russian Communists as expounded by Neuberg. His work, *The Armed Uprising*, became a field manual for Chinese Communists in staging urban and rural uprisings in 1928 and in subsequent years. All Communist secret documents seized by the Chinese Government showed that the organization of "Action Committees" in the different localities, the agitation among the masses, the "notices" and "orders" issued during armed uprisings, were all taken from Neuberg's manual.

In the cities the Chinese Communists formed the "Red Labor Union" as the workers' basic organization. They also organized, under the General Labor Union, a "General Strike Action Committee" for every trade in order to foment political strikes. They further organized Red vanguards to give their party members military training so as to prepare them for armed uprisings. In the villages, following the example of the Kombyed or Poor Farmers' Corps in Soviet Russia, the Chinese Communists organized farmers' committees, took arms from the local militia and turned them over to the farmers' army. In this way they practiced a sort of "dictatorship of farmers' unions." Then a so-called Military Council of Workers and Farmers combined urban and rural armed bands to form a "Workers' and Farmers' Revolutionary Army" to "fight for initial victory in several provinces or in just one province."

Besides learning the Russian technique of armed uprisings from Neuberg, the Chinese Communists also adopted the methods of violence employed by roving armed brigands in Chinese history. According to the *Brief History of the Growth of the Chinese Red Army*, which the Chinese Communists have used as a manual for the training of their troops, the Communist roving brigands originated in 1927 on the Hunan-Kiangsi border.* There were originally two brigand leaders there, named Wang Tso and Wang Wen-tsai. When Mao Tse-tung's Red Army reached that region, he linked up with them.

Thereafter, all the rural uprisings staged by the Chinese Communists were described as the "duties of Red Army"— murder, arson, extortion, fund-raising, and agitation among the masses. Their political program consisted of "killing the landlords, redistributing their land, arming the masses and establishing a Soviet regime." When Li Li-san developed his policy line, the Communists only believed in the principle of "the cities leading the villages," and the armed uprisings they instigated in the rural areas still aimed at the capture of the big cities. During this period the form of mob violence used was primarily that of Soviet Russia. Following the "liquidation" of the Li Li-san policy line in September 1930 the idea of "besieging the cities with villages" began to take hold among the Chinese Communists. Thus, the hit-and-run tactics of the armed roving brigands became the Communists' main form of violence.

Chinese villages, however, are self-governing bodies with clans as basic units. Members of the same clan are blood kins-

* In the Chinkangshan (hills) in the Lohsiao Range.

men and members of different clans are related by marriage. After generations of friendly dealings and mutual assistance, there are strong bonds of sentiments even between the landlords and the tenants. When the Chinese Communists sought to foment class struggle and instigate uprisings in the otherwise peaceful villages of China they found propaganda and agitation alone inadequate to achieve their purpose. They had to resort to such tactics of roving armed bands as robbery, kidnapping, killing of the victims, destruction of entire villages and the abduction of able-bodied people. In particular, they used the local riffraff and lawless elements to massacre landlords and rich farmers. They created a reign of terror among the masses and caused hatred between landlords and tenants. Before setting fires to the homes of landlords and rich farmers they encouraged the poor people to help themselves to whatever they could lay their hands on, thus deliberately creating conflicts between the rich and the poor. At the same time they let the fires burn down the homes of the poor as well so that they could force the homeless to join them and become part of their roving bands.

Whenever the Communist troops entered a village or a rural town they would resort to burning, killing and pillaging, and set the people against one another. When they withdrew they would carry off all the able-bodied men in the area, leaving behind only the old and the infirm, women and children. Even the latter would be subject to the control and watch of the Communist underground. As a result they dared not talk to Government forces, much less to cooperate with them.

In territories under their control the Communists' grip over the people and the blockade of information were exercised through a combination of primitive and modern forms of torture so as to achieve the maximum effect of immorality, violence and terror. The tortures they inflicted on their victims were solely aimed at giving them the severest pain without killing them outright and at inflicting on them mental as well as physical injuries. According to reports filed with the Government by the victims, the Communists practiced as many as seventy-two different kinds of torture.

Anti-Communist Campaigns after the Mukden Incident

In December 1930 and again in May 1931 the Government launched two inconclusive military drives against Communist rebels in the mountainous regions of Hunan and Kiangsi. The third campaign which lasted from July to October, 1931, was proceeding satisfactorily when the unprovoked Mukden Incident* occurred on September 18, 1931. This compelled the Government to transfer forces, committed to quelling the rebellion, to North China for redeployment.

Meanwhile, the Chinese Communists and their fellow travelers took advantage of the Japanese aggression in Manchuria by instigating students in Peiping, Shanghai and Nanking to converge on Nanking on the pretext of making petitions but actually to embarrass the Government in every way possible. They also sowed seeds of suspicion between the Government and the local authorities by declaring: "Unless Chiang goes, it is impossible to fight Japan."

Through their propaganda and intrigue, they created a crisis which threatened to lead to national disunity. In the interest of the nation I felt it incumbent upon me to tender my resignation in December.

Thenceforth the Chinese Communist troops coordinated their actions with the quickening pace of Japanese aggression against China. This was tantamount to subjecting the Government to a pincer attack both from within and without.

When on January 28, 1932, the Japanese Navy attacked Shanghai, the Communists immediately utilized the situation to extend their Soviet areas in Hunan, Kiangsi, Kwangtung

---

* Japanese troops attacked Mukden, capital of Liaoning province in Manchuria.

and Fukien provinces. They set up a so-called Soviet Provisional Central Government at Juichin, and occupied numerous districts on the Honan-Hupeh-Anhwei borders and in central and southern Hupeh with a view to encircling Wuhan. The areas overrun by the Chinese Communists extended over seven provinces,* covering over 100,000 square kilometers. Conditions in these areas became completely disorganized and the people were all terror-stricken. Like a prairie fire, the Communist reign of terror spread. People both in and outside the Government, faced with external aggression on the one hand and Communist menace on the other, unanimously demanded that I resume my post and continue to lead the nation in this hour of danger. Upon the termination of hostilities in Shanghai, I announced it as my policy to make internal pacification a prerequisite to resistance against external aggression.

On June 18, at a Five-Province** Communist-Suppression Conference held at Kuling, concrete plans were decided on for a fourth campaign. This was to begin with actions against Communists in the three provinces of Honan, Hupeh and Anhwei. In November Government troops routed those in the border regions. The Communists under Hsu Hsiang-chien fled westward into northern Szechwan. Meanwhile, Ho Lung's hordes in western Hupeh were also forced to flee toward Hwofeng. In January 1933, when a decisive victory was practically in sight, the Japanese troops invaded Shanhaikwan.*** This was followed by the Battle of the Great Wall in March. Once again the Government had to send troops to North China, and the fourth major campaign against the Chinese Communists, which was already under way, had to be called off.

With the Battle of the Great Wall over, I again called a

* Hunan, Kiangsi, Chekiang, Fukien, Hupeh, Honan and Anhwei.
** Honan, Hupeh, Anhwei, Hunan and Kiangsi.
*** A mountain pass along the Great Wall.

military conference in October 1933 at Nanchang to formulate plans for a fifth campaign against the Communists in Kiangsi. This time the campaign was to be conducted on the basis of 30 per cent military effort and 70 per cent political effort. A strict economic blockade was to be enforced against the Communists. Forts and pillboxes were to be built to cut the Communists' lines of communication. Roads were to be constructed as Government troops advanced. By the summer of 1934 the Communist area in five provinces* had been reduced to the mountainous regions in southern Kiangsi with an area of less than 2,000 square kilometers. This was only one-fiftieth of what the Communists had under their control in 1932.

By October 1934 the so-called Soviet district in southern Kiangsi was in a very precarious situation as a result of the steady increase of the Government's military pressure and the tightening of the economic blockade and also of the drop in food production and the loss of farming population in Sovietized districts following the introduction of farm collectivization. Finally, they had either to flee or face annihilation.

Communist Troops' Flight Westward

Earlier, during the Battle of Shanghai in 1932 against the Japanese, the Chinese Communists, carrying out instructions of the Communist International, resolved that the high tide of revolution had arrived and attempted to storm big cities along the Yangtze. Whether or not such a military adventure would succeed was the subject of repeated disputes both in the Russian Communist Party and in the Chinese Communist Party. Once again Moscow dispatched Lominadse to China to survey conditions in the Communist districts. In his report after his return to Russia, Lominadse expressed the belief that the

* Hunan, Kiangsi, Hupeh, Honan and Anhwei.

Chinese Communists' Sovietization policy would almost certainly end in failure. He suggested that the Chinese Communists should abandon their base in Juichin and flee toward Szechwan in the West in preparation for a prolonged struggle. Stalin did not accept this suggestion. By 1934, subjected to repeated encirclement attacks by Government troops, the Communists collapsed in eight guerrilla districts. The remnants had to get away in small groups. This marked the end of the directive given by the Communist International at its Sixth Plenary Session for the Chinese Communists to stage armed uprisings, to set up a Soviet regime and to start an "agrarian revolution."

Hsu Hsiang-chien's men fled to northern Szechwan and attempted to enter Shensi. Headed off by Government troops and the local forces in Szechwan, his men moved into western Szechwan instead, while Communist units under Mao Tsetung reached Kweichow in their flight. Failing to occupy Kweiyang,* Mao and his remnants sneaked across the Tatu River to join Hsu Hsiang-chien's men in western Szechwan.** Mao and Hsu met at Mao-Erh-K'ai, but as they could not agree on their next move, they split up again. Hsu moved deeper into western Szechwan. Meanwhile Chu Teh, who had fled westward with Mao, turned toward Yunnan. As to Mao and Peng Teh-huai, they took their remnants northward and finally reached northern Shensi, where they joined with the local Communists under Liu Tse-tan. At the end of this long flight there were only some 5,000 armed Communists left. From the military standpoint, they no longer constituted a serious threat.

Surrender of the Communists and Their Political Offensive

The Chinese Eastern Railway Incident of 1929, engineered by the Russians, and the Mukden Incident of 1931, per-

* Capital of Kweichow province.
** At Moukung and Sungpan.

petrated by the Japanese militarists, clearly indicated that the Chinese Republic would have to blaze a bloody trail between Russia and Japan before its independence and freedom could be insured. Though the dispute over the Chinese Eastern Railway was settled temporarily as a "local incident," China still found herself sandwiched between two forces. This was because the Chinese Communists, upon Moscow's instructions, had coordinated their armed uprisings with aggression by the Japanese militarists.

We have seen how in the face of the Government's strategy of encirclement the Communists had to break up their forces and try to escape in small numbers. Militarily speaking they came to a dead end early in 1935. Whereupon they tried to save themselves by political means. Their slogan was: "Co-operation between Kuomintang and the Chinese Communist Party to resist Japan and save the nation."

At the Communist International's Seventh Congress held in Moscow between July and August 1935, Georgi Dimitrov made a report on the "United Front." Regarding China, he suggested that a "comprehensive anti-Japanese and anti-Imperialist United Front" be formed. As this was Stalin's policy decision, it became a Congress resolution as a matter of course and on this the Chinese Communists based their subsequent actions.

Meanwhile the Chinese Communists who had fled to Szechwan and Kweichow ran into serious difficulties. On August 1 Chu Teh and Mao Tse-tung issued a declaration from Mao-Erh-K'ai, proposing an "Anti-Japanese People's United Front" and demanding the formation of a so-called National People's Coalition Defense Government.

In February 1936 Chu Teh and Mao Tse-tung, with a view to forestalling the consequences of a serious famine in northern Shensi, sent Liu Tse-tan's units known as "Red Army's Anti-Japanese Vanguards" across the Yellow River into western Shansi's food-producing areas only to be defeated by Government troops along the Tungpu Railway. Liu Tse-tan himself was killed in action. Chu Teh and Mao Tse-tung, realizing that they were in no position to undertake any more military adventures, decided to surrender. They approached the Government for "cessation of hostilities and negotiations for peace."

The Neutralist Tactics of the Chinese Communists

On September 18, 1935, in a statement commemorating the fourth anniversary of the Mukden Incident, a so-called Shanghai Anti-Japanese National Salvation Grand Alliance posing as neutrals, blazed abroad the slogan: "Let us stop the civil war and unitedly resist Japan." Similar neutral organizations quickly sprang up and spread among the youths, students and intellectuals in all the big cities in the country.

In Peiping, for instance, professors and students in a number of universities and colleges paraded in the streets in December 1935 in protest against "Self-Rule for Hopei and Chahar Provinces." This was started as a patriotic movement but it came to be utilized by the Communists to advance their neutralist tactics. In North China alone there were more than thirty such organizations.* Uniformly, they proclaimed in their publications the "People's Front" as demanded by the Communist International. This was true not only in Peiping and Tientsin but also in Shanghai and other cities.

It was the purpose of the "People's Front" to isolate the Government and its forces so that the Chinese Communists could continue to exist, expand, and rearm for a comeback. It advocated: "Resist Japan and save the nation." This showed more clearly than ever that the intention of the "People's

---

* The "North China Joint Association for National Salvation," the "North China People's National Salvation Grand Alliance," the "Peiping-Tientsin Students National Salvation Amalgamated Association," and the "Peiping-Tientsin Cultural Circles National Salvation Association," etc.

Front" in precipitating a war with Japan was to give the Chinese Communists a respite during which they could gather strength.

Fighting a Two-Front Diplomatic War

The Government's success in its fifth major campaign against the Communist forces had averted the danger of having to fight on two military fronts simultaneously, but as events developed it still had to fight on two diplomatic fronts: against Japan and against Russia.

After the Mukden Incident the Japanese militarists set up the puppet regime of "Manchukuo," in Manchuria. Then in a series of moves they created "self-rule" in Inner Mongolia, set up a special area in East Hopei and imposed a special status upon Hopei and Chahar provinces with a view to their eventual detachment from the Chinese Government.

In a pamphlet entitled "Friend or Foe?" issued in the autumn of 1934 I warned Japan that if her militarists should fail to mend their ways by abandoning plans of aggression against China, any conflict between the two nations would only bring disaster to both. Time and again I clearly stated: "Japan must realize what evil forces Kuomintang is confronted with, and what repercussions might result in East Asia from the triumph of these evil forces." Unfortunately the Japanese militarists completely ignored my advice and continued to apply pressure upon the position of the Government for their own military ends.

On February 26, 1936, a group of young Japanese army officers staged a *coup d'état* in Tokyo. Later on the Hirota cabinet combined all the different plans of aggression against China into a conglomerate policy embracing three demands of "neighborly friendship, joint defense against Communism, and economic cooperation." This policy was used as a basis for negotiations with the Chinese Government. It was very clear then that if we rejected those principles it would mean war. On the other hand, if we accepted them, it would mean the end of China as an independent nation. This was our diplomatic front vis-à-vis Japan.

Also after the Mukden Incident Moscow repeatedly expressed to our Government its desire to resume diplomatic relations. An agreement to this effect was announced by Dr. W. W. Yen and Maxim Litvinov in Geneva on December 12, 1932. But there was to be no improvement in Sino-Russian relations for several years. In fact, cases of Soviet infringement on China's sovereign rights continued to occur from time to time. In March 1935 Soviet Russia sold the Chinese Eastern Railway to the puppet regime of "Manchukuo" over China's protest. This provided added impetus to Japanese aggression. In the spring of 1936, after Japan had brought up Hirota's Three Demands, I felt that we should take positive steps to negotiate with Russia. Chang Chun,* then minister of foreign affairs, held a number of discussions with Bogomoloff, the Soviet ambassador, with a view of finding a way of safeguarding peace both in the East and in the West through joint effort. On March 12, however, the Russo Mongolian Mutual Assistance Pact was announced. Bogomoloff tried to stop a Chinese Government protest by making a scene at our Foreign Office. He even threatened to disclose the contents of his secret conversations with Chang Chun. Despite this episode, the Chinese Government still lodged a serious protest with the Soviet Government on April 5.

Soviet Russia's external activities were double-barreled. Its Foreign Office was doing its utmost to bring about a relaxation of the precautionary measures other nations had taken against her and was pursuing "peace diplomacy." In the meantime, the Communist International was carrying on the antiwar movement and other subversive activities against the Western nations in the name of "anti-Fascism." Its Far East-

---

* Chang Chun is now secretary-general of the President's Office.

ern policy was likewise double-barreled. The Soviet Government adopted a neutral attitude toward the Sino-Japanese conflict and, in fact, tried hard to reach a compromise with Japan. The Chinese Communists, however, working through the so-called Anti-Japanese and National Salvation Grand Alliance and other similar organizations, called upon the Chinese Government to stop the campaign against them and to resist Japanese aggression together. Simultaneously they sponsored a movement for China to enter into an alliance with Russia. This was our diplomatic front vis-à-vis Russia.

The international situation in which China found herself at the time was not simply one of struggle between Japan and Russia. To be more specific, what Japan wanted was "joint defense against Communism." She did not ask for joint measures to deal with Soviet Russia. Nor did the movement sponsored by the Communists and their front organizations in favor of an alliance with Russia give any assurance that Russia would join China in opposing Japan. In fact, Japan and Russia shared a common objective: They both intended to isolate us from the Western powers, especially from the United States, so that we would be an easier prey to them.

Though Japan and Russia both had the same territorial design on China, they could still easily come to a compromise over the partition of China if it should become necessary for them to resist the Western powers, particularly the United States. Consequently, if China agreed to become a Japanese satellite by accepting Hirota's Three Demands, or if she accepted the German mediation after the outbreak of the Sino-Japanese War and came to terms with Japan, it would be hard to tell whether Japan would later advance northward or southward. It would be just as hard to tell whether Moscow would choose to fight Japan so that she could dominate China for herself or whether she would seek to coerce China, follow a neutral line and goad Japan to move southward if the Chinese Government should conclude an alliance with Russia.

In short, had China either yielded to Japan or aligned herself with Russia, the Western democracies would have been the losers and the history of World War II would have been different. Either course would have endangered both our national existence and world peace. For these reasons my final decision was that China's foreign policy should be one of promoting cooperation among the democratic nations within the framework of the League of Nations. It was also decided that efforts should be made to improve relations with Russia. In October 1936 Dr. T. F. Tsiang* was appointed ambassador to Russia succeeding Dr. W. W. Yen, with instructions to carry on active negotiations with Russia so long as they were conducted on a basis of equality.

Conclusion of the Sino-Russian Nonaggression Pact

The Marco Polo Bridge Incident** on July 7, 1937, which touched off our War of Resistance against Japan, had the effect of accelerating negotiations with Russia. On August 21 China and Russia signed a Nonaggression Pact, of which the principal provisions were:

Article 1. The two High Contracting Parties solemnly reaffirm that they condemn recourse to war for the solution of international controversies, and that they renounce it as an instrument of national policy in their relations with each other, and in pursuance of this pledge they undertake to refrain from any aggression against each other individually, or jointly with one or more other Powers.

Article 2. In the event that either of the High Contracting Parties should be subjected to aggression on the part of one or more third Powers, the other High Contracting Party obligates itself not to render assistance of any kind, directly or indirectly, to such third Power or Powers at any time during the entire conflict, and also to refrain from taking any action or entering into any agreement, which may be used by the aggressor or aggressors to the disadvantage of the Party subjected to aggression.

* Now China's permanent delegate to the United Nations.
** Japanese attack on the famous bridge south of Peiping.

China was the victim of Japanese aggression and fought Japan for eight long years during which the Sino-Soviet Non-aggression Pact should have been the basis of peaceful co-existence between the two countries. Let us see to what extent Moscow carried out the terms of this pact and what "peaceful coexistence" meant in practice.

The Sian Incident

To go back to the time when war with Japan seemed in-evitable, the Chinese Government tried to reach a settlement with the Chinese Communists at home. My view was that the Communist armed forces must be disbanded before the Com-munist problem could be considered as a political issue and solved as such. At the end of 1934, shortly after the success-ful completion of the fifth campaign against the Communist forces, I designated Chen Li-fu to handle this problem.

Earlier, in 1931, Ku Shun-chang, leader of the Chinese Communist secret service, had surrendered to us. This en-abled the Government to uproot all Communist secret organs in Nanking and Shanghai. Their so-called Central Commit-tee was broken up and had to move to Communist territories in southern Kiangsi for reorganization. In the autumn and winter of 1935 Chen Li-fu reported to me that through a friend's introduction Chou En-lai had approached Tseng Yang-fu, a Government representative in Hongkong. Chou hoped that the Government would designate someone to con-duct negotiations with the Communists. All Chou reportedly wanted was to stop the fighting at home and to resist Japan together; there were no other conditions. Chou wrote to Chen Kuo-fu and Chen Li-fu on September 1, reaffirming this position of the Chinese Communists.

On May 5, 1936, the Chinese Communists issued a circular telegram calling for "cessation of hostilities and holding of peace negotiations." Whereupon, Chou, as a representative of the Chinese Communist Party, and Pan Han-nien, as a representative of the Communist International, came to Shanghai to meet Chang Chun. At first I was somewhat doubtful of Pan's status. After some checking Chen Li-fu found out that Pan was in possession of a secret code for communicating with the Communist International. I felt that whether his status was true or not was immaterial. Therefore I did not press the matter. Later Pan came to Nanking to negotiate with Chen Li-fu. The Government put up to the Chinese Communists the following four points:

1. Abide by the Three People's Principles.
2. Obey Generalissimo Chiang Kai-shek's orders.
3. Abolish the "Red Army" and integrate it into the National Army.
4. Abrogate the Soviets and reorganize them as local governments.

After protracted discussions they finally accepted these four points. Understanding had been reached on practically all the issues. I was then in Sian. All that remained to be done was to get my final approval as soon as I was to return to Nanking.

During this period the Communists had started a propaganda offensive for "peace," and made Shensi province their first objective. They had established contact with Chang Hsueh-liang and Yang Hu-cheng, two military commanders in Shensi. Leaflets advocating "Fight the Japanese instead of the Communists" had made their appearance among the Manchurian Army under Chang. Meanwhile, there had even been reports that both Chang and Yang had formed ties with the Chinese Communist Party. In Sian, capital of Shensi, the two commanders had done their best to shield Communist elements and front organizations. As a result, both the "Third Party" and the "National Salvation Association" openly engaged in reactionary propaganda. Unless timely measures were taken, the situation could lead to a rebellion. Therefore I went to Sian in the hope that my presence there would constitute a stabilizing factor. It was also my plan to call all officers to a conference at the end of the year, at which I would announce the Government's policies on the continued prosecution of the military campaign against the Communists and on the question of armed resistance against Japan. I had every intention to expose the Communists' peace offensive so that these officers would not be taken in.

On December 12, in the dead of the night, I was suddenly seized in Sian by men under Chang Hsueh-liang and Yang Hu-cheng. I instantly realized that these two men must have acted under the strong influence of the Chinese Communists. Therefore, when Chang came to see me in the quarters where I was detained, I simply admonished him by saying: "Either for your own sake or for the sake of the nation, the only thing for you to do is to repent at once and escort me back to Nanking. You must not fall into the trap set by the Communists. Repent now before it is too late."

In these circumstances Chang did not dare to bring up the eight demands that they had prepared. All he said was that the situation was complicated and that it was not as simple as I had put it. He begged me to control my anger and hear him through. I cut him short and forbade him from touching on any political subjects. It was not until the third day that Chang finally mumbled, partly to persuade and partly to implore, the so-called eight demands he and the others had previously agreed upon among themselves. He also said that all I had to do was to sign my name and he would at once escort me back to Nanking. In reply, I said: "So long as I am a captive, there can be absolutely no discussion." At the time I thought that even if Chang and the others should come to their senses the Communists would seize upon this rare opportunity either to force me to accept the demands or to kill me. For to the Communists this meant life or death. As I was prepared to sacrifice myself if necessary, I flatly refused to discuss any political conditions with the rebels. The Government likewise ignored the preposterous demands made by Chang and Yang and promptly decided to send an army against them.

On December 22 my wife suddenly arrived in Sian. The first thing I said to her when we met was: "For the past ten days the rebels have been putting all kinds of pressure on me. Were I to accept their terms they would send me back to Nanking. You have come to be with me in my hour of peril. I believe you have done this out of consideration for our national interests and not for personal reasons alone. National interests must come first. If the rebels should ask you to persuade me to sign any terms you must resolutely refuse. We would rather die than accede to these demands." I am proud to say my wife was equally and similarly determined. She would never persuade me to do anything against my principles. "I am here to share your fate," she avowed. Three days later, on Christmas Day, we safely returned to Nanking without having to subscribe to any conditions.

The whole story behind this sensational incident, however, became known only much later. The initiative came from Chang Hsueh-liang and Yang Hu-cheng was the author of the kidnapping idea. Contacts between Chang and Yang and the Communists had been established six months earlier, and Chang was already in an advanced state of collusion with the Communists. Lest the Government get wind of their secret contacts, most of Chang's negotiations with the Communists were carried on in Yenan in northern Shensi, which at the time was garrisoned by troops under Chang's command.

A week before the incident Chang Chi-lan, a Chinese newspaper editor who was himself a revolutionary in the earlier days, came to see me at Hwachin Hot Springs, on the outskirts of Sian. In the course of a general discussion we came to the unrest reportedly in existence in Chang's Manchurian

Army as a result of negotiations with the Communists in northern Shensi. He said that these rumors could be a trick on the part of the Communists to sow suspicion between the Government and Chang Hsueh-liang, and he suggested that the situation be watched closely. I replied: "Being a native of northern Shensi, you are naturally more concerned with this problem even than others. Please tell me whether your correspondent in Yenan has sent you any important news lately." He affirmed that there were many rumors but he would not place too much credence in them. He spoke hesitatingly and evasively. Finally he expressed the opinion that if left alone these rumors would probably die in due course. Whereupon I came to the point and asked him a direct question: "Speaking of rumors, could it be that you, too, have heard of Chang Hsueh-liang's secret negotiations with the Communists in Yenan?" Somewhat taken aback, he answered "Yes," adding, however, that he did not think that this could be true.

In analyzing the news Chang Chi-lan said that if Chang Hsueh-liang were really sincere in his support of the Government for united resistance against Japan, he would have frankly reported to the Government and in no circumstances would he have gone over the Government's head to establish contacts with the Communists. Hence, he continued, the said rumor could be a Communist device to cause misunderstanding between the Government and Chang Hsueh-liang. In conclusion, he said, however, that in view of all these rumors it would be wise to take precautions. When I heard this, I realized the situation was serious. He added that special attention should be paid to one particular development, i.e., people in Sian were saying, "Let us stop fighting the Communists and resist the Japanese together." He said that from observations derived from his visit in Sian for the past ten days, he felt that this problem was more important than any others of the moment. He asked me what I thought. I replied that the Government's consistent policy to resist Japan had been reaffirmed following the successful conclusion of the military campaign against the Communists in Kiangsi the previous year. I pointed out, however, that what the Communists wanted was not united resistance against Japan but the cessation of military drives against them. In other words, "united resistance against Japan" was merely a means to an end. The problem which merited careful study was how to make the Communists really resist Japan with the rest of the nation.

I also suggested to Mr. Chang that his paper should explain this to the general public so that the people would all understand what the Government was trying to do. He asked whether he could pass on my remarks to his friends in Sian first. I said: "Please do. Furthermore, I intend to call all senior officers in the area to a conference in the middle of the month when I shall take up this question for discussion."

Later, during the days of my captivity, Mr. Chang's paper used my conversation with him at Hwachin Hot Springs as material in leaflets air-dropped over Sian asking Chang Hsueh-liang and Yang Hu-cheng and the Manchurian Army to call off their revolt.

Communist front organizations, namely, the "Third Party," the "National Salvation Association" and the "Students' Federation" carried out the initial reactionary propaganda to instigate rebellious actions by Chang Hsueh-liang and Yang Hu-cheng. While these neutralist elements were not Communists, the latter made use of them. As a matter of fact, the Communists did not want them in their party, because their purpose would be better served by having these people follow a neutralist course or speak in the name of the "Third Party." Not being Communists, these people were able openly to spread rumors not only among the civilians but also among the armed forces. They even subjected Chang Hsueh-liang and the troops under him to an intensive propaganda, and they kept on provoking Chang, who, being torn between "suppression of the Communists" and "resistance against Japan," finally succumbed to this incessant offensive by the neutralists. Chang Hsueh-liang, on his part, never would admit that he had been influenced by Communist instigations. He said he was merely anxious to fight Japan so as to avenge the loss of Manchuria, and his original idea was to make use of the strength of the Communists to fight Japan.

Chang Hsueh-liang, in his own account of the events leading up to the Sian Incident, said that he had fallen for the Communist intrigue not because it was particularly effective but because of the existence of internal contradictions in our own midst. This had created an opening for Communist infiltration. Chang recalled how he had assumed military command when he was still in his twenties, how he had taken part in civil wars, and how he had succeeded in turning erstwhile foes into friends. He himself originally had fought the Government and how finally for the sake of national unity he had declared his allegiance to the Government. He thought the Communists could be dealt with in the same way, since they were also Chinese. While because of certain differences today they were the enemy, tomorrow they could become friends if both sides had a common national objective. He regretted that he had not made a thorough study of the Communist Party and hence lacked the correct understanding but there were others who had made the same mistake. Since his major premise was wrong, all his subsequent moves were also incorrect.

Also according to Chang Hsueh-liang's own account, following his talks with me in the first two days of my detention, he realized that in view of my firm attitude and strong determination not to be coerced, there was no hope of carrying out his original plan. Meantime disagreements between him and the others broke out. It soon became clear that the situation was not as simple as they had envisioned it to be at first. What particularly upset him was the Government's decision to launch a punitive expedition against him and the other rebels. He became all the more aware of the seriousness of the situation as it threatened to get out of hand. On the third day of the incident he decided to send a plane to Yenan to bring Communist representatives to Sian to discuss matters of cooperation with the view of securing Communist participation in a joint military affairs committee to be composed of representatives of the Manchurian Army, the Northwest Army (under Yang Hu-cheng) and the Communist Army. This new turn of events enabled the Communists and their front organizations to attain their objective of placing Chang and Yang under their control.

The Declaration on Joint Effort to Face the National Crisis

In February 1937 Ku Chu-tung, director of the Provisional Headquarters at Sian, began to reorganize the Chinese Communist forces. Questions concerning party and political affairs would be left for Chou En-lai to take up again when he came to Nanking, but all discussions were still to be based on the same four points that were discussed before the Sian Incident. On February 10 the Chinese Communist Party's Central Committee sent a telegram embodying the results of the negotiations to our Party's Central Executive Committee during its Third Plenary Session, proposing the following four principles:

1. The Chinese Communist Party is to stop throughout the country all its plans of armed uprisings aimed at overthrowing the National Government.
2. The Soviet regime is to be renamed the Special Area Government of the Republic of China; the Red Army is to be renamed National Revolutionary Forces under the direct command of the Central Government and of the National Military Council in Nanking.

3. Thorough democratic systems through general elections are to be carried out in the Special Area.
4. The policy of land confiscation is to cease and the Common Program of the Anti-Japanese National United Front is to be resolutely enforced.

On February 21 our Party's Central Executive Committee adopted at its Third Plenary Session the "Resolution for Complete Eradication of the Red Menace." This resolution, meant to counter the four principles brought up by the Chinese Communists, comprised the following four points:

1. The organization and command of the nation's armed forces must be unified before there can be any effective control and operation. The simultaneous existence of armed forces that follow entirely incompatible political ideologies is impermissible. Therefore, the so-called Red Army and its units under various specious names should be completely abolished.
2. The unitary administrative power is a prerequisite to national unification. The existence of two administrations side by side is impermissible. Therefore, the so-called Soviet government and other organizations detrimental to unification should be completely abolished.
3. Communism is absolutely incompatible with the Three People's Principles which are dedicated to saving the nation and the people. It is against the interests of the Chinese people, their opportunity of livelihood and their way of life. Therefore, it must cease its operation.
4. Class struggle is based on the interests of a single class. Its method is to divide society into so many opposite classes and then set them hating and killing one another. It necessarily resorts to fighting over the control of the masses and to armed uprisings, resulting in social disorders and general sufferings. Therefore, it must cease.

After the outbreak of the Sino-Japanese War, the Central Committee of the Chinese Communist Party issued a declaration expressing its readiness to face the national crisis with the rest of the nation. This declaration contained four pledges as follows:

1. As Dr. Sun Yat-sen's Three People's Principles answer the needs of China, the Chinese Communist Party will fight for their complete realization.
2. The Chinese Communist Party will abolish all its policy of armed uprisings and its Sovietization movements against the Kuomintang regime, and will stop its program of dispossessing the landlords through violence.
3. The Chinese Communist Party will abrogate its existing Soviet government and hereafter practice democracy so as to unify the administrative power of the country.
4. The Chinese Communist Party will stop calling its armed forces the Red Army, abolish their existing military designations, integrate them into the National Revolutionary Forces, subject them to the jurisdiction of the National Military Council of the National Government and await orders to march to the front to fight the Japanese.

In response to this declaration I issued a statement on February 23 in which I said:

The Chinese Communist Party's declaration is a proof that national consciousness has triumphed over all other considerations. The points contained in the declaration such as abandonment of the policy of armed uprisings and Sovietization movements, and abolition of the Soviet area and of the Red Army, are all essential conditions for mobilizing the nation's strength for resistance against aggression. The reference to its readiness to fight for the realization of the Three People's Principles goes further to show that all of China's efforts are directed toward one purpose.

Since the Chinese Communists have given up their preconceived ideas and recognized the importance of national independence and national interests, we hope they will sincerely fulfill their pledges. Furthermore, we hope that like everybody else in the country they will contribute their strength to the nation's defense against aggression under a unified command so as to complete the task of National Revolution.

At the time of my statement I really believed that the Chinese Communists had repented and were sincere in their expressed readiness to join the rest of the nation in the fight against aggression. Besides, even when directing military campaigns against the Communist troops I regarded them as Chinese and hoped that eventually they would become loyal to the nation again. It was also my belief that with adequate vigilance and precautions they could be kept in line. So long as they would give up armed insurrection they could work with other political parties for China's revolution and national salvation. That was why from the beginning of the Government's military operations against the Communists in 1930 till 1936 I had used military force and political means simultaneously. I took the Chinese Communist Party's declaration as evidence of the effect of the Government's moral influence. Meanwhile, all patriotic and farsighted people in the nation also took it as the successful outcome of Government's policy, and as a good augury for victory in the nation's War of Resistance.

No one could have foreseen that in their subsequent actions the Chinese Communists would go completely against their solemn pledges. I, too, was overconfident in my judgment, and this led to tragic consequences afterward. They proved that they cannot be expected to have any sense of loyalty to their own country. They are not capable of having any national consciousness. This experience has taught us a bitter lesson. Though it has been a matter of great humiliation to me personally to recount, it may not be without some value to the free world in its present struggle against Communism.

Reorganization of Communist Troops by the Government

The National Military Council issued an order on August 22, 1937, appointing Chu Teh and Peng Teh-huai commander and deputy commander, respectively, of the Eighth Route Army of the National Revolutionary Forces. The said army, composed of three divisions with a total strength of 20,000 men, was assigned to the Second War Area in northern Shansi under General Yen Hsi-shan's command.

In the meantime, Liu Tsu-han and Chang Kuo-tao were appointed chairman and vice-chairman, respectively, of the Shensi-Kansu-Ninghsia Border Area Government.

Later, Communist troops under Yeh Ting and Hsiang Ying, south of the Yangtze River, were reorganized into the New Fourth Army, with Yeh as commander and Hsiang as deputy commander. This army, composed of four columns with a numerical strength of over 10,000 men, was assigned to the Third War Area under General Ku Chu-tung's command.

Kuomintang's "Resolution for the Complete Eradication of the Red Menace," the four pledges of the Chinese Communists, and the integration of the Communist troops into the National Revolutionary Forces were to become the basis of "peaceful coexistence" between Kuomintang and the Chinese Communists during the Sino-Japanese War. Now let us see how the Chinese Communists made use of all this for expansionist purposes behind the façade of "peaceful coexistence."

The People's Political Council and the Program of Resistance and National Reconstruction

In July 1937 when the policy of sustained resistance against Japan was being formulated, the Government called a conference for this purpose at Kuling* to which representatives of various political parties as well as a number of nonparty lead-

* A well-known mountain resort in Kiangsi.

ers were invited. When the major hostilities broke out the Government set up a National Defense Advisory Council composed of leaders of the Young China Party, the National Socialist Party, the Chinese Communist Party and various cultural organizations. They were to advise the Government. On July 6, 1938, the People's Political Council was established. It was composed of representatives of various political parties, ethnic minorities, professions and geographical regions. At its first conference it adopted the Program of Resistance and National Reconstruction, which affirmed:

1. The Three People's Principles as the highest guiding principles in national salvation and reconstruction.
2. The over-all authority of the supreme commander.
3. As a foreign policy, China's support for the international peace organization and the promotion of international cooperation in a spirit of independence and sovereignty.
4. The principles guiding the establishment of wartime democratic institutions and the adoption of measures for wartime political, economic and cultural enterprises.
5. The policy of cultivating the people's morale and safeguarding China's culture.
6. The Program as the basis of peaceful existence among the various political parties.

The People's Political Council could be described as China's wartime parliament, to which the Government submitted reports on military and political affairs at regular sessions and, in case of important developments, at emergency sessions, for the purpose of soliciting its members' views and enlisting their support. Though the People's Political Council's proposals were only for the Government's reference and adoption at its discretion, all important resolutions became laws and were duly promulgated by the Government for enforcement.

This is how the Chinese Communist representatives behaved in the council:

1. They used the council as a platform for propaganda to make the people believe that they were firm in their determination to resist Japan and that the Communist forces were heroic fighters.
2. They persuaded some of the councilors, who either belonged to other political parties or had no party affiliations, to be neutral when the Communists attacked the Government, and to blame the Government in any armed conflict between Communist and Government forces.
3. Whenever they failed in their propaganda, or when the councilors in general withheld their support, the Communists would boycott the council, or walk out in the middle of a session, in an attempt to sabotage or obstruct the council's proceedings.

Nevertheless, the People's Political Council won the confidence of the nation at large and the Program of Resistance and National Reconstruction provided a rallying point for national solidarity during the war.

Mao Tse-tung's Gestures at the Beginning of the War

In the autumn of 1937 when Chu Teh was leading the Eighth Route Army out of northern Shensi,* Mao Tse-tung, in a speech to the troops at Yenan, said in part as follows:

The Sino-Japanese War gives the Chinese Communists an excellent opportunity to grow. Our policy is to devote 70 per cent of our effort to our own expansion, 20 per cent to coping with the Government, and 10 per cent to fighting the Japanese.

This policy is to be carried out in three stages. During the first stage we are to compromise with Kuomintang in order to ensure our existence and growth. During the second stage we are to achieve a parity in strength with Kuomintang. During the third stage we are to penetrate deep into parts of Central China to establish bases for attacks on Kuomintang.

* Communist base wherein lies Yenan.

In October the Communists' Central Political Bureau, in a resolution on "The Future of the War of Resistance and the Chinese Communists' Line of Action," laid down the following programs:

1. To expand and to strengthen the United Front by removing the veils covering secret Communist organizations and activities and by extending regional operations to a nationwide scale for the purpose of obtaining for the Communist Party a legal and equal competitive status.
2. Force being the determining factor in China's politics, emphasis should be put on expanding the Communist Party's armed forces in the course of the War of Resistance to lay the foundation in the struggle for political power in the future.

This was the Chinese Communists' line of action marked out at the outset of China's war with Japan, which they studiously followed during the eight ensuing years. They had a supreme director in the person of Stalin, chief of the Russian Communists. The principle that Soviet Russia's interests were always put above those of the Chinese Communists themselves was amply proved by their actions.

In November 1937, at the time of the Nine-Power Conference in Brussels, Stalin unexpectedly received Chang Chung, counselor of the Chinese Embassy in Moscow, and confided in him that he thought that China was fighting hard and well. If the situation should become unfavorable to China, Soviet Russia might declare war on Japan.

In 1938 a tripartite alliance of Japan, Germany and Italy was fast taking shape. Moscow looked upon China's war with Japan as something which could relieve it of anxiety in the East and hoped very much that the Sino-Japanese War would be prolonged. After the fall of Nanking and when the Japanese were driving toward Wuhan, Soviet Russia's close friendly attitude toward China and the material aid given us, which was motivated by this hope, was reflected in the Chinese Communists' attitude toward the Government. In his letter to me dated June 10, Stalin expressed his "firm faith" in China's ultimate victory. In September the Chinese Communist Party's Central Committee held its Sixth Plenary Session at Yenan. Chou En-lai did not even wait for the session to finish before he came to see me in Wuhan with a letter from Mao Tse-tung, which said in part:

At the Sixth Plenary Session of our party, it was generally felt that the War of Resistance is about to enter upon a new stage, which will be characterized by greater difficulties on the one hand, and by greater progress on the other. The task before the nation is to unite the people, consolidate and expand the anti-Japanese front, persevere in our war efforts, mobilize new strength, overcome difficulties and prepare for a counteroffensive.

We also deem unity and solidarity during this period as of greater importance than during any previous period. The only way before us is for various political parties and factions, and the people as a whole, to exert their utmost under your leadership, in guarding against and destroying the enemy's schemes of subversion, removing the people's pessimistic feelings, in heightening their national consciousness, in fortifying their faith in the ultimate victory, and in adopting such wartime policies as are needed at this new stage. Only thus can we achieve our object of forestalling the enemy's offensive and preparing our own counteroffensive.

At this juncture the interests of Kuomintang and of the Chinese Communist Party are identical, and this is also an important factor in our long war and lasting solidarity. I am of the firm belief that only a lasting solidarity between the two parties is capable of sustaining a long war. However ferocious he may be, the enemy will be defeated in the end, for our nation of 450,-000,000 people will be able to surmount all difficulties and gather strength during this long and bitter struggle, to expel the enemy in a counteroffensive, and to establish our nation as a strong power in East Asia. This is my view which I trust is shared by your good self.

The general tenor of this letter, paying as it did lip service to "lasting solidarity between the two parties" and "unity and solidarity of the Chinese nation," sounded so unlike the Chinese Communists that it aroused my suspicion. I knew Mao Tse-tung's call for "lasting solidarity" would be a cover for many substantive demands to come. Sure enough, Chou En-lai soon afterward made the following four proposals to Kuomintang: (1) To stop all inter-party strife; (2) To permit Chinese Communists to become members of Kuomintang, or to permit some of them to join first and, if the results are good, to allow the rest of them to follow suit later; (3) To abolish all Chinese Communist youth organizations and allow all members of these organizations to join the San Min Chu I Youth Corps;* and (4) To permit all Chinese Communists who join Kuomintang or the San Min Chu I Youth Corps to retain their membership in the Chinese Communist Party.

The Chinese Communists were again trying to infiltrate Kuomintang on a large scale. In view of our painful experience between 1924 and 1927 we decided never to allow ourselves to be deceived again. But despite our rejection I continued to hope that the Chinese Communists, as a result of the national spirit and national consciousness that had been aroused by the war, and under the pressure of popular sentiments and public opinion, would keep their pledges and make their contributions to the war effort under the National Government's leadership.

Stalin's Change of Attitude

The Chamberlain-Daladier visit to Munich further whetted Hitler's appetite for aggression. Europe was on the verge of an explosion. On March 10, 1939, Stalin suddenly declared at the 18th National Congress of the Russian Communist Party: "A new imperialist war is entering its second year. This war extends from Shanghai in the East to Gibraltar in the West. It involves 500,000,000 people." He stressed that henceforth

---

* The Three People's Principles Youth Corps.

Soviet Russia must rely on her own strength to ensure her security. He also said that Soviet Russia would strive together with other nations to preserve peace and to establish friendly relations with neighboring countries. This speech was the signal for Stalin's change of tactics from the "United Front" to "defense of the Fatherland."

Stalin's speech obviously had the effect of encouraging Nazi aggression. On March 14 Hitler carved up Czechoslovakia, and soon afterward annexed that country altogether. Subsequently Stalin carried on secret negotiations with Germany and, at the same time, conducted open discussions with Britain and France. It was our Government's hope that Soviet Russia's negotiations with Britain and France would succeed in preventing a major outbreak in Europe.

Sun Fo, president of the Legislative Yuan, was then in Moscow. On June 16, at the time of the signing of a Sino-Russian commercial pact, he forwarded a letter from me to Stalin. In this letter I said I reposed hope in the cooperation between Britain and Soviet Russia. Stalin, in his reply of July 9, said in part: "If our negotiations with the European countries should produce satisfactory results—which is not impossible—this may be an important step toward the creation of a bloc of peace-loving nations in the Far East as well. Time is working favorably toward the formation of such a bloc."

The meaning of this passage is ambiguous. What he called "negotiations with the European countries" and "a bloc of peace-loving nations," could be taken to mean a coalition of Britain, the United States, France and Russia which would be the kind of coalition we had hoped for. Yet his remarks could also mean a coalition of Germany, Japan, Italy and Russia. That would be something the Japanese militarists and German Nazis wanted.

Apparently it was not Stalin's wish that there should be excessive misgivings in our midst, for he added:

As a result of the now two-year-old war with China, Japan has lost her balance, has started to be nervous and is hurling herself recklessly now against England and now against Soviet Russia and the Outer Mongolian Republic. This is a sign of Japan's weakness. Such conduct on Japan's part may unite everyone against her. From Soviet Russia Japan has already received the counterblows she deserves. Britain and the United States are waiting for an opportune moment to do harm to Japan. And we have no doubt that before long Japan will receive another counterblow from China, one that is a hundred times mightier.

On the surface, this sounded like a compliment to our war effort. Besides, it mentioned the Russo-Japanese clash at Nomanhan as proof of Russia's anti-Japanese feelings. Actually his reference to Japan's attacks on "Soviet Russia and the Republic of Outer Mongolia" camouflaged the beginning of Russo-Japanese negotiations. Besides, the part about Outer Mongolia conflicted with China's sovereign rights in that area.

On August 23 Stalin openly concluded the Russo-German Mutual Assistance Pact with Hitler, thereby hastening the outbreak of the war in Europe. In April 1941 he concluded a neutrality pact with Japan.

The Chinese Communists' Change of Attitude

The International Communists had carried on their "United Front" activities under "anti-Fascist" slogans. Now Soviet Russia, "fatherland of Socialism" suddenly turned round and signed a Mutual Assistance Pact with Germany to precipitate a war between the latter and the Western democracies. This made it necessary for the international Communists not only to cease their anti-Fascist movement but also to cooperate with Nazi espionage organizations to sabotage the Western nations' war preparations and operations in the name of opposing an "Imperialist War." The Chinese Communists, toeing the Moscow line, adopted the following measures:

1. In the diplomatic field the Chinese Communists praised the Russo-German Pact as a victory for Soviet Russia's foreign policy. On September 1 Mao Tse-tung, in an interview with the *Hsinhua Daily News,* a Chinese Communist organ, said, in his opinion, "The said pact upsets the intrigue of Chamberlain and Daladier and the international reactionary capitalist class to provoke a war between Soviet Russia and Germany, upsets the encirclement of Soviet Russia by the reactionary bloc of Italy, Germany and Japan, solidifies the peace between Soviet Russia and Germany and secures further progress of Socialist reconstruction in Soviet Russia."

After the outbreak of the war in Europe the Chinese Communists openly condemned it as an Imperialist war. On September 14 Mao Tse-tung, in a speech entitled "The Second Imperialist War" delivered in Yenan, clearly stated that "regardless of whether it is Germany, Italy or Japan, or whether it is Britain, the United States or France, all Imperialist nations directly or indirectly taking part in this war could only have one objective which is that of the Imperialist counter-revolution against the interests of the people." The political views he expressed were "oppose the Imperialist War, and organize a Revolutionary War." That is why the Chinese Communists were openly opposed to American and British "Imperialism" during this period. They attacked the Government for its policy of cooperation with the United States and Britain, and once again started a movement for an alignment with Soviet Russia. They also tried to turn our National War of Resistance against Japan into a so-called "Revolutionary War" which is just another name for civil war.

2. In the military field the Chinese Communists' strategy of devoting 70 per cent of their effort toward their own expansion became more obvious than ever. In reality, it was a side current in the international antiwar movement instigated by Moscow. Meanwhile, Mao Tse-tung tried to carry out the

third stage of his plan worked out earlier in the war to develop the Communist Party's strength.

In September 1937 the 18th Group Army* entered Shansi. Soon afterward it began to take independent actions in setting up two military districts, one on the Shansi-Hopei-Chahar border, and the other on the Shansi-Hopei-Honan border. Furthermore, it continued to pour into the great plains of Hopei, Shantung and Honan. Everywhere it went it attacked and absorbed local armed forces and anti-Japanese guerrilla units who were under the Government's command and added them to its own numerical strength. Its troops under Lu Cheng-tsao, which had entered central Hopei, surrounded and attacked the Government's anti-Japanese forces led by Chang Ying-wo at Po Yeh, while its troops under Ying Jen-fu, which had entered the Hopei-Shantung border region, attacked the Government's 53rd Mobile Force at Yehshan and killed its commanding officer, Sun Chung-wen. In the meantime, Communist forces under Liu Po-cheng and Hsu Hsiang-chien disarmed local militia in central Hopei and western Shantung, attacked the Hopei and Shantung provincial governments to make it generally impossible for them to perform their functions.

After March 1939 the attitude of the Chinese Communists worsened. They marked out a special area on the Shensi-Kansu-Ninghsia border where they set up a special area local government. In addition they planned insurrections at other places. In the east their "Shantung Column" crossed into northern Kiangsu and resorted to violence. Their 18th Group Army in Shansi established a Border** District Government at Wutai, while in southern Shansi they instigated a revolt of Government troops.

On June 10, 1939, I sent for Chou En-lai and Yeh Chien-

---

* New name for the Eighth Route Army.
** Shansi-Hopei-Chahar-Suiyuan.

ying* and cautioned them accordingly. I said the Chinese Communists should faithfully abide by their own pledges, obey Government orders, enforce laws of the state and settle local incidents.

In January 1940 Ho Ying-chin, the Government's chief of the general staff, told Yeh Chien-ying that the Chinese Communists must stop adding to their numbers and marking out military districts without authorization. The Communists' demand was that the 18th Group Army be expanded to comprise three armies of nine divisions and that the Shensi-Kansu-Ninghsia border district be not only maintained but even enlarged. The discussions bogged down.

Following this, Government forces in Hopei** were forced by the Chinese Communists to evacuate the province, while troops in Shansi east of the Yellow River were also subjected to Communist attacks with the result that there was great confusion in the whole of that province. In Shantung Government forces in the western part of the province were forced to retreat to the north of the Yellow River. Furthermore, the Communist troops spread from western Shantung over to eastern Honan and northern Anhwei in an attempt to link up with units of the New Fourth Army then moving northward from south of the Yangtze River.

On July 16, 1940, the Government, with a view to preventing more clashes in various parts of the country, worked out an arrangement with the Communists represented by Chou En-lai and Yeh Chien-ying. This agreed arrangement was later handed to Chou En-lai, who took it to northern Shensi on July 24, for observance by Communist field commanders. Meanwhile, all Government forces were ordered to avoid conflicts with the 18th Group Army and the New Fourth Army. Important points in the arrangement were:

* Yeh was then the Communist chief of staff.
** Under Lu Chung-lin and Chu Huai-ping.

1. The Shensi-Kansu-Ninghsia Border Area (to comprise eighteen counties by approval) was to be renamed the Northern Shensi Administrative Area, and placed temporarily under the Executive Yuan but subject to the direction of the Shensi provincial government.

2. The areas of operations for the 18th Group Army and the New Fourth Army were to be redefined. The Hopei-Chahar War Area was to be abolished, and the two provinces of Hopei and Chahar, plus that part of Shantung province north of the Yellow River, were to be assigned to the Second War Area, of which Yen Hsi-shan was to remain as commander and Chu Teh, a Communist, as deputy commander, to direct military operations in accordance with orders of the National Military Council.

3. Both the 18th Group Army and the New Fourth Army were to be entirely moved to the above-designated areas within one month after receipt of orders.

4. The 18th Group Army was to have three armies of six divisions, plus three supplementary regiments, with permission to add two more supplementary regiments. The New Fourth Army was to be reorganized into two divisions.

The New Fourth Army Incident

Though the High Command's order to avoid conflicts was uniformly obeyed by Government troops, the same could not be said of the 18th Group Army. In August 1940 Communist troops in western Shantung moved into southern Shantung to attack the seat of the Shantung provincial government. Shen Hung-lieh, governor of Shantung, desirous of averting a head-on clash, withdrew from Lutsun. Meanwhile, units of the New Fourth Army crossed the Yangtze River from the south to attack two towns* which were then under the control of

* Jukao and Taihsing.

the Kiangsu provincial government at a time when troops there were engaged in battle with the Japanese. The New Fourth Army continued its attack until the provincial seat of government was transferred elsewhere.

In view of the serious situation created by the Communist attacks on Government troops in Shantung and Kiangsu, the High Command, through General Ho Ying-chin, dispatched a telegram on October 19 to the New Fourth Army's commander setting the end of November as the deadline for his units to arrive at the new area of operations north of the Yellow River.

On December 9 I personally issued an order to Chu Teh, Peng Teh-huai, Yeh Chien-ying and Hsiang Ying for all units of the 18th Group Army south of the Yellow River to move to the north before December 30, and for all units of the New Fourth Army south of the Yangtze River to move to the north before December 31 and to cross the Yellow River northward by January 31 of the new year.

The New Fourth Army refused to move northward as ordered. Instead, it made plans to control the triangular area formed by Nanking, Shanghai and Hangchow. On January 5, 1941, its units even attacked the Government's 40th Division at Sanshih. Whereupon Ku Chu-tung, commander of the Third War Area, took disciplinary action by disbanding the Communist forces between January 6 and January 14. On January 17 the National Military Council ordered the cancellation of the New Fourth Army's designation. Yeh Ting, who was captured, was turned over to the military court for trial.

The Russo-Japanese Neutrality Pact

In March 1941 Yosue Matsuoka, Japan's foreign minister, went to Moscow after a visit to Germany. The Soviet deputy foreign minister told the Chinese ambassador in Moscow that

Stalin had received Matsuoka for purely protocol reasons. On April 11 A. S. Panyushkin, Soviet ambassador to China, assured the Chinese Government that Soviet Russia would not sacrifice the interests of a friendly country for selfish considerations and that the Soviet Government was only extending to Matsuoka the usual diplomatic courtesy. Two days later, on April 13, the Russo-Japanese Neutrality Pact was announced.

In this pact, Japan recognized the so-called Republic of Outer Mongolia in exchange for Soviet Russia's recognition of so-called Manchukuo. This was not only detrimental to China's territorial sovereignty but also violated the Sino-Soviet Agreement of 1924 and the Sino-Russian Nonaggression Pact of 1937. The sanctity of treaty obligations meant nothing to the Russian Communists.

The German-Russian War and the Chinese Communists' Attitude

The war which broke out between Soviet Russia and Germany in June 1941 forced Stalin to change his attitude again, and Mao Tse-tung had to change his accordingly. During this period, the Chinese Communists' relations with the Government were fairly stable.

In August 1942 German forces penetrated deep into the Caucasus and were approaching the Volga River. In September they reached the outskirts of Stanlingrad. From October to November, the Russian and German troops fought from house to house, street to street, in the city of Stalingrad itself. On October 13 Mao Tse-tung sent Lin Piao to see me at Sian. The latter did his best to assure me of the Chinese Communists' support for the Government's Program of Resistance and National Reconstruction* and of their sincere desire for "complete unification and lasting solidarity." Lin said:

* Adopted in 1938, the second year of the Sino-Japanese War.

Mao Tse-tung has time and again told me that henceforth our two parties should "move closer toward each other and merge into one body" in order that we could proceed from the existing "sincere cooperation" to "complete unification and lasting solidarity." Such slogans represent the mature thoughts of the Chinese Communists in general. They have appeared in our Declaration of July 7, and have become a code of political action on the part of the Communist party as a whole, which no one can change.

Although the Chinese Communists believe in Communism, they know it cannot be put into practice in China in ways prescribed by Engels, Marx, Lenin and Stalin. What they advocated and did is definitely not applicable to China.

As to the programs of revolution and national reconstruction as laid down in Dr. Sun's Three People's Principles, and the policies which the Central Government has adopted for resistance and national reconstruction, the Chinese Communists take no exception to them whatsoever.

At present, because of our different ways of doing things, it may still be difficult to forge a complete entity. We can only strive in accordance with the Three People's Principles and the Program of Resistance and National Reconstruction, hoping that we do not go against the people's wishes in our advance together toward the common goal of resistance through solidarity and national reconstruction through unification. It is the expectation of the Chinese Communists that a solid foundation for final victory will be laid under your leadership.

Mao Tse-tung's attitude this time was again a reflection of Moscow's policy toward China. In October of the same year Panyushkin returned to Russia for consultations. When he came back he brought a letter from Stalin. Dated December 11, it expressed Stalin's hope for peaceful coexistence, obviously a blueprint for Mao Tse-tung's views on the same subject. It contained the following important points:

"The friendship of our two peoples has been manifested during the most difficult trials. It will be strong and sincere for a long time to come.

"After the victorious completion of the war, this friendship will unquestionably serve as a firm basis for collaboration be-

tween our two peoples in the building of a lasting peace for
the whole world."

Soviet Aggression in Outer Mongolia and the Annexation of Tannu Tuva

In June 1944 while the Russo-German War was raging in
Europe, Soviet Russia annexed Tannu Tuva, part of China's
territory in Outer Mongolia. It will be recalled that the
Karakhan Declaration of July 15, 1919, clearly stated that
Soviet Russia abandoned her special rights in Outer Mongolia.
Yet in 1921 Russian troops in Siberia invaded Outer Mongolia
on the pretext of pursuing the White "Guardists." In July of
the same year Russian troops entered Ulan Bator (Urga).
Shortly afterward the "Mongolian People's Revolutionary
Party," a creation of the Russian Communists, set up a so-
called Mongolian People's Revolutionary Government. In
August Russian troops from Siberia entered Tannu Tuva,
where a puppet government was set up and a Russia-type
"constitution" promulgated. Soon Tannu Tuva became Soviet
Russia's first satellite.

Article 5 of the Sino-Soviet Agreement of May 1924 stipulated that "the Soviet Government recognizes Outer Mongolia as a part of the territory of the Republic of China, and
respects China's sovereignty in the said territory." The Soviet
Government also agreed to hold discussion with the Chinese
Government for the withdrawal of Soviet troops from Outer
Mongolia.

In July of the same year, however, Moscow instigated the
puppet regime of Outer Mongolia to hold a Soviet-style "People's Representative Congress," to promulgate a Soviet-type
"constitution," and to rename the territory the "Mongolian
People's Republic." Thus, in one stroke, Soviet Russia set at
naught the stipulations in the Sino-Soviet Agreement of 1924.
Soon afterward Outer Mongolia became Soviet Russia's second satellite.

On June 20, 1941, when German troops invaded Soviet Russia, the puppet regime in Tannu Tuva convened its great Huruldan (parliament) and declared war on Germany on the side of Soviet Russia. On August 17 the same year, also upon Soviet Russia's direction, it petitioned Moscow for Tuva's incorporation into the Soviet Union. On October 13 the Supreme Soviet approved Tuva as an autonomous regime of the U.S.S.R. Thus, from a Soviet satellite Tannu Tuva became a region of Soviet Russia. This process of absorption set a precedent for Soviet Russia in handling other satellites subsequently.

Sinkiang's Return to the National Fold

When Japan occupied Manchuria and followed it up by exerting pressure on Hopei and Chahar, Russia was busily encroaching upon Sinkiang in the Northwest where she infiltrated its local administration and exploited its economic resources. After the Soviet-instigated *coup d'état* in Sinkiang on April 12, 1933, which put Sheng Shih-tsai at the head of the local administration, Soviet Russia steadily stepped up her military aggression and political domination over the province.

In January 1934, when Ma Chung-ying's troops laid siege to Tihua (Urumchi), Soviet Russia sent Red Army units into Sinkiang to help Sheng against Ma. This was her first step toward the military control of Sinkiang. In 1938 Soviet Russia, on the pretext of preventing Japanese aggression, sent a regular Red Army unit known as the "Red Eighth Regiment" into Hami. This completed her scheme of putting Sinkiang under her military control and cutting off Sinkiang's communications with other parts of China.

In Soviet Russia's aggression in Sinkiang military domination went on side by side with economic exploitation. In 1935, working through the Soviet-Sinkiang Trading Company, she concluded a 5,000,000 gold roubles loan agreement with Sheng

Shih-tsai. The Chinese Government's efforts to prevent the signing of the agreement were in vain. In 1938 Soviet Russia induced Sheng Shih-tsai to go to Moscow, where he joined the Communist Party. After this Soviet control over Sinkiang became stronger than ever. Soviet personnel were found in government organs throughout the province. In November 1940, after the conclusion of the Russo-German Mutual Assistance Pact and at a time when the war in Europe was rising in its tempo, Soviet Russia sent a secret envoy to Tihua to compel Sheng Shih-tsai to sign an agreement leasing to her Sinkiang's tin mines. Using the mining concession as a pretext, she grabbed rights to build railways and highways, to install telephones, to set up radio stations, to carry on surveys, to prospect for mineral resources, to build houses and barracks for Russian personnel and for Russian troops to take up garrison duties throughout the province. The duration of this agreement was set at fifty years. This constituted an indisputable proof of Soviet intentions to annex the whole of Sinkiang.

Earlier I have mentioned that Mao Tse-tung's remnants fled northwestward from Szechwan in August 1935. They were really heading for Sinkiang, where they hoped to obtain material supplies from Soviet Russia. It was only because they were intercepted by Government troops on the Shensi-Kansu border that they turned toward northern Shensi to join the local Communists under Liu Tse-tan and Kao Kang.

Sinkiang is part of China's territory. It has long been one of the Chinese provinces. As a strategic base in the heartland of Asia, it can contribute toward peace and security in Asia and elsewhere in the world only when it remains under the complete jurisdiction of the Republic of China. Though the Chinese Government had to devote its entire strength to prosecuting the war against Japan, it tried its best to safeguard China's territory, sovereignty and administrative integrity in the great Northwest. It was determined to prevent Soviet

Russia from having a free hand in her aggressive designs in Sinkiang, and to keep the Chinese Communists from opening an international route to Soviet Russia, for such a turn of events would alter the entire situation in Asia and pose a threat to world peace.

After Soviet Russia had increased her pressure on Sinkiang early in 1941, Sheng Shih-tsai began to feel the threat to his personal safety. During April 1942 Soviet consular officials and secret agents plotted a *coup d'état* in Sinkiang to over-throw Sheng and set up a Soviet puppet regime instead. In August of the same year I made an inspection trip to the provinces of Shensi, Kansu, Ninghsia, and Chinghai in the Northwest and asked my wife and General Chu Shao-liang to fly to Tihua, the provincial capital of Sinkiang, so as to bring messages of cheer to the people and troops there and to discuss with Sheng matters pertaining to the protection of China's territory and sovereignty as well as the return of ad-ministrative authority to the Government. Following the mission, Sheng took advantage of the Russo-German war to return to the fold of the Government to which he reaffirmed complete allegiance. Soviet Russia sent its deputy foreign minister to Tihua to ask Sheng to fulfill his promise made in 1934 to enforce Communism in Sinkiang and threatened Sheng with serious consequences for breach of this undertak-ing. Sheng stood firm. The Soviet emissary had to return to Moscow crestfallen.

In January 1943 officials appointed by the Central Govern-ment to military and political positions arrived in Sinkiang to assume office. In the main the task of regaining control over Sinkiang was practically completed. Then the Chinese Government called upon Soviet Russia to withdraw her Red Eighth Regiment from Hami, her guards from the aircraft assembly plant at Toutengho on the outskirts of Tihua, and also all Soviet organs from Sinkiang, in order to restore China's administrative integrity and sovereignty in that province.

Soviet Russia delayed until April 1943 before she agreed to effect the withdrawals. In June Chinese Government troops entered Hami. This happened at the time of the dissolution of the Third International, when Soviet Russia was putting on a tactical smile for the benefit of the antiaggression nations.

But Stalin was utterly ruthless. He knew that the situation in Sinkiang was already beyond control. He ordered Panyush-kin to send the Chinese Government a memorandum on June 16, 1943, in which he described Sheng Shih-tsai's actions against Soviet Russia as "illegal and hostile." Meanwhile, he gave the Chinese Government a copy of Sheng's secret agreement with Soviet Russia. His motive was clearly to destroy the Chinese Government's confidence in Sheng and, at the same time, to make Sheng feel uneasy in his relations with the Central Government. As a matter of fact, when Sheng decided to revert allegiance to the Government, he had made a complete report on the existence of this agreement. The failure of Stalin's intrigue to sow discord between Sheng and the Government only went to show his treachery.

After the Government took over Sinkiang, Moscow at once instigated the nomadic Kazakhs in Soviet Russia and in the Altai Mountain district in Sinkiang to start raids on the border to provide a pretext for Soviet aggression. In August 1944 Soviet secret agents in Tihua resumed their rabble-rousing activities, which almost brought on a revolt. This was averted only by the magnanimous attitude of the Government, which brought about a fair settlement. Soon afterward the situation returned to normal.

Sheng Shih-tsai was transferred and given a post in the Central Government, then at Chungking, and all military and political affairs in Sinkiang passed under the direct control of the Government just like any other province in the country. The Russians realized that they could no longer cause trouble in Tihua. In November that year they used armed Russian secret agents and some local Communist elements to launch a surprise attack on the city of Ili* and to set up a puppet regime there with the name of the "Eastern Turkestan Republic." The rebels also attacked and occupied our airfield and other military positions.

In 1945 officials of the Soviet Consulate-General at Tihua once again resorted to "peaceful coexistence" both in attitude and in tactics, and urged the Ili rebels to ask the Sinkiang provincial government for a peaceful settlement. In order to secure temporary stability the provincial authorities agreed to let the rebel leader join the provincial government as its deputy chairman. The Central Government did this out of a desire to remove the cause of local discontent. But Moscow merely marked its time. In 1949, when the war against the Communists in Central China was turning against the Government, rebel elements who had been previously admitted into Sinkiang's "coalition government," rose against Masud, a Uigur leader, as chairman of the provincial government. This miniature "coalition government" was to become the prototype for similar setups which the Russian Communists installed in various satellite countries after World War II.

The Outbreak of the Pacific War and the Abrogation of Special Rights in China by the U. S. and Britain

Japan launched her sneak attack on Pearl Harbor on December 7, 1941. On the same day she attacked the Philippines, Hongkong and Singapore. The outbreak of the Pacific War brought China, the United States and Britain together as comrades-in-arms. This also sealed the fate of the Japanese aggressors.

On January 1, 1942, China joined the United States, Britain, Soviet Russia and other nations, totaling twenty-six, in the Washington Declaration reaffirming the principles of the Atlantic Charter and also pledging joint prosecution of the

* Ili is a city in western Sinkiang.

war until final victory was won. There was now only one war, one alliance, and one outcome. China's task was not only to work with the allies for a common settlement of the Japanese problem, but also to join the allies in establishing a lasting world peace.

On October 9 of the same year, the American and British Governments notified the Chinese Government that being desirous of strengthening their friendship and cooperation with their Chinese ally, they had decided to relinquish their extraterritorial and related rights in China, and that they would submit draft agreements for new treaties in the near future. On the following day, October 10, which is China's National Day, the United States and Britain simultaneously issued formal statements to this effect.

In announcing this news at the National Day celebration mass meeting in Chungking, I said: "The bondage imposed on us by the foreign powers through unequal treaties for the past century has been removed at last. Dr. Sun's dictum in his last testament on 'the abolition of unequal treaties' has been fulfilled. Henceforth, we should redouble our effort to strengthen ourselves in every way so as to stand on our own feet as really independent and free citizens; only thus can we hope to build a really independent and free nation and prove ourselves a worthy ally."

This achievement inspired greater confidence in our ultimate victory and raised our hopes to greater heights than ever in the success of national reconstruction.

Because of this development, Moscow's policy toward China underwent a complete change. Prior to this the Russian Communists had hoped that China would keep on fighting, thereby stopping Japan from moving northward, while the Chinese Communists sought, above all, to develop their armed forces and to enlarge their territorial control. This would pave the way for the eventual partition, if not the total conquest, of China, which was their objective. Now Stalin began to plot how to deprive China of the fruits of victory and to stop China's rise as an independent, united and strong nation.

Mao Tse-tung, of course, had to make preparations on behalf of Moscow for this change of policy. His first aim was to make sure that the abolition of extraterritorial rights in China by the United States and Britain would not turn the heart of the Chinese people to such an extent as to make them move closer toward the Western democracies.

Moscow and the international Communist parties knew that the good will created by the Soviet Government's renunciation of Russia's special rights in China in 1919 was a crucial factor in the formation and growth of the Chinese Communist Party. Such an important announcement by the United States and Britain at a time when China was still in the throes of her war with Japan would necessarily constitute a great hindrance to the Russian Communists' present and future designs on our country. Furthermore, it made a great mockery of their propaganda. For this reason, they and their Chinese stooges were determined to undermine the Government's international position and to neutralize the wholesome effect which China's friendship for her allies and the new treaties of equality would have on the Chinese people.

One of the things they did was to spread rumors among members of the American military advisory mission and through their own diplomatic missions abroad to the effect that the Chinese Government was carrying on secret negotiations with Japan for cessation of hostilities. Their purpose, of course, was to make the United States discontinue its aid to our Government and to bring about a collapse in our war effort which, after all, had been their objective all along.

The Chinese people, however, were fully appreciative of this historic friendly move on the part of their American and British allies. They were determined to back up the Government's policy of waging the war to the very end. They were not taken in by the Russian propaganda which, in fact, gave them an insight into their real motives. Consequently, insofar as the Chinese people were concerned, it did not have any effect.

In their propaganda, it may be recalled, the international Communist parties and other fellow travelers stigmatized the conclusion of new treaties of equality by Britain and the United States as "a policy of appeasing China's ruling class." They described the move as an attempt "to prevent the Chinese Government's surrender to Japan." They also insinuated that it was a deliberate effort "to enhance the prestige of the Chinese Government and to help it control the country after the war." Most representative of this line of malicious propaganda is Israel Epstein's book *The Unfinished Revolution in China*. This was purposeful slander of the Chinese Government, and at the same time an insult to our allies.

On January 11, 1943, the new Sino-American and Sino-British treaties of equality were promulgated. Chinese people in all walks of life showed considerable enthusiasm in discussing various problems of postwar reconstruction. Our Government formulated a directive for first-stage economic reconstruction in the postwar period. I personally proposed a ten-year postwar reconstruction plan in which I called on the people to concentrate their will and strength for the sake of victory as well as for the sake of building up China, once the war was over, as a united, democratic and modern nation by making good use of our independent status and by welcoming foreign capital and technical cooperation. My call won the unanimous support of the people, but it was subjected to vicious attacks by the international Communists. This was natural because if we should exercise our independence and full sovereignty and succeed in developing our rich resources and in raising our people's standard of living through cooperation with our Western allies on a basis of equality and reciprocity, and in building China into a modern and democratic nation to share shouldering the responsibility of maintaining world peace, it would be something which neither Moscow nor its instrument of aggression in China, namely, the Chinese Communists, could tolerate. They felt they must take action to obstruct and to sabotage it.

Resumption of Negotiations with the Chinese Communists

By the end of December 1942 Russian troops had pushed German forces out of Stalingrad. On February 1, 1943, the Russians began to clear the Caucasus of German troops. Meanwhile the Chinese Communists again became arrogant and their troops in Kiangsu and Shantung renewed their attacks on Government forces.

Remnants of the former New Fourth Army, taking advantage of a battle then under way between the troops under the command of Governor Han of Kiangsu and the Japanese at Lienshui, inflicted heavy losses on the 112th Division under Han's command. In the meantime the 18th Group Army subjected Government forces in Shantung under Yu Hsueh-chung to sudden attacks.

On March 28 Chou En-lai and Lin Piao called on General Ho Ying-chin, chief of the general staff, to present four demands. They were:

1. A legal status for the Chinese Communist Party.
2. Expansion of the Communist forces to four armies of twelve divisions altogether.
3. Conversion of the Northern Shensi Border District into an administrative area and reorganization of other areas.
4. Postponement of the transfer of Communist forces from south of the Yellow River to areas of operations designated by the Government till the end of the war.

In reply General Ho Ying-chin reiterated the principles laid down in his message of October 19, 1940. Chou En-lai said the Communists accepted the principles but asked that negotiations be resumed on the timetable set for the actual transfer and on the numerical strength of the Communist forces.

It was clear that Chou En-lai and Lin Piao were not sincerely seeking a solution. For that reason further talks could serve no useful purpose at all.

The Communists' Disciplinary Movement in Preparation for a Volte-Face

On February 1, 1942, Mao Tse-tung started a "Cheng Feng" or disciplinary movement in Yenan. It turned out to be a basic task in the Chinese Communists' preparation for their subsequent all-out rebellion. During the war, national consciousness and confidence in the Government had reached an unprecedented height in China. Since the Chinese Communists were aiming at sabotaging the war and opposing the Government they must first eradicate any vestige of national consciousness from the minds of individual Communist members. In order to do this they must destroy the people's traditional morals and sentiments and, further, their humane spirit which is at the root of all morals and ethical sentiments. During this movement the Chinese Communists turned their attention to correcting what they deemed as unorthodox trends in education, in party organs as well as in the field of literature and art, and to re-evaluating subjectivism, dogmatism and formalism through self-criticism and self-examination. They made ruthless attacks on nationalistic thoughts and liberal thinking. They asked their party members "to overcome national consciousness with class consciousness" and even "to replace human nature with class nature." One Wang Shih-wei was severely criticized (finally he disappeared) for having said, "Stalin is a great man but he is inhuman." Indeed, "to replace human nature with class nature" was the first purpose of the movement.

As many as 30,000 Communist cadres took part in discussions during the movement. Between Mao Tse-tung's report on the movement in February 1942 and the Literature and Art Forum in Yenan in May 1943, the senior Communist cadres underwent ideological training for four months. Throughout the training a second purpose, "Maoism" and "Mao Tse-tung's monolithic leadership," were emphasized.

"Dissolution" of the Communist International

On May 22, 1943, Moscow announced the dissolution of the Communist International. This came as a great surprise to the world. I also mistook it to be an expression of the Russian Communists' sincere desire for cooperation with the United States, and not just a deceptive gesture. As the Communist International was the command post for Communists in countries outside Russia and was the center of their common faith, I felt that if its dissolution by Stalin was a deception it would mark the complete bankruptcy of him as a world figure. Henceforth no one would believe him, or the Russian Communists for that matter, again, in whatever they might do. But the truth soon became clear to me.

Outwardly, Stalin's dissolution of the Communist International was intended to counter the tripartite anti-Communist alliance of Germany, Japan and Italy, and to promote the solidarity of the anti-Axis democratic front. In reality, however, it proved to be another of Stalin's political maneuvers and propaganda tactics. It was also the revival of his international intrigue following the victory at Stalingrad. Now that the Communist International had been dissolved, Moscow could deny any responsibility for such intrigues and brutal acts as the Communists in other countries might perpetrate upon its orders.

The truth is that following the adoption of the "United Front" resolution by the Communist International at its

Seventh Congress in 1935, such organizations as the Labor International, the Youth International and the Women's International under the Communist International had all become regional organizations under various new names in order to facilitate their work among the masses. Now the Communist International itself would go underground. Its announced dissolution was entirely Stalin's political gesture and propaganda stunt while adhering to his "United Front" stratagem.

In the Russian Communists' world-wide strategy China remained their first objective. For the sake of their onslaught against China they took steps to cover up the Chinese Communists' direct subordination to Moscow. Subsequently the disciplinary movement at Yenan produced a slogan for the "China-nization of Marxism." It also pointed out that Mao Tse-tung's ideology is "Chinese Marxism." This was in preparation for the dissolution of the Communist International to come. Let us note that the Chinese Communists' disciplinary movement lasted from March to May, 1943, and that the "dissolution" of the Communist International was announced in May of the same year.

From this moment onward the International Communists and their fellow travelers no longer referred to the Chinese Communists in their propaganda as an ordinary Communist Party or as an instrument of Soviet Russia, but as "a democratic party" of Chinese farmers and "agrarian reformers." Also from this moment onward Moscow and Yenan began to launch violent political attacks against the Chinese Government.

Meanwhile the American Communist Party had its name changed to that of a political association to camouflage its real function as Soviet Russia's secret agent. Moscow's principal assignment for American Communists and their fellow travelers was a twofold one: directly, to damage the Chinese Government's prestige and jeopardize the Sino-American friendly relations by influencing the American Government

and American public opinion, and, indirectly, to publicize the
Chinese Communists by exaggerating their contributions to
the current war effort, their strength, their "land reforms,"
and "New Democracy," and by portraying "democratic freedoms" and "happiness and progress" in Communist areas in
northern Shensi as if Utopia had become a reality there.

Rogov's Correspondence—Origin of the "Two Chinas" Theory

On August 8, 1943, Moscow's *War and the Labor Class*
magazine published a long article criticizing the Chinese Government. The article, written by Vladimir Rogov, Tass correspondent in China, alleged that there were "appeasers,
defeatists and surrenderists" in the Chinese Government
scheming to prevent military reforms and industrial reconstruction, and that this had reduced China's combat strength.
The article went on to say that "they fomented conflicts and
incidents, including armed clashes, doing their best to disrupt
military cooperation between Kuomintang and the Chinese
Communist Party, and to instigate actions with a view to
persecuting and destroying the Eighth Route Army and the
New Fourth Army." It also pointed out that "civil war" would
soon break out in China. This led people in and outside the
American Government to believe that there were "die-hards"
in Kuomintang bent on fomenting civil war. The Tass agency
had actively paved the way in its propaganda for the complete change-over by the Chinese Communists. Rogov's article
was reprinted in the American *Daily Worker* and also in two
or three other papers. It was quoted by the Chinese Communists' *Hsinhua Daily News* which said "the Chungking
authorities were subjected to severe criticism by public opinion in allied countries for their reactionary actions and
measures."

The July 14, 1943, issue of the *Far Eastern Survey*, published by the Institute of Pacific Relations, carried an article by T. A. Bisson entitled "China's Position in the Allied War." It said there were two Chinas, a "democratic China," meaning areas under Chinese Communist control, and a "feudalistic China," meaning the Republic of China. The "two Chinas" talk in international circles today is the repetition of an old tune first played by American Communists and their fellow travelers as early as thirteen years ago.

Thereafter international Communists worked overtime to turn American public opinion and American diplomacy against the Republic of China and Chinese Government. Such adjectives as "corrupt," "incompetent," "reactionary" and "dictatorial" were flung on our Government and on me personally. Their aim was to sabotage relations between China and the United States so as to isolate China. The Sino-Japanese War was then at its most difficult stage. They wanted it to fall short of victory so as to enable the Chinese Communists to seize power. This was Moscow's plot, but few could see it at the time.

Two Wars Merging Into One

When major hostilities broke out in Shanghai in August 1937 the Soviet consulate-general there moved from Hongkew to the French Concession. Following the conclusion of the Russo-German Mutual Assistance Pact in August 1939, which was followed by the outbreak of war in Europe, the same consulate moved back to Hongkew, at that time already under Japanese military control. The close liaison between the Japanese military secret service and the Soviet consulate in Shanghai went on uninterrupted despite the Russo-German War. Wang Ching-wei's puppet regime at Nanking was actually established with Soviet Russia's blessing, because the Soviet consulate-general, working through the Japanese military secret service, had intimated that at a proper moment Moscow would accord it recognition.

The basis of the secret understanding between Japan and Soviet Russia was the partition of China's territory between them. When war broke out in Europe in September 1939 secret service agencies maintained by Japan's general staff in Shanghai at once initiated negotiations with Wang Ching-wei on the "setting up of a Government." The "Principles for the Readjustment of New Relations Between Japan and China" proposed by Japan was an exposé of Japanese militarists' plan for carving up China. In North China they used the puppet state of "Manchukuo" as a base for their Continental Policy and proceeded therefrom to slice off the so-called "Mongolian Autonomous Area" and the "North China zone of close collaboration" covering Shansi, Hopei and Shantung provinces. In Central China the Japanese militarists used the Kiangsu-Chekiang plain as a base and then moved up the Yangtze River until they reached Ichang. In South China they used Taiwan and Hainan Island as bases and Fukien and Kwangtung as the outer fringe for their Oceanic Policy.

Outer Mongolia, Sinkiang, Tibet and the northwest region west of Tungkwan* were to be allotted to Soviet Russia. These were the conditions proposed by Japan and agreed to by Soviet Russia. I was not surprised when I received this information, but it was my belief that Soviet Russia's ambitions definitely would not stop there. This move on the part of the Japanese militarists, therefore, only betrayed their naïveté. In January 1940 the secret document containing the "Agreement for the Readjustment of New Relations Between Japan and China" was published in Hongkong papers. This exposed the intrigues of Japan and Soviet Russia for the partition of China. The Japanese-Russian Neutrality Pact of April 1941 was but a small part of this grandiose scheme. There could no longer be any question about the support

* Tungkwan is a mountain pass along the Lunghai Railway in Shensi province in China's northwest.

which the Soviet consulate-general in Shanghai had given to Wang Ching-wei's puppet regime.

During the battles in western Hunan and in western Hupeh at the end of 1943, and again during the battle along the southern section of the Peiping-Hankow Railway in 1944, the Chinese Communists tipped off the Japanese secret agents in regard to the Government's plans of deployment and operations. It was the Chinese Communists' intention to induce the Japanese forces to penetrate deep into southwest China, then the main base of China's resistance, so that they themselves would have a chance to break out of the Government blockade and to extend their control to the northwest. They were prepared to go even a step further by launching a pincer attack together with the Japanese against the Government's military bases in Szechwan and Kweichow provinces. Thus, behind the intensive propaganda offensive which the International Communists had launched against the Chinese Government, preparations were steadily going on for an all-out military offensive against the Government forces.

This kind of secret coordination was not confined to Chinese Communists and Japanese forces. Actually there was similar coordination between Soviet Russia and the Japanese in their aggression in China. In March 1944, when the Japanese launched a large-scale military drive ranging from the Peiping-Hankow Railway to the Canton-Hankow Railway, Chinese Communist forces attempted to break into Kansu in the hope of opening a direct line of communication between Yenan and Soviet Russia. During the same year the Soviet consulate-general at Tihua instigated a series of incidents in Sinkiang.

This then is the real substance of the "peaceful coexistence" that was tried out between China and Soviet Russia and between Kuomintang and the Chinese Communist Party. It is also the inside story of how two wars, Japan's direct and open war against China and Soviet Russia's indirect and clandestine war against China, became merged into one.

Negotiations—The Third Round

In 1943, as a result of a summer offensive, Soviet Russia succeeded in recovering two-thirds of the territory previously occupied by the Germans. The beginning of Germany's final defeat was already discernible. It was during this period that Stalin formulated his entire policy for the postwar world. He began to project himself into the future and correlate his plans accordingly. He refused to attend the Cairo Conference* although in December of the same year he went to Teheran to meet Roosevelt and Churchill, where he rejected Churchill's proposal for the opening of a second front in the Balkans but obtained allied agreement on landings on the French coast. Stalin's first-round victory in his world strategy already spelled the doom of countries in Eastern Europe.

In January 1944 Russian troops raised the siege at Leningrad. In February and March they recovered Kiev and pushed westward from the Dnieper to the Dniester. They also routed the German army in the Crimea. The Chinese Communists on their part began to take positive steps to launch an all-out political offensive against the Government.

During the discussions held in Sian in 1944 the Chinese Communists steadily raised their demands as time went on. Finally the talks underwent a complete change in substance. From these talks one could clearly discern the direction in which the Chinese Communists were moving in their all-out political offensive.

In his talks with Wang Shih-chieh, a Government delegate, from May 4 to May 8, Lin Tsu-han, a Communist delegate, brought up seventeen points which did not differ much from the Communist demands presented on two previous occasions.

* President Chiang met American and British Allied leaders at Cairo.

He asked for four armies of twelve divisions and the transfer of Chinese Communist troops to designated areas only after the end of the war. The border district was to be converted into an administrative area under the Executive Yuan instead of under the Shensi provincial government. The Government was to accord the Chinese Communist Party a legal status and to release "political prisoners." And in addition he asked— and this was something new—for the removal of the Government's military blockade around the Shensi-Kansu-Ninghsia border area.

On January 4, 1945, Lin Tsu-han suddenly presented a twelve-point memorandum stating "the Chinese Communists' views for the settlement of certain urgent problems," which almost completely overthrew what had been agreed upon in previous discussions. By the new terms submitted by Lin, the Communists demanded:

1. Five armies of sixteen divisions.
2. That the Government recognize the "popularly elected anti-Japanese local administrations" in the Shensi-Kansu-Ninghsia border area and in North China as legitimate local governments and also the various measures which these local administrations considered necessary for the prosecution of the war.
3. That the Government allow the Chinese Communist forces to maintain the status quo in their garrison areas during the war, and to leave the question of their transfer for discussion after the war.

Concerning the border areas, they made the following new demands:

1. Regarding arms, ammunition and medical supplies furnished by Allied countries, the Government is requested to distribute them to all Chinese armed forces on a fair basis, and both the 18th Group Army and the New Fourth Army should each receive a rightful share.

2. The Government is requested to instruct military and political organs to remove their military and economic blockade around the Shensi-Kansu-Ninghsia border area and various anti-Japanese bases.

In addition, as a propaganda move, the Chinese Communists made the following obviously insincere demands concerning the "political situation in general," posing as the defenders of freedom:

1. The Government is requested to enforce democracy, to guarantee freedom of speech, freedom of publication, freedom of assembly, freedom of forming associations and freedom of person.
2. The Government is requested to lift the ban on political parties, to recognize the legal status of the Chinese Communists and anti-Japanese parties and factions, and to release political prisoners.
3. The Government is requested to carry out genuine local self-government by the people.

The Stilwell Affair—Chinese Communists' Opposition to General Wedemeyer

I particularly wish to make clear two points in connection with these new Communist demands: first, the distribution of allied military aid to China, and second, the removal of the Government's blockade around the Communist border area. These were the real issues in the Stilwell affair.

General Joseph Stilwell was assigned to China by the United States to direct military operations against the Japanese in northern Burma. I was appreciative of his services and ordinarily I had confidence in his proposals on various matters. It so happened that when he was in the China-Burma Theater of War, the American Communists and their fellow travelers were busy in their propaganda depicting the Chinese

Communists as "agrarian reformers" and as elements of a "patriotic democratic party," and defaming me as a die-hard and reactionary Fascist. General Stilwell was one of those influenced by this propaganda. He had mistakenly believed that the Chinese Communist forces would obey his command. He asked me to have the Government and Communist troops re-equipped on an equal basis, to send the Communist forces into battle and at the same time to use in operations against the Japanese the Government troops immobilized in Shansi and Shensi because of the Chinese Communists' threat to revolt.

I regret to say that he had no idea whatsoever of the Chinese Communists' schemes. He did not believe that the Communists had tried to sabotage China's National Revolution upon Moscow's instructions in the past. Nor did he foresee what the Chinese Communists would do, once they were re-equipped and sent out of the "border area," to impede China's war effort and overthrow the Government. General Stilwell's subsequent dispute with me was created entirely by the Communists and their friends. It almost caused disruption of Sino-American military cooperation in the China-Burma Theater.

When General Stilwell first came to China I should have confided in him all the facts about Soviet Russia's intrigues and her real aims in China's revolution and in the war. He might have had a better understanding of the situation and taken appropriate precautionary measures. I regretted very much that I did not do this, but I thought he had just come to China and we had not had time to build up a relationship of mutual trust between us. On this point it might be said that I made a mistake. To this day my heart still aches over this unfortunate affair.

In October 1944 General Albert C. Wedemeyer succeeded General Stilwell as commander of U. S. forces in the China Theater and concurrently chief of staff to the China Theater

Headquarters. General Wedemeyer devoted himself to matters relating to the military counteroffensive, leaving the
Chinese Communist problem to Ambassador Patrick Hurley
to handle.

General Wedemeyer, however, made a study of the real
situation concerning the Chinese Communists in order to get
at the root of the trouble. He also analyzed Ambassador
Hurley's experience in negotiating with the Communists and
reviewed General Stilwell's tour of duty in China in order to
get a proper perspective. Therefore, he acquired a good
knowledge of the Chinese Communists' scheme and did not
fall for their propaganda or their attempt to surround him.
This explains the perfect cooperation between the United
States and China in military and political affairs and the excellent accomplishments during the period of Ambassador Hurley's and General Wedemeyer's service in China.

In May 1945, in making plans for the counteroffensive,
General Wedemeyer toured North China where he visited
the fronts in Shensi and Suiyuan. He passed through Yenan
but he declined the Communists' invitation to stop over and
call on Mao Tse-tung. General Wedemeyer was one of those
who understood the Communist intrigues at the time and incurred their wrath as a result.

Early in 1946, when the United States was mediating in the
dispute between the Chinese Government and the Chinese
Communists and taking a hand in the reorganization of the
Chinese Communist forces, General Wedemeyer had to leave
China and return to America.

Chinese Communists' Military
Expenses and Political Capital

The Chinese Communists and their international "comrades" had accused the Government of discriminating against
the 18th Group Army by not treating it in accordance with

its expanded numerical strength nor on a same footing with Government troops. Actually, as approved by the Government, the 18th Group Army was composed of three armies of six divisions, plus five supplementary regiments, and the Government had issued funds to it on that basis on an equal footing with Government troops. The Chinese Communists, however, never used the funds for the purpose for which they were intended. Instead, they used them to subsidize their front organizations and cultural bodies in carrying on their subversive activities against national unity and the war effort. For instance, money needed by the Chungking *Hsinhua Daily News*, the chain of *Life* bookstores in various places, and such periodicals as *Masses* and the *Liberation Weekly*, the Anti-Japanese University in Yenan, the North Shensi College, all came from military funds which the Government had given to the Communists for the maintenance of the 18th Group Army. As to funds and food provisions needed by Communist forces in other places, they obtained them by illegal methods from people in the "Special Area" or "Border Districts," and through "Land Reform Struggle" and the manufacturing and peddling of morphine, and through various forms of taxes, levies and requisitions.

The second source of revenue for the Chinese Communists to finance their political warfare was illicit trade between Japanese occupied areas and free (Government-controlled) areas. During the war the Government took steps to blockade the Japanese-occupied areas. The Chinese Communists, however, conducted smuggling through five different routes:

The first route was from Paotow to northern Shensi via Suiteh, and from northern Shensi to eastern Kansu and Ninghsia. The "anti-Japanese stores" in Suiteh and the "Kwang Hwa Stores" in Yenan were the principal Communist organs that handled the buying and selling of Japanese goods.

The second route was through the crossing points along the Yellow River in the northern Shensi border area. Japanese

goods coming across through these ferry points garrisoned by
the 18th Group Army poured into areas west of the Yellow
River and eventually into the central and southern parts of
Shensi province for profitable distribution.

The third route was from Tsinan in Shantung westward to
northern Honan and southern Shansi.

The fourth route was from Wuhu above Nanking on the
Yangtze westward to western Anhwei and Hupeh and
Kiangsi.

The fifth route was from Pengpu north of Nanking westward to northern Anhwei and western Honan.

Profits from smuggling provided the Chinese Communists
with funds to help finance their propaganda and organization
warfare and subversive activities against the free (Government-controlled) areas.

One of the items which the Chinese Communists handled
in their smuggling activities, and which not only violated the
Government's ban but also harmed the people's general health,
was opium. This came from two sources:

First, it came from production centers in Japanese-occupied
areas, especially Jehol, and entered the free (Government-
controlled) areas through routes and river crossing points
garrisoned by the 18th Group Army. The Chinese Communists collected a passage levy of 8 fapi* for every ounce
of opium.

Second, it came from the Shensi-Kansu-Ninghsia Special
Area where the farmers were ordered to plant poppy by the
Chinese Communists who would send men to collect the
opium when the poppy was ripe, and shared the crop with
the growers either on a 30-70 or on a 40-60 basis, depending
on the fertility of the land in question. Whatever amount the
farmers were allowed to keep was also purchased by the
Chinese Communists at a fixed price.

It is, therefore, obvious that there is no truth in the Chinese

* Fapi was the Chinese legal tender at the time.

Communists' accusation that the Government had withheld or reduced funds for the support of the 18th Group Army.

Negotiations—The Fourth Round

While the war was still raging, the Chinese Communists stepped up their all-out political war against the Government after the third series of negotiations. On November 7, 1944, General Patrick Hurley flew to Yenan in the company of Lin Tsu-han. On November 10 he returned to Chungking with Chou En-lai, bringing with him an "agreement" he had initialed with Mao Tse-tung. This agreement showed what were the Chinese Communists' political conditions:

1. The Chinese Government, Kuomintang, and the Chinese Communist Party should cooperate so as to defeat Japan with unified Chinese armed forces at an early date and to rebuild the country.

2. The existing National Government should be reorganized into a coalition government, to be composed of representatives of all anti-Japanese parties and of nonpartisan political bodies; a new democratic policy should be promulgated and reforms should be instituted in military, political, economic and cultural enterprises; and the National Military Council should be reorganized into a Coalition National Military Council, to be composed of representatives of all anti-Japanese armed forces.

3. The Coalition National Government should endorse Dr. Sun Yat-sen's principles, establish a government of the people, by the people, for the people, adopt pertinent measures to promote progress and democracy, uphold righteousness and freedom of faith, freedom of publication, freedom of speech, and freedom of assembly and association, the right of making appeals, freedom of person, the right of domicile, and to put into practice the freedom from fear and freedom from want.

4. The Coalition National Government should recognize the legal status of Kuomintang, the Chinese Communist Party, and all anti-Japanese organizations.

This "agreement" was full of such terms as "democracy," "freedom," "peace" and "progress" which found a ready reception in the democratic nations. Furthermore, it listed "New Democracy" and "coalition government" as two of the conditions. Since the betrayal of Poland and the *coup d'état* in Czechoslovakia, such slogans no longer had any meaning. They are nothing but Moscow's formula of enslaving other countries though at the time we had yet to see its application in Eastern Europe.

I decided to reject the part of the agreement about "coalition government." As to the other points, I felt there was room for discussion. Upon his return to Yenan, however, Chou En-lai wrote to General Hurley to say that the Central Authorities of the Chinese Communist Party did not approve of all the points that had been discussed.

Negotiations—The Fifth Round

In the latter part of January 1945 the Chinese Communists again sent Chou En-lai to Chungking. The negotiations which ensued were entirely for the purpose of political propaganda with "coalition government" as its main thesis. The Communist attitude was worse than ever. In their propaganda they not only attacked the Government but also unjustly accused Mr. Patrick Hurley of collusion with the Chinese Government because of his declaration that "the United States will not give arms to Chinese political parties that possess armed forces." Thus, Hurley also became a target of Communist attacks.

The fifth round of negotiations achieved no more concrete result than the previous talks. It came to an end in May.

The Enforcement of Constitutional Government

Dr. Sun's teachings about the National Revolution had two parallel objectives. Externally, China was to attain independence and equality with other nations; internally, a foundation was to be laid for democratic government and for the implementation of the Principle of People's Livelihood. "Political tutelage" under our Party's guidance was only meant as an intermediate stage between military rule, necessary for the achievement of the revolution, and the final goal of constitutional government. Had it not been for the Sino-Japanese War, the National Assembly would have been convened and a constitution adopted as early as 1937.

During the years 1944 and 1945, though the Sino-Japanese War had entered into its most difficult phase, victory was already in sight. There were spirited discussions of the question of postwar reconstruction in Chungking, our wartime capital. My decision was to advance the timetable for the enforcement of constitutional government in order to establish democracy and to prepare for our postwar programs. On March 1, 1945, in my speech to the Association for the Promotion of Constitutional Government, I announced that the Government was prepared to convene the National Assembly on November 12 of that year when the period of political tutelage would be terminated and a constitution promulgated. The question of convocation of the National Assembly was discussed by the People's Political Council at its session on July 7. The Chinese Communists, however, refused to attend despite the fact that the session was going to decide on concrete measures for a democratic rule. As a countermeasure they made preparations for the calling of a so-called Liberated Area People's Representative Assembly. Constitutional democracy is anathema to Communism.

*Chinese Communist Attempts During
Sino-Soviet Negotiations*

At the Yalta Conference in February 1945 Stalin had scored what might be described as a complete victory in the second round of a diplomatic tussle against the United States and Britain. He won his points over the Polish question, the question of allied occupation of Germany and the question of veto power in the United Nations Charter. In particular, China's sovereignty in Outer Mongolia and administrative integrity in Manchuria were sacrificed in return for Soviet Russia's entry into the war against Japan. Meanwhile, in Stalin's over-all intrigue against the Chinese Republic, left-wing Americans were allowed to continue to intensify their vicious propaganda against China and against me personally, all this at a time when Chinese Communists and their front organizations were told by Moscow to carry on with their political subversion and armed insurrection.

In June of the same year, when China and Soviet Russia were negotiating the Treaty of Friendship and Alliance, the peace preservation corps at Tenghwa in northern Shensi, upon the instigation of Chinese Communists, occupied the county seat and clashed with Government troops there. In the meantime, in eastern and western parts of Chekiang and in southern and northern parts of Suiyuan, Communist forces renewed attacks on Government troops. This was used as fresh propaganda material by the American Communists and their fellow travelers in accusing the Chinese Government of "starting a civil war," and in asking the American Government to stop sending military supplies to China.

End of the Second Period of "Peaceful Coexistence"

The foregoing is an account of the development and the final outcome of renewed cooperation and "peaceful coexistence" between China and Soviet Russia and between

Kuomintang and the Chinese Communists during the war years from 1937 to 1945. The earlier submissive attitude of the Chinese Communists at the time when they sued for peace, their four pledges of September 22, 1937, at the beginning of the Sino-Japanese war, and Mao Tse-tung's lip service to "lasting solidarity," "sincere cooperation" and "complete unification"—all these turned out to be preliminary steps to an armed rebellion and political subversion toward the end of the war.

The Chinese Communists apparently had hoped to seize power at the time by resorting to the same tricks successfully employed by the Russian Communists in 1917 when they overthrew the provisional government through propagating defeatism among the Russian people. The Chinese Communists failed because the Government had maintained its firm control on the military situation, and because of the attainment of victory in China. Of over-all importance was the factor of the moral and spiritual strength of the people which the Government was able to mobilize throughout the war. But once the war was over, Moscow immediately unleashed its comprehensive plan to conquer China from without and subvert her from within.

CHAPTER THREE

OUTCOME

The Third Period (1945-1949)

The unexpectedly early termination of war and the surrender of Japanese troops with their arms to the Government deprived the Chinese Communists of a chance to seize power while the war was still on.

Both the Russian and Chinese Communists once again harped on the old tune of "peaceful coexistence" to hamstring the Government troops and to harm Sino-American cooperation. But during the period of the past thirty years, thrice the relations between China and Soviet Russia had been marked alternately by peace and rupture of relations. The final outcome was the fall of the Chinese mainland behind the Iron Curtain to become the Soviet Empire's base of operations against Asia and other parts of the world. The story is worth retelling.

The Chinese Government's Acceptance of Japanese Surrender

On August 10, 1945, Japan sent a note of surrender to the Allies through the good offices of Switzerland and Sweden. The note said: "The Japanese Government is ready to accept the terms enumerated in the joint declaration which was issued at Potsdam on July 26, 1945, by the heads of the Governments of the United States, Great Britain and China and later subscribed to by the Soviet Government, with the understanding that the above declaration does not comprise any demand which prejudices the prerogatives of His Majesty as a sovereign. The Japanese Government sincerely hopes that this understanding is warranted and desires keenly that an explicit indication to the effect will be speedily forthcoming."

On August 11, on behalf of the Allies, the United States requested Switzerland to transmit a reply to the Japanese Government wherein the procedure of surrender was outlined. The note ended with the declaration that, "The ultimate form of the Government of Japan shall, in accordance with the Potsdam Declaration, be established by the freely expressed will of the Japanese people."

At the Cairo Conference I maintained that the question of preserving or abolishing the Japanese monarchy should be left entirely to the Japanese people themselves whose wishes in this regard must be respected by all allies. President Franklin D. Roosevelt understood my point of view and agreed with me. Upon the conclusion of hostilities, all the Japanese troops overseas surrendered by order of their emperor. In Japan, because of the traditional revered position he held, law and order was maintained without any incident.

The China Theater's area for accepting Japanese surrender covered the Chinese Republic, Taiwan and Indo-China (Vietnam) north of the 16th degree North Latitude. I assigned General Ho Ying-chin, commander-in-chief of Chinese Ground Forces, to take charge of all matters concerning Japanese surrender. Altogether 1,283,200 Japanese troops surrendered in the China Theater

It will be recalled that the Allied Headquarters had assigned to Soviet Russia the duties of accepting the surrender of Japanese troops in Manchuria. On August 8 Soviet Russia declared that a state of war with Japan would exist as from August 9, which was only one day before Japan's offer to surrender or six days before hostilities practically came to an end. Soviet troops entered Manchuria, Jehol and Chahar only three days before the Japanese actually laid down their arms. This marked a new starting point in Soviet Russia's aggression against China and in Chinese Communists' subversion against the Government after World War II.

The Chinese Communists' "Seven Orders of the Day" and Six Demands

Upon receipt of Japan's declaration of surrender, the National Military Council of the Chinese Government immediately asked all armed forces in the country to wait for orders and carry out all decisions pertaining to the acceptance of surrender in accordance with Allied agreements. In its orders to the 18th Group Army the National Military Council specifically instructed all its units to remain where they were and to await orders, and, for those committed to combat duties, to abide by orders of their respective war area commanders. In no circumstances were they to make any unauthorized moves.

But the Communists did not obey the orders of the High Command. Chu Teh, in the name of the "Yenan Headquarters," issued "Seven Orders of the Day," directing Communist forces in various places to resort to all-out violence. The military movements indicated in Chu's "orders" were:

1. "In coordination with the Soviet Red Army's entry into China": (a) troops under Lu Cheng-tsao were to move from Shansi and Suiyuan into Chahar and Jehol; (b) troops under Chang Hsueh-shih were to move from Hopei and Chahar into Jehol and Liaoning; (c) troops under Wan Yi were to move from Shantung and Hopei into Liaoning; (d) troops under Li Yung-chang were to move from Hopei and Jehol into Liaoning and Kirin; and (e) Korean Communist troops were to enter Manchuria together with the others.

2. "In coordination with the entry of Outer Mongolian troops into Inner Mongolia, Suiyuan, Chahar and Jehol": (a) troops under Ho Lung were to move northward from Suiyuan; and (b) troops under Nieh Yung-tseng were to move northward from Chahar and Jehol.

3. All troops in Shansi were "placed under Ho Lung's unified command to occupy the area along the Tatung-Pucheng Railway and in the Fen River Valley."

4. In order to seize or sever "all principal arteries of communication" in the country, "all Communist troops along the Peiping-Liaoning Railway, the Peiping-Suiyuan Railway, the Peiping-Hankow Railway, the Tatung-Pucheng Railway, the Tsangchow-Shihchiachwang Railway, the Chengting-Taiyuan Railway, the Paitsing Railway, the Taotsing Railway, the Tientsin-Pukow Railway, the Lunghai Railway, the Canton-Hankow Railway, the Shanghai-Nanking Railway, the Nanking-Wuhu Railway, the Shanghai-Hangchow Railway, the Canton-Kowloon Railway, the Chaoho Railway, and troops on both sides of important roads in other Liberated Areas were to go actively into attack."

On August 17 the Chinese Communists, again through Chu Teh, presented a set of six demands to the Government:

1. "In accepting the surrender of Japanese and puppet forces and in concluding agreements or treaties for the purpose, the Government should consult first the Anti-Japanese People's Armed Forces in Liberated Areas in order to reach unanimity of views.

2. "All Anti-Japanese People's Armed Forces in Liberated Areas and in occupied areas should have the right, on the basis of the terms of the Potsdam Declaration and the procedure as laid down by the Allies, to accept the surrender of Japanese and puppet troops and to take over their arms and supplies.

3. "The Anti-Japanese People's Armed Forces in Liberated Areas and in occupied areas, should have the right to send delegates to take part in accepting Japanese surrender and in administering affairs after the enemy's surrender.

4. "All Anti-Japanese People's Armed Forces in Liberated Areas should have the right to designate representatives to attend the peace conference and United Nations meetings.

5. "Generalissimo Chiang should be asked to stop civil war by assigning troops in Liberated Areas to accept the surrender of Japanese and puppet troops they have surrounded in their areas, and by assigning Government troops to accept the surrender of Japanese troops they have surrounded in their own areas.

6. "An all-party conference should be called at once to form a democratic coalition government to effect democratic political and economic reforms."

The purpose behind Chu Teh's "Seven Orders of the Day" and six demands was perfectly clear. It was to take independent actions to disarm Japanese and puppet troops, to occupy and disrupt lines of communication and to extend their area of control so as to join forces with Soviet and Mongolian troops pouring into Manchuria, Jehol, Chahar and Suiyuan. At the same time by demanding the formation of a "coalition government," they gave their military tactics support in the form of a political offensive.

Program of Peaceful Reconstruction

During the eight years of war, China mobilized 14,000,000 of her people, of whom 3,200,000 became casualties. The war cost China $1,464,300,000,000, in Chinese currency. These figures do not include the heavy losses in life and property sustained by the people in general. Naturally the people wanted to see demobilization and the beginning of reconstruction as soon as possible. Now that Japanese Imperialism had been defeated and unequal treaties between China and the Western powers had been abrogated, there was every reason to expect success in our dual task of revolution and reconstruction. Therefore, on the day victory was announced, the Government disclosed a definite Program of Peaceful Reconstruction to guide the nation in external relations and internal administration

Our foreign policy has always been to strive for general security and a lasting peace. At the end of World War I Dr. Sun said: "Those who make the nations help one another will triumph, while those who seek personal interests or the interests of one nation alone will go into oblivion." At the end of World War II I resolved on guiding our foreign policy in accordance with the following principles:

1. As one of the authors of the United Nations Charter and one of the four original sponsors of the United Nations Organization, China should stand for the preservation of peace and justice and remain a firm supporter of the United Nations.

2. We should not be vindictive toward Japan. Instead, we should adopt a magnanimous policy and work for the conclusion of a peace treaty with Japan.

3. We should try our best to find a way of living in peace with Soviet Russia. We knew that after Japan's defeat, as far as Asia was concerned, Soviet Russia would be the only aggressive power and the only source of external threat to China. Peaceful coexistence in the real sense between China and Soviet Russia would, therefore, be a factor of basic importance to peace and security in Asia.

4. Regarding Korea, we should abide by the Cairo Declaration and assist her so that she becomes independent and unified in order to safeguard peace and security in East Asia.

OUTCOME

5. As for Thailand, we wanted to see her recover her pre-war independent and equal status and establish normal and friendly relations with the Republic of China.

6. During the war the Republic of China twice had to send troops into Burma, but out of respect for our ally's sovereign rights, and in full accordance with international good faith, the Chinese Expeditionary Forces in Burma would be withdrawn the moment their duties in the Burma Theater could be brought to an early end.

7. The Republic of China, by agreement among the Allies, had sent troops into Indo-China to accept the surrender of Japanese forces north of the 16th degree North Latitude. We have no territorial or other demands to make in Indo-China. Our only hope was that it would become self-governing and independent. Therefore, upon the acceptance of the surrender of Japanese forces in that area, and the restoration of law and order, the Chinese troops there should be withdrawn.

8. Regarding Hongkong, which had been included in the China Theater, the Republic of China would not take advantage of the acceptance of Japanese surrender to prejudice international cooperation or to affect its friendly relations with Britain. No Chinese troops were allowed to infringe on British rights in Hongkong.

In domestic policy, our over-all objective being to build up a modern democratic and unified nation, our plans were guided by the following principles:

First, we wanted to bring about a democratic and constitutional rule. During the Sino-Japanese War we had planned to convene the National Assembly on November 12, 1945, to adopt a constitution. The plan miscarried on account of the obstructions engineered by Communists and in particular by the Democratic League, a Communist front organization. After victory the Government decided to convene the National Assembly on May 5, 1946, in order to terminate the period of political tutelage and to initiate a completely constitutional government.

Secondly, we wanted to safeguard national unification. All troops should be integrated into the National Army and there should be no more personal or party armies. Party differences should be settled on the floor of the legislature in accordance with democratic procedure and constitutional practices. There should be no more resort to force in settling political disputes.

Thirdly, we wanted to use foreign capital and technical assistance to develop our natural resources and to raise the people's standard of living. In particular, we should offer our resources in Manchuria to the whole world as China's contribution to the betterment of human welfare.

On September 3, 1945 (VJ-Day), I set forth our Program of Peaceful Reconstruction by declaring:

At this juncture when war ends and peace begins, we and our allies are bringing to a close a dangerous situation which has been caused by half a century of Japanese aggression. We are trying to build a lasting peace and security for East Asia and for the world at large. We should, by maintaining friendly relations with our neighbors and stability at home, proceed to heal the wounds of war, restore law and order, aid our suffering brethren in the recovered areas, bring solace to the dependents of those who had fallen or were wounded in the war, provide medical care for the sick and cause peace and tranquillity to prevail throughout the country. Furthermore, in order to ensure that all our sacrifices have not been made in vain, we should at this time work out a pattern for constitutional government and lay a firm foundation for national unity.

In the past, top priority went to the prosecution of our war and the winning of victory. From now on, our efforts should be directed toward unification and democracy. Only by implementing our program of national reconstruction and carrying out Dr. Sun's Three People's Principles could we augment our national strength and improve the standard of living of the people. This will be the greatest final victory we have been striving and praying for in our fifty years of revolution and eight years of war.

All measures subsequently taken by the Chinese Government both externally and internally were in accordance with this program, but the Chinese Communists and their international comrades continued with intrigue to sabotage our constructive effort.

Signing of the Sino-Soviet Treaty of Friendship and Alliance

On February 11, 1945, the United States, Britain and Soviet Russia had concluded a secret agreement at Yalta. The Republic of China was not represented at the discussions. We were, therefore, not bound legally by the said agreement. But it would be unrealistic to deny the influence which American policies toward Soviet Russia and China had exerted on Sino-Soviet negotiations in the spring of 1945.

When T. V. Soong, then minister of foreign affairs, went to San Francisco to lead China's delegation to the United Nations Conference in April 1945, he took with him as guidance in negotiations with Soviet Russia a brief outline which was based on the Sino-Soviet Agreement of 1924 and the Sino-Soviet Nonaggression Treaty of 1937. This represented a conscientious attempt on our part to find a way to "peaceful coexistence" between the two countries in the postwar period. We did not expect Soviet Russia to disregard both agreements and lay claims on all the special rights and interests which Czarist Russia had seized in China up to 1904.

For the sake of peace, during the Moscow negotiations we had to make the following important concessions at the expense of our rights and interests:

1. Recognition of Outer Mongolia's independence and self-government.
2. Joint operation of the Chinese Changchun Railway.

3. Declaration of Dairen as a free port and the exemption of customs duties on goods entering the free port from abroad for through transit to Soviet territory on the Chinese Changchun Railway and on goods coming from Soviet territory on the said railway into the free port for export.

4. Joint use by the two countries of Port Arthur as a naval base.

In return, Soviet Russia made the following undertakings in the treaty and in the various annexes attached thereto:

1. The Government of the U.S.S.R. agrees to render to China moral support and aid in military supplies and other material resources, such support and aid to be entirely given to the National Government as the Central Government of China.

2. The Government of the U.S.S.R. regards the Three Eastern Provinces (Manchuria) as part of China, and reaffirms its respect for China's full sovereignty over the Three Eastern Provinces and recognizes their territorial and administrative integrity.

3. As for recent developments in Sinkiang, the Soviet Government reaffirms that it has no intention of interfering in the internal affairs of China.

4. Regarding the question of withdrawal of Soviet troops which had entered China following the U.S.S.R.'s participation in the war against Japan, Stalin declared that these troops would begin to withdraw three weeks after the Japanese surrender and this withdrawal would be completed within three months at the latest.

The Sino-Soviet Treaty and its various annexes together with Stalin's pledge should serve as the logical yardstick with which to study Soviet Russia's subsequent performances in diplomacy and military affairs, and also as a pointer to future developments.

Talks with Mao Tse-tung in Chungking

Simultaneous with its negotiations with Soviet Russia for the conclusion of the Sino-Soviet Treaty of Friendship and Alliance, the Government was holding renewed discussions with the Chinese Communists, hoping to find a formula for peaceful coexistence with them. After Japan's offer to surrender I sent three messages to Mao Tse-tung inviting him to come to Chungking. On August 27 Ambassador Patrick Hurley flew to Yenan and the following day brought Mao Tse-tung back.

Altogether, Government delegates and Communist representatives held five meetings in forty-one days. On October 10 the minutes of the conversations were published. The important points follow:

1. Concerning the basic policy on peaceful national reconstruction: (a) "As the Sino-Japanese War has been brought to a victorious conclusion, China is now on the threshold of a new era of peaceful national reconstruction. Concerted efforts should be made under the leadership of President Chiang Kai-shek on the basis of peace, democracy, solidarity and unity for lasting cooperation in order to avoid civil war, for building up China as an independent, free, rich and strong nation and for full implementation of the Three People's Principles. (b) "Nationalization of the armed forces, political democratization and equality and a legitimate status for political parties, as advocated by President Chiang, should be the road to take toward peaceful national reconstruction."
2. Concerning the question of political democratization: "The Government is to convene a Political Consultative Conference, to which representatives of all parties and nonpartisan leaders will be invited, to exchange views on affairs of the state and to discuss questions relating to the

Program of Peaceful National Reconstruction and the convocation of the National Assembly."

3. Concerning the National Assembly: It was mutually agreed that questions regarding delegates to the National Assembly, the organic law of the National Assembly, the election law and the draft constitution, over which no agreement had been reached, would be taken up by the Political Consultative Conference for settlement.

4. Concerning the nationalization of armed forces: The Chinese Communists proposed that the Government should reorganize the entire Chinese armed forces, decide on its implementation area by area, re-demarcate the military zones and formulate a system of conscription and replenishment with a view to unifying the military command. Under this program the Chinese Communists would be prepared to have their troops reduced to twenty or twenty-four divisions and to move their troops to be so reorganized for concentration in areas north of the Lunghai Railway and in northern Kiangsu and northern Anhwei. The Government said a nation-wide military reorganization program was being planned and it would consider reorganizing the Chinese Communist forces into twenty divisions. "In order to formulate concrete plans regarding all the questions mentioned in this section, it was agreed that a Committee of Three should be formed."

5. On accepting Japanese surrender: The Communists asked that the area of accepting surrender should be re-demarcated. In reply, the Government said that the participation of Communist forces in accepting Japanese surrender could be considered following their compliance with the Government's orders.

In his speech on the eve of his departure from Chungking for Yenan, Mao Tse-tung, according to an account in the

October 9th issue of the Communist *Hsinhua Daily News*, said:

China today has only one road before her. It is peace. Peace is everything. All other considerations are mistaken.

In working together, Kuomintang, the Chinese Communist Party and other parties and factions need not fear difficulties, as these can all be overcome in conditions of peace, democracy, solidarity and unity under President Chiang's leadership, and upon the implementation of the Three People's Principles.

Although Mao Tse-tung said that he would harbor no other ideas, the Communists were in fact having just such considerations. What were these? Subsequent developments provided the best answer to this question. Less than a month after his return to Yenan Mao Tse-tung tore up the foregoing agreements and pledges completely.

Communist Obstruction to the Acceptance of Japanese Surrender

The forty-one-day-long discussions in Chungking, which attracted nationwide attention, were used by the Chinese Communists as a smoke screen to cover up their activities in the field. What were those activities? According to an account in the October 17th issue of the Communist *Hsinhua Daily News*, the Communists had seized as many as 200 cities during the month from September 11 to October 11; had put under their control numerous points along the Tsingtao-Tsinan Railway, the Tientsin-Pukow Railway, the Lunghai Railway, the Peiping-Suiyuan Railway, the Peiping-Liaoning Railway, the Tehchow-Shihchiachwang Railway, the Peiping-Hankow Railway and the Taoching Railway, thereby obstructing the main communication lines in North China and Central China; had threatened shipping along the coast from Shanhaikwan in the north to Hangchow in the south, along the section of the Yellow River from Wanchu to Wucheh.

along the Yangtze River in Kiangsu and Anhwei provinces, and also along the Grand Canal.

After September 11 Government troops were busy accepting the surrender of Japanese troops in various parts of the country. In thirty days and eleven areas they disarmed 1,255,-000 Japanese forces who were later all repatriated to Japan in accordance with stipulations of the Allied Headquarters. The Chinese Communists, however, detained nearly 30,000 of the Japanese troops they had disarmed in Chahar, Hopei, Shantung and in northern Kiangsu.

While obstructing the acceptance of Japanese surrender by Government troops, the Chinese Communists launched a vigorous anti-American propaganda campaign throughout the country.

American forces had fought side by side with Chinese Government troops in the China Theater. When the war ended they assisted the latter in accepting the surrender of Japanese armed forces. Both during and after the war the help of the American forces was sincerely appreciated by the Chinese people. The Chinese Communists, however, charged that by assisting the Government in accepting Japanese surrender in Tientsin, Chinwangtao, Peitaho, Tsingtao and Yentai (Chefoo), the Americans were "interfering in China's internal affairs."

The Communist propagandists insinuated that while Russian troops were being withdrawn from Manchuria, American troops were being landed in North China to help the Government carry out its "antidemocratic policies." One purpose of this propaganda was to arouse public opinion in the United States and to force the American Government to withdraw its troops from the China Theater. Another purpose was to prevent Government troops from going to North China to accept Japanese surrender, especially to stop them from going to Manchuria to re-establish Chinese authority in that region.

Meanwhile, what were the Chinese Communists doing while this propaganda was sweeping over the world?

1. They destroyed lines of communication. All trunk and branch railways in North China were subjected to destruction not once but several hundred times. The sections most extensively damaged would take months to repair.
2. They breached the Yellow River dikes. In the Taikung area in Honan province alone they flooded an area of several hundred square kilometers.
3. They dynamited or dismantled a number of mines in Hopei, Shansi and Honan provinces.
4. They set fire to or otherwise damaged factories. In Shansi province alone they destroyed more than 500.
5. They razed to the ground a large number of villages and rural towns in Kiangsu, Shantung and Honan provinces.
6. They perpetrated massacres. The most barbarous mass killings occurred in Kalgan.
7. They pressed able-bodied men into their armed forces. In areas under the Communist control no one between fifteen and forty-five years of age was spared.
8. They expanded their area of control. From September till December, 1945, the Communists had increased the number of counties in their so-called Liberated Areas from 70 to more than 200.
9. They issued vast quantities of "Anti-Japanese Currency Notes" and "Border Area Currency Notes" and forced them upon the people, thereby sabotaging the nation's monetary system.

Soviet Russia's Treaty Violations in Manchuria

Articles 2 and 5 of the "Agreement Regarding Relations Between the Chinese Administration and the Commander-in-Chief of the Soviet forces after the entry of Soviet troops into the Three Eastern Provinces of China (Manchuria) during the joint military operations against Japan," which formed part of the Sino-Soviet Treaty of Friendship and Alliance, read as follows:

Article 2: A Chinese National Government representative and staff will be appointed for the recovered territory, whose duties will be:

(a) To establish and direct, in accordance with the laws of China, an administration for the territory cleared of the enemy.

(b) To establish cooperation between the Chinese armed forces, both regular and irregular, and the Soviet forces in the recovered territory.

Article 5: As soon as any part of the recovered territory ceases to be a zone of immediate military operations, the Chinese National Government will assume full authority for the direction of public affairs.

The Soviet forces took advantage of the Japanese surrender and entered Manchuria, where they disarmed and detained the Japanese as prisoners of war. But Ambassador Hurley informed us on August 30 that Stalin had told Averell Harriman, then American ambassador in Moscow, that "to date, the Soviet forces have not established any contact with the Chinese Communists," and that "the Soviet forces have not discovered any Communist guerrillas in Manchuria." Eventually the Soviet forces turned all the Japanese arms they had seized in the area over to the Chinese Communists.

On October 1 Petrov, the Soviet ambassador, notified our Government that the Soviet Government had decided to start withdrawing their forces from Manchuria early that month, and asked our Government to send a representative to Changchun before October 10 to discuss with General R. Malinovsky matters concerning the transfer of garrison duties from the Soviet forces to the Chinese. Our Government sent

Hsiung Shih-hui, director of the Northeast Headquarters, to Changchun, and also notified Petrov that we had decided to ship troops by way of Dairen, where they would land to take over as the Russian forces began to withdraw.

On October 5 a message was received from Fu Ping-chang, Chinese ambassador in Moscow, saying that the Russian Foreign Office had informed him: "As Dairen is a port for goods and not for troops, the Soviet Government is resolutely opposed to any troops landing at Dairen." Thus, our original plan to land troops at Dairen had to be abandoned. After his arrival at Changchun, Hsiung Shih-hui had two talks with General Malinovsky on October 13 and 17, when he brought up the Chinese Government's plans for landing troops at Hulutao and Yingkow instead. General Malinovsky replied he had no comments on this matter. But when the first units of our troops landed at Hulutao on October 27 they were fired on by Chinese Communist forces. No landing was possible and as a result they had to turn back to Tsingtao. Finally, they were re-routed to Chinwangtao where they landed and followed the Peiping-Liaoning Railway toward Shanhaikwan.

On November 5 Malinovsky informed Hsiung Shih-hui that Hulutao had been occupied by the Communists and that the latter had also entered Yingkow. He could not, therefore, be responsible for the landing of Chinese Government troops at Yingkow. He added that the Soviet troops would start moving northward on November 10 and that they would not be responsible for conditions in areas thus evacuated. He rejected all our proposals for the organization of local militia units and the dispatch of liaison officers to accompany our representatives to the various provinces and cities in Manchuria on take-over missions. By this time Chinese Communist units had moved to Manchuria from Shantung by sea and had taken Antung. On November 11 they had even entered Changchun, where the Northeast Headquarters was located. About the same time Communist forces began making preparations for combat in Mukden.

Soviet Russia's Occupation of Outer Mongolia and Invasion of Jehol and Chahar

As related above, when Soviet Russia went to war with Germany in June 1941 the puppet regime in Tannu Tuva immediately declared war against Germany. Not long afterward Tannu Tuva was annexed to form part of the Soviet territory. By August 1945 Moscow applied the same formula to Outer Mongolia. On August 11, two days after Soviet Russia's declaration of war against Japan, the puppet regime in Outer Mongolia also declared war against Japan. On February 13 the following year, Soviet Russia and Outer Mongolia signed a new treaty whereby Outer Mongolia, while nominally still independent, actually became part of the Soviet territory.

Following Soviet Russia's declaration of war against Japan her troops invaded Manchuria. Following Outer Mongolia's declaration of war Mongol troops invaded our Chahar province. On August 23, under the cover provided by the Soviet and Mongol forces, Chinese Communist troops entered Kalgan. The Russian and Chinese Communists proceeded to create a movement for "Inner Mongolian autonomy." In the name of their Outer Mongolian puppets, Soviet troops sent arms and ammunition to "Inner Mongolia," and despatched a so-called "Soviet-Mongolian Military Mission" to Kalgan to train and equip the Chinese Communist forces. In January 1946 there was convened a so-called Eastern Mongolian People's Representatives Conference at Kekengmiao south of Hsinan to set up an "Eastern Mongolian People's Autonomous Government." In April of the same year a conference of the Eastern and Western Mongolian puppets was held at Chengteh at which the "Eastern Mongolian Autonomous Government" was absorbed into a "Joint Association for the

Promotion of the Inner Mongolian Autonomy Movement." All these maneuvers were to stage an "Inner Mongolian People's Representatives Conference" for the purpose of establishing an "Inner Mongolian Autonomous Regional Government" at the time when the Chinese Government convened the National Assembly.

Later, on June 5, 1947, under the cover of Soviet planes bearing the Red Star insignia, Outer Mongolian troops in the Paitaishan area on the Mongolia-Sinkiang border invaded Sinkiang province. Fighting flared up again in January 1948 and lasted for four months. The Chinese Government lodged repeated protests with the Soviet Government. Moscow countered by accusing Chinese troops of invading Outer Mongolia.

In the Sino-Soviet Treaty of Friendship and Alliance of August 1945 China accepted Soviet Russia's demand for Outer Mongolia's independence out of a desire to maintain friendship and a lasting peace between herself and Soviet Russia. The Chinese Government's policy toward Outer Mongolia has always been one of treating it on an equal basis with other ethnic components in the country. If Outer Mongolia should be genuinely independent and become a buffer and a guarantee for Sino-Soviet nonaggression, then the price China paid in agreeing to Outer Mongolia's independence, though extremely heavy, would still be worth it.

Upon Moscow's instigation, the puppet regime in Outer Mongolia fomented uprisings in Inner Mongolia and caused disturbances in Sinkiang. In the series of incidents which broke out in Sinkiang, Outer Mongolia became Soviet Russia's tool for aggression. This puppet regime of Outer Mongolia does not represent the Mongolian people; it is now a Soviet instrument for aggression against China and threatens peace in Asia. In no circumstances can it be considered an independent and self-governing country.

Stalin's Actions

By August 1945 Soviet Russia's violations of her treaty undertakings and her territorial ambitions in Jehol, Chahar and Manchuria and her directives for the Chinese Communists to betray the country had all been exposed. As to the atrocities such as pillaging and raping committed by Soviet forces against our people in Manchuria, I have no heart to relate them in detail here.

Having seen through Russia's treachery and her designs on Manchuria, we decided to withdraw the Northeast Headquarters and all personnel charged with take-over duties from Changchun back to Shanhaikwan.

On November 15 our Ministry of Foreign Affairs informed Soviet ambassador Petrov of this decision. At the same time I sent a message to President Harry S. Truman, pointing out that Soviet Russia's treaty violations and bad faith in Manchuria not only were detrimental to China's territorial integrity and unification, but also constituted a serious threat to peace and order in East Asia, and that the only way to prevent any further deterioration of the situation would be for China and the United States to take positive and coordinated actions. In reply President Truman assured me that he would work out some suitable measures in close cooperation with me.

Following the announcement of our decision to withdraw the Northeast Headquarters from Changchun, the Russians suddenly modified their attitude and appeared friendly. They also declared that the take-over program could proceed in accordance with the Sino-Soviet Treaty of Friendship and Alliance and that they anticipated no difficulty which could not be solved through discussions.

Nevertheless, I adhered to my decision of withdrawing the Northeast Headquarters to Shanhaikwan. All Government troops assigned to Manchuria went there by land, moving on both sides of the Chinchow-Shanhaikwan Railway. On November 26 they arrived at Chinchow and took possession of Hulutao. Thereupon I ordered them to halt and not to press onward to Mukden. The Government's decision was not to proceed with the take-over program but to leave the Russians in illegal occupation of the area in violation of the treaty, and to see what they would do to solve the Manchuria question, on which world peace and security depended.

During this period the Russians time and again expressed friendliness. In the meantime the United States generously offered to put a large number of ships at our disposal to transport Government troops to Manchuria by sea to expedite the implementation of the take-over program. I modified my original decision and acted accordingly. On December 5 Malinovsky said he would like to discuss with us the question of liaison as our Government troops pushed eastward from Chinchow to Mukden. On January 26, 1946, Chinese Government troops entered Mukden.

It was at this point that Stalin took the unusual step of inviting my son Ching-kuo to visit Soviet Russia. On December 25 Ching-kuo left for Moscow as my personal representative and returned to China on January 14, 1946. In his two talks with Ching-kuo, Stalin spoke of his hopes for peaceful coexistence between China and Russia and between Kuomintang and the Chinese Communist Party. He also expressed himself in favor of cooperation between China, the United States and Soviet Russia, but said he was opposed to the introduction of any third power's influence into Manchuria. He urged China to adopt an independent policy, leaning neither to one side nor to the other.

Finally, Stalin expressed the hope to Ching-kuo that I would visit him in Moscow or arrange to meet him at a suitable place somewhere on the Sino-Soviet border. I believe this was Stalin's real purpose in inviting Ching-kuo to Russia. I consulted General George Marshall, U. S. special envoy to China.

His reply was: "Anything that can help relations between China and Russia, I am for it." I felt that no useful purpose could be served by going into details. I decided to decline Stalin's invitation in a courteous manner.

On May 5, 1946, N. Roshin, the Soviet Embassy's military attaché, contacted Ching-kuo to say that he had received instructions from Moscow to see him. The two met on the following day. It transpired that Stalin had renewed his invitation to me to go to Moscow preferably following Molotov's return from Paris. On May 7 Moscow wired Roshin again, asking him to get a definite reply from me.

I felt that if I should accept the invitation the only road before us in diplomacy would be to follow the Russian Communists' consistent strategy toward China, i.e. cooperation between Kuomintang and the Chinese Communist Party, the joint establishment of a coalition government and complete dependence on Soviet Russia. All these represented steps in Moscow's scheme of "peaceful transformation" for China. Once we should start on this road it would mean the end of China's national history and culture and her status as an independent country.

On the other hand, if I should turn down the invitation it would of course disappoint Stalin. As a result he might become more ruthless in his support of his Chinese puppets in carrying out aggression against China. Unfortunately, world public opinion had already come under the influence of the Communist International's propaganda. Most of the democratic nations had chosen to appease Soviet Russia in the Sino-Soviet dispute. In the circumstances then prevailing, whichever foreign policy we might adopt, be it pro-Russia or pro-Anglo-American, the consequences would not be difficult to imagine.

Finally, after a thorough discussion with the senior members of the Government and the Party, it was unanimously decided that China's permanent national interests and her people's fundamental welfare, instead of the shifting world conditions of the moment, should be the basis of our foreign policy. Even such great sacrifices as China has been forced to make under the Sino-Soviet Treaty of Friendship and Alliance have failed to satisfy Soviet Russia. Obviously nothing short of complete domination of China would satisfy Stalin's appetite. Therefore, before Soviet Russia gave any indication of the possibility of Sino-Soviet cooperation by fulfilling her obligations under the Treaty, there was no point for me to meet Stalin.

This was at a time when the crisis, starting from Manchuria, was fast developing into a threat to the East Asiatic mainland and the western Pacific. It was generally felt that only by Sino-American cooperation could this crisis be averted. Of course Moscow knew that, in order to occupy Manchuria and help the Chinese Communists in their rebellion, it must begin by undermining Sino-American relations and isolating China.

A hidden international current was already lashing at Sino-American relations, and China was already being isolated. It was no longer possible for China and the United States to work out a joint policy toward Soviet Russia on the basis of our common interests. Consequently the only thing we could do was to disregard what attitude and policy the Western nations might or might not adopt toward us, and to be prepared, in consonance with our own independent policy, to go it alone, if necessary, in combatting Soviet aggression to the bitter end. It was on such considerations that I decided to turn down Stalin's second invitation.

Later, an official of the American Embassy asked me about "the two requests for a meeting" which I was supposed to have made to Stalin and which the latter had turned down. It was only then that I told him the whole story. That it had been rumored as my request was typical of Stalin's maneuver. If I had accepted the invitation Stalin would have been able to exploit it to the fullest extent in fomenting misunderstandings between China and the United States.

Stalin's Proposal—Neutralization of China

Moscow not only sought to harm China's relations with the United States, but also attempted to manipulate China's foreign and domestic policies. On several occasions Stalin expressed the following views to the Chinese Government:

1. In explaining his relations with the Chinese Communists, he hoped that China would not think of Soviet Russia and the Chinese Communists as if they were identical. He said that, politically, he had no connection with Chinese Communists. Such sympathy as the Russian Communists might have shown toward the Chinese Communists was the sort of sympathy they had expressed toward Communists in all countries. He admitted that Soviet Russia once did have a resident representative in Yenan, who, however, had since been recalled. He said he had refused to agree to the Chinese Communists' sending troops into Manchuria.

2. Stalin not only asked China to bar third powers from Manchuria but also expressed the hope that China would adopt an "independent policy." He criticized the United States for helping Japan to recover and asked China to take positive measures together with Soviet Russia for joint defense against Japan. He also hoped that China would readopt its earlier policy of 1924 favoring an alignment with Soviet Russia and the admission of Chinese Communists into Kuomintang. What he meant by an "independent policy" favoring neither one side nor the other, was really a neutralist policy, which could only end in China's isolation insofar as her relations with the other countries were concerned, and would leave us no choice but to lean completely on Soviet Russia.

3. He said Soviet Russia's moral and material help to China would not be given to the Chinese Communists but to the

Chinese Government toward the latter's support. If the Chinese Government thought it unnecessary, Soviet Russia would not care to take part in attempts to solve problems between Kuomintang and the Chinese Communist Party. Stalin hoped that the Chinese Government would make more concessions to meet the Chinese Communists' demands. He suggested that Kuomintang and the Chinese Communists would "compete in peace."

4. He emphasized that after World War II he visualized there would be no world war for twenty to thirty years.

This was the neutralist tactics which Soviet Russia tried to apply in China in 1946, the year after victory. It was also obviously Stalin's stratagem vis-à-vis the free world in general. His intentions were perfectly clear. If I had adopted what he chose to call an "independent policy," regarding ourselves as a bridge between the United States and Soviet Russia and between the East and the West by taking a neutralist stand, and formed a "coalition government" with the Chinese Communists through Moscow's mediation, the whole country would then have become a Soviet satellite through "peaceful transformation." Soviet Russia would then have succeeded in controlling China as a whole without shedding a single drop of blood and would have not only conquered Asia by peaceful means but also converted the Pacific Ocean into a Russian lake. That was why I firmly rejected all Stalin's proposals.

Propaganda Offensive by the International Communists

The aggressors in Moscow knew that in order to conquer China in the military field, first of all they would have to defeat the Chinese Government in the field of public opinion and diplomacy in the United States. At the same time they also knew that unless they overthrew the pro-American Chinese Government and replaced it with one of Chinese Communists, it would be impossible to carry out their scheme and secure the expulsion of American influence from China and the fulfillment of their ambition to establish hegemony in Asia.

The Government was free to choose between force and peaceful means and either one would have solved the Chinese Communist problem. I chose the road of peaceful reconstruction. I had every confidence in being able to keep the situation under control and to put down a Communist insurrection if there should be one. The Chinese Communists, of course, knew that in either case, peaceful reconstruction or mobilization for a suppression campaign, the Government could deal them severe blows and even wipe them out altogether. Consequently, operating in foreign countries as well as in China under Moscow's direction, they used the cloak of "peaceful coexistence" to conceal their armed insurrection, which in turn was used to strengthen and intensify their political offensive. This put the Government in a difficult position where it could neither have peace nor wage a war.

At the time few people had a clear understanding of the basic nature of the Chinese problem.

Politically, the Chinese Communists' insurrection was in fact Soviet Russia's war of aggression against China. It was the Chinese Communist forces who started this war, but the instigation had come from Moscow. Yet the international Communists, in an attempt to mask the ugly face of aggression, unanimously pronounced it as "civil war" and accused the Chinese Government of having started it.

Legally the Chinese Government, like the government of any other democratic nation, would have no alternative but to take steps to suppress the insurrection in order to preserve the political and social order. This was the duty of the Chinese Government and it was also its authority. Yet the international Communists, in their propaganda ostensibly against "civil war," succeeded in making people both in and outside China lose sight of the Government's duty and authority, mistake it for a Chauvinist and aggressive-minded Fascist regime and defame it as such. At the same time left-wing liberals in the West believed that the Chinese Communists had launched the insurrection for the sake of democracy and agrarian reform.

As American attitude toward the China problem was of vital importance; it was necessary for the Chinese Government, first of all, to win international understanding. It had for the time being no choice but to remain on the defensive and to permit the Communists to take the initiative in order to convince the world where responsibility rested. Result: insurrection rapidly spread. Eventually the Government lost its power to maintain law and order in the country, and in due course the Communist military might grew to constitute a real menace to world peace.

Neutralist Maneuvers by the Communists

While the international Communists were busy manufacturing "civil war" in China on the one hand and pushing their "anti-civil war" political and propaganda offensive on the other, the Chinese Communists once again resorted to neutralist tactics. The so-called Anti-Japanese National Salvation Grand Alliance, formed before the Sino-Japanese War, joined forces with several other political groups to form the so-called Democratic League. After the war the League extended its scope of activities again in a neutralist garb. In October 1945, in a manifesto issued at the end of its extraordinary national congress, it openly admitted its neutralism in the following words:

"Since its inception, the Democratic League has taken an independent and neutral stand in making incessant efforts toward bringing about national peace, unification and solidarity."

The manifesto also disclosed that the Democratic League was engaged in propaganda both for and against "civil war" on behalf of the Chinese Communists. For it said:

"The situation in China today is one in which Kuomintang and the Chinese Communist Party are opposed to each other. Since the Japanese surrender this opposition has increased the danger of civil war. If this trend is not completely reversed, it will be idle for China to talk about peace, unification and solidarity, let alone democracy."

The Democratic League's proposal for a settlement was an endorsement of the Chinese Communists' view on the formation of a "coalition government." For the manifesto said:

"The Democratic League has consistently believed that a national democratic coalition government is the only road to peace, unification and solidarity. It is also the only way for the nation to work together in concerted efforts for national reconstruction."

Since the situation then existing was "one of opposition between Kuomintang and the Chinese Communist Party," what could be more popular for anyone to do than to strike an independent and neutral stance and work for China's "peace, unification, solidarity and democracy?" In this propaganda offensive all wavering politicians and disaffected military men and those who were not farsighted politically, and others who had no clear knowledge of Soviet Russia's aggression and the Chinese Communists' subversive activities, thought they had found a political future for themselves.

Imperceptibly the Chinese Communists succeeded in isolating the Government and the neutralists at the same time. The latter, having no adequate knowledge of China's National Revolution nor of Communism, were a confused lot. They did not know any difference between right and wrong and failed to distinguish between good and bad. Most of them were only interested in political maneuvering and in personal gains. They tried to maneuver between the Government and the Chinese Communists. They calculated that even if the Chinese Communists should gain the upper hand, they could still so manipulate the situation as to obtain a handsome reward for their services. At any rate they reckoned that they would have plenty of chance to promote their own interests. The neutralists never anticipated that as soon as the tide of war had turned against the Government and they themselves were shut behind the Iron Curtain, they would have lost all their usefulness to the Chinese Communists and would have to place themselves completely at the mercy of the Communists.

During 1946, on account of the Political Consultative Conference and American mediation, appeasement was very much in the air and the neutralists became more active than ever. The camouflage of neutralism and democracy thus provided the Chinese Communists with a cover under which to intensify their military action, extend their infiltration and disorganize the anti-Communist forces, and finally to foil the Government's policy of mobilization for their suppression. These tactics proved to be far more effective than if the Chinese Communists had acted in their own name.

The Beginning of American Mediation and the First Cease-Fire Order

On December 15, 1945, President Harry S. Truman made a statement on America's policy toward China. On the same day General George C. Marshall, as special envoy, set out for China to carry out his mission.

For the seventh time the Chinese Government sat down with the Communists at the conference table. The previous six series of talks having all ended in failure, people both in China and abroad naturally were not optimistic about the outcome of the seventh one either.

On December 17, following my first interview with General Marshall, one American general asked me what I thought of the future prospects of the peace talks now that General Marshall had come to China as mediator. I replied, "The key to this question is in the hands of Soviet Russia. You have to get your answer from Moscow." In return, I asked him, "Do you think Moscow would agree to let the United States succeed in its mediation efforts between Kuomintang and the Chinese Communist Party?" He said, "Why don't you tell this to General Marshall?" I said, "This is not the time. I'll wait and see." I was hoping then that by virtue of his great prestige, General Marshall might succeed in his mission.

After six meetings held between January 7 and 10, 1946, the Committee of Three, composed of a Government delegate, a Communist delegate and General Marshall, agreed on a cease-fire. On January 10 both the Government and the Communists issued orders to their respective commanders in the field. Principal points in the order were:

1. All combat activities should cease at once.
2. All military movements should cease. This, however, should not affect Government troops moving into or inside Manchuria to re-establish Chinese authority there.
3. All destructive and obstructive activities against lines of communication (including postal service) should cease at once.
4. To carry out the cease-fire order, an Executive Headquarters should be established in Peiping, to be headed by a Committee of Three, representing the Chinese Government, the Communists, and the United States. All its instructions and orders should be unanimously agreed to by its members and promulgated by the Executive Headquarters in the name of the chairman of the Government.

The Political Consultative Conference

The Political Consultative Conference was convened on the day the cease-fire orders were issued. In my opening address I said with all sincerity:

"The Government is prepared to accept any resolution that may be reached at this conference, so long as it helps national reconstruction, benefits the people's welfare and aids in the progress of democracy in the country."

At the same time I announced that the Government had decided to take adequate measures to safeguard the people's freedoms, respect the legal status of political parties, implement the program of local self-government, hold general elections and release political prisoners.

The Government delegate at the conference was the first one to propose the expansion of the governmental structure to the effect that before the convocation of the National Assembly, the Government would admit members of other political parties and nonpartisan leaders in its State Council and also in its Executive Yuan (Cabinet) as part of its preparations for constitutional rule.

The Political Consultative Conference reached five agreements after twenty-one days of deliberations. Principal points in these agreements were as follows:

1. On Government Reorganization:
   (a) The State Council should have forty members, to be chosen by the chairman of the Government from among members as well as non-members of Kuomintang.
   (b) The State Council should adopt ordinary resolutions with the approval of more than one-half of the state councilors present. In case of resolutions involving changes in administrative programs, they should be approved by two-thirds of the state councilors present.
   (c) Members of the various political parties as well as nonpartisan leaders would all be eligible for appointments as heads of ministries and commissions in the Executive Yuan and as ministers without portfolio.
2. On the Program of Peaceful National Reconstruction:
   The Program of Peaceful National Reconstruction should guide the Government in its administration after the reorganization and expansion of its structure and be-

fore the enforcement of constitutional rule. This program should make elaborate provisions concerning the people's rights, adopt comprehensive measures concerning political, military, diplomatic, economic and financial, educational and cultural, relief and rehabilitation matters and overseas Chinese affairs under the following four headings:

(a) The Three People's Principles should be observed as the supreme guiding principles in national reconstruction.

(b) The entire nation should unite under President Chiang and work for the realization of a united, free and democratic New China.

(c) President Chiang's views on political democratization, the nationalization of all armed forces and an equal and legal status for all political parties should be regarded as the path leading to peaceful national reconstruction.

(d) Political means should be used to resolve political disputes in order to ensure the peaceful development of the nation.

3. On Military Affairs:

The resolution on military affairs fell under four headings, namely, principles relating to the building up of the national army, principles relating to military reorganization, measures concerning control of armed forces by the civil branch of the government and measures for military reorganization and integration.

The important principles to be observed were the following:

(a) The armed forces should belong to the State.

(b) All political parties should be banned from engaging in any overt or covert activities among the armed forces.

(c) The National Military Council should be reorganized into a Ministry of National Defense under the Executive Yuan, in which there should be set up a Military Planning and Development Committee consisting of representatives from various circles in the country.

(d) The Subcommittee of Three on Military Affairs should, in accordance with the original plan, move speedily to work out details for the reorganization of the Chinese Communist forces and to complete their integration at an early date. Government troops should, in accordance with the original plan of the Ministry of War, be reorganized into ninety divisions within six months. When these two reorganization plans were completed, the nation's armed forces should be unified and reorganized again into fifty to sixty divisions in all.

4. On the National Assembly:

The Government had originally decided to convene the National Assembly on November 12, 1945, to terminate the period of political tutelage. It was postponed on account of stiff opposition put up by the Chinese Communists and the Democratic League. On this question the Political Consultative Conference had reached an agreement, which comprised the following important points:

(a) The National Assembly would be convened on May 5, 1946, and the function of the first National Assembly would be to frame a constitution.

(b) The number of regional and vocational delegates would remain at 1,200. For Taiwan and Manchuria, 150 new regional and vocational delegates would be added.

(c) The number of delegates from political parties and of prominent civic leaders would be increased to 700. The question of apportionment would be decided later.

5. On Proposed Revisions to the Draft Constitution:

The Political Consultative Conference proposed twelve

principles for revising the Draft Constitution (usually referred to as the May 5th Draft Constitution), which was promulgated by the Government before the war. A Draft Constitution Re-Examination Committee would be formed to prepare modifications in accordance with the proposed principles of revision. Views from various sides should be taken into consideration.

Formulas for the Reorganization and Integration of the Armed Forces

According to the five agreements reached, the question of military affairs would be discussed by a Conference of Three and the Subcommittee on Military Affairs. On February 9 the Conference of Three met to discuss the resumption of communications and the full text of its agreement was published by the Government. From February 14 to 25 the Subcommittee on Military Affairs held five meetings and agreed on a Basic Formula for the Reorganization and Integration of Chinese Communist Forces into the National Army. The principal points in this formula were:

1. In the Agreement of October 10, 1945, and during the Political Consultative Conference, the Chinese Communists asked that their forces be reorganized into twenty divisions. It was agreed in the Basic Formula that during the first period of twelve months Government troops would be reduced through reorganization from 354 divisions to ninety divisions, and during the same period the Chinese Communists could retain eighteen divisions. During the second period of six months the Government could keep fifty divisions and the Chinese Communists ten divisions. Government troops would maintain a ratio of five to one vis-à-vis the Communist troops.
2. In integrating Chinese Communist forces into the National Army it was agreed that during the first period four group

armies would be formed, each to be composed of one
Government army and one Communist army. During the
second period divisions would be similarly integrated to
form armies. Thus, of a National Army of twenty armies,
six would be composed of mixed Government and Communist forces.
3. Regarding geographical distribution of Communist and
Government forces, it was agreed that during the first
period, in North China, in addition to the four group
armies of combined Government and Communist forces,
the Government would station three more armies; in Manchuria, five Government armies and one Communist army;
in Central China, one Communist army and nine Government armies. During the second period there would be
seven Communist divisions and ten Government divisions
in North China; fourteen Government divisions and one
Communist division in Manchuria; ten Government divisions and three Communist divisions in Central China.

Following the cease-fire order, the promulgation of measures for resumption of communications, the conclusion of
agreements on the reorganization and integration of Communist forces into the National Army, the establishment and
functioning of the Executive Headquarters, and the five agreements reached at the Political Consultative Conference, it was
generally thought that the nation could begin peaceful reconstruction at last and that the people could return to their
native places to live and work in peace again.

General Marshall, too, thought that one phase of his mediation mission had come to an end. Soon afterward he returned
to Washington to report to his government. The Chinese
Government, on its part, was determined to reorganize its
forces. No matter whether the Chinese Communists would
carry out the various agreements or not, it would proceed
with their faithful implementation according to the prescribed

methods and procedures. What about the Chinese Communists?

American Mediation and Neutralism

The first time General Marshall was about to return to the United States I said to him and General Alvan C. Gillem that the Chinese Communists looked upon their armed forces as their "revolutionary capital." Although the plans for military reorganization and integration were to their advantage, actually the integration of the Communist forces into the National Army would be as difficult to achieve as "to negotiate with the tiger for its skin." If we really hoped that the Chinese Communists would carry out this military integration plan we would have to rely upon God to make them "turn pretenses into realities."

After General Marshall had left for the United States the Chinese Communists tore up the cease-fire agreement by pouring troops into Manchuria, thus setting at naught the cease-fire agreement and extending the area of their rebellion. When he returned to China I said to him: "The United States, in her present efforts to assist in the peace talks between Kuomintang and the Chinese Communists and to mediate in their military conflict, could succeed only by coordinating her policies with China's policies. Particularly, there should be mutual understanding between the American and Chinese Governments so that the Communists would have no chance to drive a wedge between us." Throughout this period I exercised the utmost forbearance in the face of the Communists' treachery and their fantastic demands, for I was determined to prevent any breach in Sino-American relations, as this could only help the Communists.

General Marshall's mediation efforts in China should be viewed from two standpoints. The position of the United States was that of a third party trying to mediate in the conflict between Kuomintang and the Chinese Communists in the interest of China's own unity. Naturally, she was sincere and also believed she was being perfectly fair. On the other hand, Soviet Russia was merely exploiting the American mediation for the sake of her "neutralist tactics." In the first place, although she had turned the arms of over a million Japanese troops to the Chinese Communists, the latter required more than a year to replenish their numbers and to complete their training before they would be ready for an all-out rebellion. For this reason, she sought to take advantage of the American mediation to gain time for the Chinese Communists. In the second place, she not only tried to utilize the American mediation to launch her customary neutralist tactics for the purpose of alienating Sino-American relations, but actually had an even larger objective in mind, i.e. to prevent the American mediation from succeeding.

From the standpoint of the Russian Communists, if General Marshall should succeed in his mediation efforts it would only mean a setback for Russia's policy toward China. Therefore, she not only wanted to defeat the American effort but also to bring about in the course of the mediation a clash and eventually a breach between China and the United States. Consequently, what Soviet Russia did during this period was to incite the Chinese Communists to ignore their own pledges by starting a rebellion on the one hand, and to carry on a smear campaign against the United States on the other. Finally, this anti-American campaign reached such a violent pitch that it became utterly fantastic. This was Soviet Russia's intrigue to sabotage the American mediation. It was her hope that after the failure of the American effort and after General Marshall had gone home, she herself could play the role as a mediator so that she could manipulate the political situation in China. As we had anticipated this, Soviet Russia did not have a chance to realize her scheme.

Incidents in Manchuria and the Second Cease-Fire Order

When Soviet troops were evacuated from Changchun on January 23, 1946, Chinese Communist troops immediately moved in. Government troops, bound by the cease-fire order, could neither resist nor attack and had to move away to avoid a clash. On February 16 the Chungking *Hsinhua Daily News* announced that there were 300,000 so-called "Democratic Allied Forces" in Manchuria. Later, a spokesman of the Chinese Communists made a four-point proposal:

1. The Government should reorganize the Northeast Headquarters, its political and economic affairs committees and the provincial governments, by asking "democratic personages," members of various political parties and nonpartisan leaders in Manchuria to take part in them.
2. The Government should recognize and reorganize the "Democratic Allied Forces" in Manchuria.
3. The Government should recognize the "self-rule governments" in various counties in Manchuria.
4. The Government should limit the number of troops sent into Manchuria to re-establish Chinese authority there.

The cease-fire order of January 10, as we saw, was not applicable to Government troops who were to move into Manchuria to re-establish Chinese authority.

In arming and helping the Chinese Communist troops to occupy various counties and cities in Manchuria following the evacuation of her own troops, Soviet Russia acted in violation of the Sino-Soviet agreement. In obstructing Government attempts to re-establish Chinese authority in Manchuria and in attacking Government troops there, the Chinese Communists acted in violation of the cease-fire order. Furthermore, judging by the Communist spokesman's statement, the Chinese Communists had no intention of abiding by any of the agreements reached by the Subcommittee of Three before January 10.

On the eve of General Marshall's first departure for the United States the Conference of Three met on March 11 to discuss the situation in Manchuria. General Marshall proposed the dispatch of field teams into the area by the Executive Headquarters with orders to supervise the cessation of hostilities. Articles 4 and 5 of his proposal contained the following provisions:

Article 4: Chinese Government troops should have the right to occupy any area necessary for the re-establishment of Chinese authority in Manchuria. It was particularly stipulated that Government troops should have exclusive administrative right in areas on both sides of the two railways mentioned in the Sino-Soviet Treaty to a depth of thirty kilometers.

Article 5: Government troops could ask Communist troops to evacuate such areas (including coal mines) as considered necessary for the re-establishment of Chinese authority. Chinese Communist troops should not enter areas evacuated by the Soviet forces.

Chou En-lai, the Communist delegate, refused to agree to Article 4. After General Marshall left, his place on the Conference of Three was taken by General Gillem and discussions continued. Chou En-lai changed Articles 4 and 5 into three articles as follows:

Article 4: In its efforts to re-establish Chinese authority in Manchuria, the Government should have the right to send troops to areas "now" being evacuated by the Soviet forces, including both sides of the Changchun Railway each to a depth of thirty Chinese *li.**

Article 5: If Government troops wish to enter areas at present being garrisoned by Communist forces, the cease-fire field teams should be consulted.

Article 6: The future demarcation of garrison areas in Manchuria should be decided separately in accordance with the Military Reorganization Plan.

* Li is about ⅓ of a mile.

When Chou En-lai took this proposal back to Yenan for instructions, it was rejected. Finally the Government and the United States made the maximum concession by deleting all revisions that had been made to Articles 4 and 5, leaving only provisions on procedures for military mediation as contained in the three articles. It was only then that Chou En-lai agreed to return to Chungking.

Thus, General Marshall's proposal, made on March 11 on the eve of his departure from China, for the dispatch of field teams by the Executive Headquarters to Manchuria, was nullified by the Communists and became totally inoperative. Subsequent talks on March 27 and on April 8 and 9 failed to produce any results.

By this time the Chinese Communists with the support of Soviet forces had further extended their rebellion, making it impossible for the cease-fire teams in Manchuria to operate. The Communists concentrated their troops at Szepingkai to block Government troops moving northward from Mukden for take-over purposes. This brought on a fierce battle which raged for a week. The 300,000 Communist troops under Lin Piao were routed by Government forces under the command of General Tu Yu-ming. More than half of the Communist effectives became casualties. The rest fled toward Harbin and Suifenho in the north. General Tu moved up from Szepingkai to Changchun on May 23. Government troops were ordered to push on along the Chinese Changchun Railway with Harbin as their target and met with practically no organized resistance. This was another decisive battle against the Communist troops since the Government's fifth campaign against them in 1934, when they were still in southern Kiangsi.

As soon as he came back from the United States General Marshall discussed with me matters concerning the cessation of hostilities and the continuation of the peace talks. Whereupon I flew to Mukden on May 21 to look over the military situation myself. Reports from the front all agreed that barring some special international complications the Chinese Communists would not be able to fight anew after the terrific punishment they had just taken at the hands of the Government forces. If the Communists would only mend their ways and carry out their undertakings under the cease-fire agreement reached in January, I would give them another chance to prove their loyalty to the nation. I issued orders for Government troops to cease pursuit and await orders.

In my letter to General Marshall written in Mukden on May 24, I stated the Government's decision to accept a truce in Manchuria. The only condition was that the Communists must abide by the cease-fire agreement, the measures for the restoration of lines of communication and the agreed formula for military reorganization and integration. Upon my return to Nanking I held several discussions with General Marshall. On June 6, in compliance with his suggestion, I issued a second cease-fire order. Government pursuit units which had already crossed the Little Sungari River and were deployed near Shuangcheng, were ordered to withdraw to Taolanchao and Tehui where they were to remain on the defensive, pending the outcome of the peace talks.

Meanwhile I issued a statement in which I said:

"I have just issued an order to all Government troops in Manchuria to stop attack, advance and pursuit as from the noon of June 7 for a period of fifteen days so as to give the Chinese Communists another chance to carry out their obligations under various agreements thus far concluded. This does not jeopardize the Government's right to re-establish Chinese authority in Manchuria in accordance with the Sino-Soviet Treaty."

During the fifteen days in question there were repeated discussions between the Chinese Government and the American delegates and the Chinese Communist delegate for a cease-fire in Manchuria and on the question of military reorganization on the basis of General Marshall's proposal. No agreement, however, was reached. On June 21 I announced an eight-day extension of my earlier order to halt advance and attack until midday June 30.

However, the Chinese Communists made even stiffer demands during the eight days, thus making it impossible to reach any agreement. The morale of Government troops in Manchuria began to suffer as a result of the negative position in which they had been placed. The second cease-fire order turned out to be the beginning of the Government forces' debacle in Manchuria. If at the time Government pursuit units near Shuangcheng, which is less than 100 kilometers from Harbin, had pressed on toward that city of strategic importance on the Chinese Changchun Railway, Communist remnants in northern Manchuria would have been liquidated and the situation throughout Manchuria stabilized. If the Chinese Communists were driven out of their foothold in northern Manchuria, Soviet Russia would have found no way to send them any more supplies and a fundamental solution to the problem of Manchuria would have been at hand. The subsequent defeat of Government troops in Manchuria in the winter of 1948 was largely due to the second cease-fire order.

The Government repeated its earlier mistake in thinking that the Chinese Communists are Chinese and are, therefore, patriotic after all, and that there was possibility of reaching a peaceful settlement sooner or later.

Soviet Russia's Looting of Factories and Mines in the Northeast

It was during this period that Soviet Russia accelerated her looting of factories and mines in Manchuria, and her intentions to monopolize the economic resources there became more obvious than ever.

After their entry into Manchuria Soviet troops immediately began to dismantle and carry away important industrial installations. On October 17, 1945, the Russians proposed to us that all factories and enterprises operated by Japan should go to the Soviet troops as war booty, that all factories and enterprises operated by the Manchukuo puppets and Chinese nationals would be handed back to the Chinese Government and that all factories and enterprises operated jointly by Japan and the Manchukuo puppets should be disposed of through formal negotiations between the Chinese and Russian Governments.

On February 1, 1946, when General Malinovsky spoke of Sino-Soviet economic cooperation, he reiterated that "the movable portions of Japan's military industries in Manchuria should be the Red Army's spoils, but as an expression of friendliness toward China, Soviet Russia is willing to share half of the proprietary rights in part of the spoils (factories and mines) with China to be operated on a joint basis." He also said: "It is hoped that the question of economic cooperation in Manchuria can be quickly settled. Soviet Russia does not wish to have any third party come in. She is particularly opposed to Manchuria being turned into an anti-Soviet base." This declaration was patently meant to oppose our Government's policy of welcoming foreign capital for the development of resources in Manchuria and also to bar the United States so that Soviet Russia alone could exploit the region.

On February 1 our Government made a counterproposal on the question of economic cooperation. We refused to recognize as valid the Russian contention that Japanese enterprises and assets in Manchuria should be considered as the Red Army's war booty. Regarding "joint operation," we indicated that it should not apply to the former South Manchurian Railway and its affiliated enterprises, hydraulic power plants, the Fushun Coal Mines, the Anshan Iron Works, aviation industry and navigation on the Sungari River. General Malinovsky said: "Soviet Russia is not willing to see Manchuria used once again as an anti-Soviet base. This plan of economic cooperation is merely a precautionary measure for our own security." He disagreed that the various factories and mines just mentioned should be excluded from joint operation.

It was at this time that Chang Hsin-fu, a special commissioner appointed by our Government to take over the mines in Manchuria, took a party of nine, including technicians and policemen, to Fushun to inspect the coal mines there. He was prevented by Chinese Communists on the scene from carrying out his duties and had to return to Mukden. While en route he was killed by Communist troops at the station in Liyen. His assassination aroused the indignation of our people, especially those in Manchuria.

The U. S. State Department sent notes to both the Chinese and Soviet Governments on February 11, stating that it would be contrary to the Open Door principle if, through Sino-Soviet joint operation of industries in Manchuria, the United States and other allies should be excluded from having an equal opportunity to take part in the development of economic resources in the region. The note also said that the final disposition of Japan's overseas properties and assets should be decided at a later date by an Inter-Allied Reparations Commission.

America's Open Door views on Manchuria were compatible with our Government's economic policies for the region. The American notes, however, did not stop Soviet Russia from plundering Manchuria of its industries and pillaging its economic resources. Talks on economic cooperation naturally got nowhere. Meanwhile, Soviet stripping of all important industrial equipment in Manchuria went on. On December 15, 1946, the U. S. State Department published a report by Edwin Pauley, American representative on the Inter-Allied Reparations Commission, on the results of his investigation in Manchuria. The report said that during the Soviet occupation, industries in the area suffered a direct loss of US$858,-

000,000, and that the losses would reach US$2,000,000,000 if they were estimated on the basis of their replacement costs and depreciation. This figure represented Soviet Russia's loot from industries and resources in Manchuria.

All-Out Attacks by Communist Troops

In May 1946 the Communist troops, in order to support their military action in Manchuria, unleased attacks on Government troops in Jehol, Chahar, Hopei and Shantung provinces in violation of the cease-fire order.

On the Jehol-Chahar Front: Despite the cease-fire order of January 10, Communist troops entered Chihfeng. Abiding by the cease-fire order, Government troops moved out in order to avoid a clash. Despite the cease-fire order of June 6, the Communists entered Chengteh. The Executive Headquarters' cease-fire team at Kalgan had to withdraw under Communist pressure on September 20.

On the Shantung Front: Despite the cease-fire order of June 6, the Communists seized Tsaochuang. The following day they occupied Tehchow, Taian, Kaomi, Kiaohsien, Nanchuan and Lantsun. At the same time they concentrated 50,000 troops at the outskirts of Tsingtao and 100,000 troops around Tsinan. Their advance on the two cities precipitated serious fighting at both places.

On the Northern Kiangsu Front: Despite the Government's declaration of June 30 on settling internal disputes by political means, the Communists threw a force of sixteen regiments against Taihsing, where Government troops suffered heavy losses. After taking the city of Taihsing, the Communists pushed on toward Taihsien and other towns on the north bank of the Yangtze River in Kiangsu to threaten the national capital at Nanking. Government troops were forced to fight back in what was known as the Battle of Northern Kiangsu.

On the Shansi-Suiyuan Front: Despite the cease-fire order of January 10, the Communists stormed and occupied

Houma and Tsining. Even after the cease-fire order of June 6, they seized twenty-two more counties, including Wenhsi, Suhsien, Hsinchiang, Yuchih, and Chiehshiu, steadily completing their encirclement of Taiyuan and Tatung. This touched off the Battle of Southern Shansi and the Battle of Tatung.

At this point the Government found it necessary to call on the Communists to evacuate Chengteh in Jehol in order to protect Peiping and Tientsin, to evacuate the Tientsin-Pukow Railway in order to restore communication on this north-south artery, and to evacuate northern Kiangsu in order to safeguard the national capital at Nanking.

Postponement of the National Assembly and the Declaration of August 14

The convocation of the National Assembly on May 5, 1946 was one of the agreements reached at the Political Consultative Conference. The Communists, however, maintained that the National Assembly should be held only after the government structure had been reorganized. As to the distribution of seats in the State Council, the Communists insisted on having fourteen seats for themselves and the Democratic League, or more than one-third of the total of forty seats, so as to have a veto on all important decisions. This unreasonable demand met with the objection of other parties, and consequently there was no agreement. In the meantime the Communists delayed submitting a list of their delegates to the National Assembly. The Government had no choice but to postpone its convocation to November 12.

The Government took the stand that the military problem must be settled before there could be any discussion of political questions. The Chinese Communists, on the other hand, used the question of Communist local administrations in northern Kiangsu as a pretext for demanding that the Political Consultative Conference take up the question in its

General Committee so as to bring about a simultaneous settlement of military and political problems. This was the main point of contention between the two sides following the postponement of the National Assembly.

On August 10 General Marshall and Dr. J. Leighton Stuart, American ambassador to China, issued a joint statement on the difficulties encountered in their military mediation effort. The statement reads:

General Marshall and Dr. Stuart have been exploring together every possibility for terminating the present growing conflict in China and for the initiation of the preliminary steps in the development of a truly democratic form of government. The desire for a peaceful solution to the political problems appears practically unanimous on the part of the people. The economic situation demands a prompt solution if a disastrous collapse is to be avoided. The fighting is daily growing more widespread and threatens to engulf the country and pass beyond the control of those responsible. Both the Government and the Communist leaders are anxious to put an end to the fighting but there are certain issues concerned in the immediate settlements involved regarding which an agreement has not been found. It appears impossible for the two parties to reach a settlement of these issues which would permit a general order to be issued for the complete cessation of hostilities in all of China. Certain of the unsettled issues relate to the military redispositions of troops. However, these apparently present less difficulty of settlement than a more fundamental issue concerning the character of local or county government to be maintained in the regions which will be evacuated as a result of the military redisposition pending a basic decision in such matters by the Constitutional Assembly.

On August 14, in order to break the deadlock, I issued a statement in which I made the following six points:

1. The National Assembly must be convened on November 12.
2. The Government will sincerely abide by the agreements reached at the Political Consultative Conference and carry

them out to the best of its ability. Regarding the Draft Constitution, all that the Government asks is that sound views be collected from all sides and that they be presented to the National Assembly for consideration so that the constitution, when formed, would be a good and practicable one.

3. On broadening the basis of government by inviting members of various political parties and nonpartisan personages to take part in it, steps of implementation will be taken at an early date, and the Government will be guided by the Program of Peaceful Reconstruction in its administration of the country.

4. Regarding the cessation of conflicts, the Government will remain bound by the original agreements and carry them out in good faith. Moreover, the Government will not ask the Communists to evacuate from all the areas they had occupied since the cease-fire order. All that it asks is that they evacuate from certain areas, where their presence has constituted threats to peace and obstacles to resumption of communications.

5. Regarding political disputes, efforts should continue to be made for their solutions. As long as the Communists faithfully carry out the agreements on cease-fire and on the resumption of communications, abide by mediation and implement the Military Reorganization and Integration Plan so that the nationalization of the armed forces will not be an empty talk, and once such a guarantee is forthcoming, the Government will be prepared to discuss with the Communists any pending problems at any time.

6. What the Chinese people need most at the moment is a chance to live and work in peace. Therefore, the Government must do its best to remove the threat to life and property and fulfill its duty to the people.

Communists' Open Rejection of the United States as the Mediator—The Virtual Termination of Mediation Effort

On September 3 I accepted General Marshall's suggestion and agreed to the creation of a Subcommittee of Five to discuss the question of government reorganization and the National Assembly, in addition to the Conference of Three which would continue its mediation effort in the military field. This was a great concession on the part of the Government, as this would enable simultaneous discussions of military and political problems with a view to their settlement through negotiations.

On September 20 the Executive Headquarters' field team at Kalgan was compelled to evacuate by the Communists. This was not only in violation of the cease-fire agreement but was a definite threat to Peiping and Tientsin, two cities of major importance to the Government in North China. For security reasons the Government had to conduct military operations against the Communist troops which had taken Kalgan by storm and against the others concentrated around it. Chou En-lai tried to intimidate General Marshall by saying: "If the Government does not call off its military action against Communist troops at Kalgan and in its environs, the Communists will regard it as the open declaration of an over-all rupture." Shortly afterward he left Nanking for Shanghai to dodge further discussions.

On October 5 I again accepted General Marshall's suggestion and ordered a ten-day halt during which the Conference of Three would discuss the military question while the Subcommittee of Five would deliberate on the political issues.

Simultaneous discussion of military and political questions was originally one of the Communists' demands. When the Government finally accepted it, they reversed their position by using the Kalgan question as a pretext. Now, after the

Government had announced a halt in the Kalgan area, the Communists raised their demands again.

The conditions which the Government brought up at this time were still based on agreements reached earlier at the Political Consultative Conference and on the Military Reorganization Plan. They were under two headings:

1. The Chinese Communists should promptly submit a list of their delegates to the State Council and another list of their delegates to the National Assembly.
2. For the implementation of the Military Reorganization Plan, the garrison areas for the eighteen divisions of Communist troops should be promptly decided and the latter should move into these areas within a definite date.

The Chinese Communists' demands were as follows:

1. There were three articles concerning military affairs:
   (a) Troops of both sides should resume their positions of January 13 south of the Great Wall and resume their positions of June 7 north of the Great Wall.
   (b) Between now and the period of military reorganization and integration, the positions of troops of both sides should be definitely fixed.
   (c) Government troops which had moved since January 13 should all return to their original positions in order to facilitate reduction through reorganization.
2. Of the eight articles on political questions, the three important ones were:
   (a) The Chinese Communists and the Democratic League must have fourteen seats in the State Council.
   (b) The Executive Yuan should be reorganized immediately following the formation of the new State Council.
   (c) After the reorganization of the government structure had been completed, various political parties would

submit lists of their delegates to the National Assembly according to the number of seats to be approved by the reorganized government.

Hoping to end the stalemate, General Marshall called on Chou En-lai in Shanghai on October 9 and asked him to return to Nanking to continue the negotiations. In response Chou presented the following demands:

1. The Government must call off its proposed attack on Kalgan indefinitely.
2. The Chinese Communists and the Democratic League should have veto power in the State Council.
3. The date of convocation of the National Assembly and the number of delegates should be settled by the General Committee of the Political Consultative Conference.

Chou En-lai also added the following points to General Marshall in a critical tone:

1. "The Chinese Communists cannot agree to the United States Government giving material aid to the Kuomintang Government at a time of civil war. They are particularly opposed to the failure of American forces to withdraw from China as promised.
2. "I have particularly noticed that every time you and Ambassador Stuart issued any statement, it was invariably after the Communists had rejected some Government terms and never after the Government had rejected Communist terms. Although your statements contained no obvious censure of the Communists, their timing has caused misunderstanding on the part of the general public."

Chou En-lai's first point was not aimed at General Marshall's mediation effort but at the presence of American forces in China. By now the Chinese Communists had ceased to look upon General Marshall as a third party, but as an enemy. In his second point Chou openly accused General Marshall of siding with the Chinese Government in his mediation effort. This was tantamount to saying that the Chinese Communists no longer had any confidence in him.

Thus General Marshall had to return to Nanking empty-handed. This meant that the Chinese Communists had already succeeded in gaining the time they needed for preparing their all-out insurrection. It also meant that Communist smiles of welcome to American mediation were no longer necessary. This signified the virtual termination of the peace talks and military mediation centered around General Marshall as a result of the Chinese Communist sabotage. As in the six previous instances the peace negotiations, which lasted for more than one year this time, also ended in failure.

The Third Cease-Fire Order and the Convocation of the National Assembly

As the Chinese Communists showed no signs of willingness to resume negotiations after the expiration of the ten-day truce, Government troops retook Kalgan. On October 16 I issued a statement on the current situation and reiterated the Government's policy of seeking a peaceful settlement. I also advocated that all military problems be solved in accordance with agreements reached in the Conference of Three. As to the question of local administrations raised by the Communists, this could be settled by the State Council after its reorganization. All these, however, were rejected by the Communists.

At this juncture, leaders of parties other than Kuomintang and the Chinese Communist Party, and nonpartisan leaders offered to mediate as "the third side." On October 25, 29 and 30 a series of talks were held. The terms which they produced were likewise rejected by the Chinese Communists. In the meantime the Chinese Communists and the Democratic

League launched anti-American movements in Peiping, Tientsin, Nanking and Shanghai.

On November 10, only two days before the National Assembly was due to open, Chou En-lai said to General Marshall: "Whether the National Assembly is merely postponed
or convened unilaterally, in either event there will be no
room for any more political discussions." Thus it became
clear that the Communists' real purpose was to prevent the
convocation of the National Assembly and the introduction
of constitutional rule.

Meanwhile, it also became very clear that they intended to
sabotage the peace talks and military mediation altogether
and to resort to armed rebellion to subvert the country. I still
hoped, however, that they had not lost all their senses and
that, in a last-minute change of mind, they might attend the
National Assembly and resume negotiations in order to save
the nation from a great disaster. Therefore, on November 11,
on the eve of the convocation of the National Assembly, I
made a final appeal to them in the hope that they would,
whether before or during the Assembly meetings, submit a
list of Communist delegates and have them take part in the
deliberations to give national backing to the launching of
constitutional rule. I issued the following statement:

It has been the Government's consistent policy to promote internal peace and national unification so that political tutelage may
be terminated and constitutional rule inaugurated. In conformity
with its wish to see a lasting peace and political stability in the
country, the Government has ordered its troops both north and
south of the Great Wall to cease all military actions except when
it is necessary to defend their present positions.

The convocation of the National Assembly is the only legal
procedure whereby the Government can hand over political
power to the people and there should be no further delay. Therefore, the Government has decided to convene it on November 12
as scheduled.

What I said in my statement of October 16 really represented
the Government's maximum concession, and I hope the Chinese

Communists will accept them in order that all outstanding problems can be settled. It is the Government's hope that the Chinese Communists will join the other political parties in following the path to democracy. Insofar as military affairs are concerned, no political parties should have their own troops, all of which should form part of the National Army.

For this reason, the Government is reserving the number of seats which the Chinese Communists and various political parties ought to have in the National Assembly and it hopes that they will decide any time during its forthcoming session to participate in enacting a constitution for the country. It is also the Government's hope that the Chinese Communists will send delegates to attend various conferences and to discuss, on the basis of points listed in my statement of October 16, measures for stopping armed conflicts, allocating garrison areas, restoring lines of communication and implementing military reorganization and integration so that they can all be expeditiously enforced.

Regarding the reorganization of the State Council, it is hoped that an agreement will be reached soon so that it can be formally put into effect. As to the Executive Yuan, since it is the body actually responsible for administration, greater caution needs to be exercised in its reorganization. For this reason, it is not proposed to effect this major change before the National Assembly adjourns.

Concerning the Draft Constitution, the Government intends to present to the National Assembly for deliberation the unfinished draft by the Draft Constitution Re-Examination Committee. Six months after the closing of this National Assembly, general elections will be held in the country in accordance with the constitution, when all political parties and the people at large can freely compete for seats in the new National Assembly which will function according to constitutional stipulations.

This means that if various political parties wished to propose changes to the constitution they could still do so in accordance with law at the next National Assembly.

By this time delegates nominated by the various parties had all arrived. The Chinese Communists were the only ones who had refused to submit a list of their delegates. The Democratic League, which had up to now posed as an independent neutral, tore off its mask and followed the example of the Chinese Communists by refusing to attend. After the opening ceremony the National Assembly decided to call a three-day recess to wait for the Communist and Democratic League delegates to turn up, but in vain.

Means and Ends of the Chinese Communists' Land Reform

While the peace talks were in progress the Communists' "land reform" was undergoing a drastic change. In one of their four pledges made in September 1937 the Communists had said that they would "stop the program of dispossessing the landlords through violence." During the Sino-Japanese War the Communists enforced in their areas a policy of reducing land rental and loan interest on the one hand and requiring their payment on the other. This was the Communists' way of using the farmers' struggle against the landlords to control both the landlords and the farmers.

At the Chinese Communists' Seventh National Congress in April 1945, Mao Tse-tung announced a land policy for the postwar period. He said, "It will begin with reduction in land rental and in loan interest and then in a series of steps seek the realization of the land-to-the-tiller ideal." This sounded reasonable, indeed. Actually, what he meant by "land-to-the-tiller" was the liquidation of landlords through class struggle which the Communists had carried out in the name of "equal distribution of land" in the days of the Chinese Soviets in Kiangsi.

In December 1946 the Communists withdrew their resident delegation from Nanking. Shortly afterward at a meeting in Yenan attended by senior cadres from various places, the Communists decided on a "thorough re-examination of the land reform program." This meant re-examination of the landlords' land, houses and other properties for equal distribution among "poor farm hands." In this movement, it was the "poor farm hands" who led in the struggle for "a major economic and political reversal."

In September 1947 the Chinese Communists promulgated an "Outline of the Land Law" which abolished the landlords' right of ownership over their lands. Poor farmers' corps became agencies for reforming the agrarian system and for land distribution. Using "equal distribution of land" and "complete reversal" as slogans, the Communists created a reign of terror in the rural areas by their numerous probes into the people's class status, thoughts, ways of doing things. They traced the farmers' ancestry for as far back as three generations.

The Communists launched such large-scale probes and stirred up class struggle by equal distribution of land because their land reform movement was at the same time a join-the-army movement. Farmers in the Communist areas were told by their unions that "henceforth members of the landlord class and feudalistic rich farmers will not be permitted to join the Eighth Route Army. Farmers must keep the arms in their own hands. Farmers should all enthusiastically join the army." In other words, the land reform movement was military mobilization.

The Chinese Communists boasted that their "land reform" was aimed at solving the problems of farmers and land. They also claimed that the so-called Farmers-Workers Alliance was to safeguard the common interests of the workers and farmers. Today they are carrying on on the Chinese mainland the same "Farmers-Workers Alliance" trick which they had used to deceive farmers in Kiangsi and Hunan provinces twenty-three years ago. The only difference is that the Communists are more ruthless today than ever before.

It should be noted that the Chinese Communists are using the "Farmers-Workers Alliance" not only to manipulate the farmers and the workers as tools in their political struggle but also to exploit them economically. Actually, their "land reform" has nothing to do with the solution of the farmers' problems or with the protection of the real interests of the workers. It will be much more truthful to say that the whole thing has been a hoax.

According to Communist theories, anyone who possesses production assets or is the principal party in a business operation and who does not make his living by selling labor, is of the propertied class. This even includes farmers and petty handicraftsmen. That was why Lenin regarded the farmers as constituting "the last propertied class." Since the propertied class is the enemy of Communism, it follows that the farmers are also the enemy of Communism. The methods the Communists use to destroy the propertied class are confiscation, joint operation and collectivization. They use the same methods against the farmers for their final elimination.

In the meantime, the Communists took note of the differences in the economic conditions of the farmers and used them as a basis for their stratagem of creating division among the farmers. It was a three-point stratagem, namely, relying on the poor farmers, unifying the middle-class farmers and hitting the rich farmers. By "relying on the poor farmers" is meant the distribution among them of properties seized from the rich farmers so as to arouse their class sentiments; by "unifying the middle-class farmers" is meant the intimidation of the middle-class farmers by the poor farmers so that they too will work for the Communists in their attempt to seize political power and to "reform" the economic system of the country.

This stratagem served the Chinese Communists well during their "land reform" and their subsequent "collectivization" movements following their all-out insurrection. But since their "agricultural collectivization" campaign moved into the period of "advanced-type cooperatives," which is another name for "collective farms," landlords and rich farmers have ceased to exist. Farmers, workers and merchants have one and all become slaves. There is now only one conflict, namely, that between the Communists on the one hand and the farmers on the other. This clash between the oppressor and the oppressed has led to the emergence of two opposing classes, namely, the masters and the slaves.

It may be recalled that in the days of the Chinese Soviets in Kiangsi and Hunan before the Sino-Japanese war, the Chinese Communists also began by using the distribution of land as a bait to secure the support of those without any property in the villages for them to persecute the landlords and rich farmers. After the distribution of land to the poor farmers and farm hands, the Communists forced the farmers to organize collective farms for the ostensible purpose of cooperation. Finally, all the farmers in the Soviet areas became serfs and all agricultural production came under the control of the Communists. This resulted in a sharp reduction in farm output. Many farmers fled, and those who could not get away lost all interest in farming. Furthermore, because of the confiscation of private property and the stoppage of trade, there was a general decline in production activities in the villages and there were increasing hardships among the farmers. In the end the Communist troops had to abandon their old base in southern Kiangsi.

This bit of history shows that the Chinese Communists, who had gained their earlier start by deceiving the farmers, will surely meet their defeat at the hands of the farmers. Today the Chinese Communists are repeating on the mainland their earlier policy of agricultural collectivization which caused their downfall twenty-three years ago. We can safely predict that they will fail again in the near future just as they did before. These are all facts which happened during the past thirty years. No amount of dialectic argument can alter the course of events.

Changes of the Neutralists—The Anti-American Movement

Before the Chinese Communists rejected General Marshall's mediation they had already directed their front organization, namely, the Democratic League, to start anti-American propaganda. By the time they did reject the mediation the League likewise changed its "peace movement" into one against the Government by tagging behind the Chinese Communists in their all-out rebellion. Soon the anti-American movement advanced from open slander to hostile actions.

As early as July 1946, when the American mediation was still in progress, Communist troops under Tsao Tse-foo forming the 53rd Regiment of their 54th Army called an Anti-American Movement mass meeting at Anping, a rural town in Hsiangho county, Hopei province. On July 28 Communist forces southeast of Anping cut off the area from the surrounding regions. All traffic was stopped. The following day a U.S. Marine Corps convoy comprising some thirty officers and men on their way from Tientsin to Peiping were fired on by Chinese Communists. The latter used rifles, machine guns and trench mortars in their ambush, which resulted in the killing of three American servicemen and the wounding of seventeen others.

Obviously, the purpose of this attack was to create an incident to support the propaganda then being conducted by the international Communists for the withdrawal of American forces in China. It was a matter of great regret that our ally, the United States, should stop its supply of arms to the Chinese Government at the very moment when the Chinese Communists began their anti-American activities. Earlier, in April, following the Chinese Communists' breach of the cease-fire agreement, the American Government had stopped its US $500,000,000 loan to the Chinese Government. Now it interrupted its military aid to China. At the same time it took no action whatever against the Chinese Communists despite their violations of the cease-fire agreement. In fact, it did not even adopt any measures in the face of Soviet Russia's arming of the Chinese Communists in Manchuria with Japanese weapons. This dealt a severe blow to the anti-Communist forces and constituted a great boost to neutralism.

The Sino-American Commercial Treaty, concluded in accordance with the spirit of the new Sino-American Treaty of January 1943 and on the basis of the principles of equality and reciprocity, was published on November 4 of the same year. The Chinese Communists directed the "Anti-American Movement Committee" in various places to oppose the new commercial treaty. In the form of forums, parades and demonstrations held in Nanking, Shanghai, Chungking, Chengtu and other places, the anti-American movement spread.

On December 24, 1946, there occurred a scandal in Peiping involving a Chinese girl student supposed to have been raped by an American soldier. This was played up by the Chinese Communists and their front organization in their propaganda. Communist agitators posing as students in Shanghai organized a "Anti-Violence Joint Association," and also sponsored a "National Anti-Violence Joint Association." They declared that, "We shall oppose the American forces as long as they remain in China." They charged that there were secret agreements between China and the United States on the stationing of American forces in China and U.S. military aid to China, and demanded the "publication of the Sino-American secret agreement." By February 1947 Communist student agitators in Shanghai formed a "Federation of Associations in Protest Against Violence by American Forces in China" as headquarters for students' anti-American activities in various parts of the country. The federation soon started a "Signature Movement by Chinese students to urge the United States to change her policy toward China."

The Chinese Communists launched the "Anti-Violence Movement" when the industrial and commercial circles in the country failed to respond to their agitation against the Sino-American Commercial Treaty. When the people in general again failed to respond to the "Anti-Violence Movement" they switched to a "Boycott American Goods" movement. This also ended in failure because the postwar market in Shanghai and other major cities was in great need of American military aid, surplus goods and UNRRA-CNRRA* supplies. The Chinese Communists' "Boycott American Goods" movement was really aimed at American aid to the Chinese Government. Although the "Boycott American Goods" movement which the Democratic League carried on in Shanghai in February 1947 was conducted along the same lines as the boycott against Japanese goods in prewar years, its only objective was "opposition to U.S. aid" and the "expulsion of American forces from China."

The American Government obliged by gradually withdrawing its troops from Peiping, Tientsin, Tsingtao and other places, and by discontinuing its military aid to China. Thus, a glorious episode of Sino-American cooperation in the cause of freedom came to an end under the attacks of the Chinese Communists and their international "comrades." The traditionally harmonious friendship which had characterized the relations between China and the United States for over a century was nearly disrupted.

Constitutional Rule and Rebellion-Suppression Going on Side by Side

Following its adoption by the National Assembly, the Constitution was promulgated by the Government on New Year's Day, 1947. The Government enacted various laws and regulations governing the general election which, it was hoped, would be held according to schedule, so that a constitutional government could be established within the pre-

* United Nations Relief and Rehabilitation Administration and Chinese National Relief and Rehabilitation Administration.

scribed period. Meanwhile, the State Council and the Executive Yuan were reorganized so that members of other political parties and nonpartisan leaders could share with Kuomintang the responsibility of governing the country.

What emerged from this reorganization was a coalition government, comprising members of the Young China Party, the Democratic Socialist Party, nonpartisan leaders and members of Kuomintang but with no Chinese Communists. It was this coalition government which later on made preparations for the general election and supervised it when it was held. Meanwhile, the Communists continued their armed revolt, thus making it necessary for the Government to launch constitutional rule and to mobilize its forces in order to put down the revolt at one and same time.

Following the issuance of the rebellion-suppression order on July 4, 1947, Government troops won in a number of individual campaigns including the capture of Yenan, the Battle of the Chimun Mountains, the Battle of the Shantung Peninsula, and the Battle of East Honan in the spring of 1948. After October 1948, when the Hsuchow-Pengpu Battle was at its critical stage and when the people and those in the Government were under the spell of Communist infiltration, there came into circulation a slogan to the effect that "Unless President Chiang goes, no American aid will be forthcoming," and that "Unless President Chiang goes, there can be no peace talks."

In these circumstances, I decided to retire from office. I did so on January 21, 1949. The moment I was gone both the armed forces and civilians on the mainland seemed to have lost a symbol of common purpose. Thus, the political situation, social order and the people's minds all fell under the Communists' invisible control. The military situation deteriorated rapidly and soon became irretrievable.

In their political activities and social movements, both the Chinese Communists and their front organizations, especially the Democratic League, had to take certain stands and were, therefore, easily identified. The same thing, however, could not be said of infiltration by these front organizations. They penetrated deep into government organs, representative bodies and civic organizations. They even joined such anti-Communist religious bodies and secret societies as the Kolaohui.* They also got hold of military men who had fought the Communists either in or outside the battlefield and politicians who acted as go-betweens between Kuomintang and the Communists. Through infiltration or encirclement they manipulated these public bodies and individuals directly as well as indirectly in order to attain their own objective.

It was generally thought that ex-militarists, ex-bureaucrats and merchants and brokers seeking profits through speculation would make poor Communists or fellow travelers. In seeking to subvert the country and to destroy the social order, the Communists found that the more degenerate these people were the more useful they would be in working for the Communists and in running their errands. Their task was to help shake the very foundation of society and demoralize the military and the civilians alike by such slogans as "oppose conscription," "oppose requisition," "oppose mobilization" and "oppose civil war."

Though the Government knew that the latter were acting as the Communists' jackals, it felt its hands were tied by democratic institutions, and as long as they operated under the cloak of "freedom" and "human rights," the Government could not take any action against these religious bodies, secret societies, underworld characters, gangsters, disgruntled politicians and profiteers who had come under the Communist grip. It was in this manner that neutralism and defeatism came to spread in the Government and in the armed forces, paving the way for Communist rumors to foment dissatisfaction, to stir up trouble and to create antagonism and disunity between

---

* A secret society in Szechwan province.

the Government and the people. The effectiveness of these subversive activities became apparent when the Government had to mobilize but found it could not do so, and suffered tragic reverses as a result.

The Purpose of Soviet Russia's Sabotage of U.S. Mediation

Reference has been made earlier to Stalin's deliberation on whether Soviet Russia should take part in mediation in China. I must add a few more details. Between the spring and summer of 1946 both the Democratic League and the self-styled independent newspapers in the country came out advocating "United States-Soviet Russia joint mediation." Later, they accused the United States of helping Japan to recover from her defeat. By putting these two views together, one accusing the United States of aiding Japan and the other suggesting United States-Soviet Russia joint mediation, one could see that behind Soviet Russia's sabotage of the American mediation was her wish to replace the United States as mediator so that she could manipulate the Chinese political situation.

In December 1946 the United States announced the end of its mediation effort in China. Shortly afterward General Marshall went back to America and the Chinese Communists openly launched a general rebellion. During the year which followed Soviet Russia and the Chinese Communists both directly and indirectly kept on asking the Chinese Government for resumption of peace talks. In the autumn of 1947, when Government troops were advancing toward Chefoo, Weihaiwei and Penglai on the southern coast of the Gulf of Chihli, their request for cessation of hostilities and resumption of peace talks became more urgent than ever.

The neutralists in the country were particularly noisy in saying, almost with one voice, that the conflict between Government and Communist troops could not be stopped except through Soviet Russia's mediation. Meanwhile, they created a defeatist atmosphere by making the general public believe that the Government's military campaign to suppress the rebels could never succeed and that Soviet Russia's mediation provided the only way out for the country.

Because of my thirty years of experience in dealing with the Russian Communists I could see what lay behind Moscow's attempt to mediate and also its consequences. If we had accepted Soviet Russia's mediation we would have become a second Poland in 1947 also by way of a "coalition government." That was why I resolutely rejected their requests and feelers on various occasions.

The Outcome of Peaceful Coexistence

When the war with Japan ended the Chinese Government signed a Treaty of Friendship and Alliance with Soviet Russia, and for a year and a half it carried on peace talks with the Chinese Communists in the hope of finding a workable formula of peaceful coexistence between China and Russia, and between Kuomintang and the Chinese Communists. Every time the Government made concessions in the peace talks, however, the Communists raised their demands. Their final objective was to occupy China for the Russian Imperialists and to turn our country of 12,000,000 square kilometers into a new colony for the Russian Empire. I have already said that the Chinese Communists made use of American mediation as part of their neutralist tactics. In other words, they saw in the American mediation a chance for the growth of neutralism, just as they had seen in the cease-fire agreement a convenient cover for their military movements. Once the cease-fire agreement was concluded, their purpose in accepting U.S. mediation had been achieved. After that they no longer considered themselves bound by any stipulations in the agreement.

On the other hand, the Government's eagerness to abide by the agreement put its troops in a passive position and made them easy prey for the Communists. Now we know that the Communists accepted American mediation in order to sabotage it and they concluded the cease-fire agreement in order to break it. This created a situation of neither war nor peace in which fighting and peace talks went on side by side. This was the practical application by the Communist International of the laws of dialectics both in its basic stratagem and in its line of action. All through the year 1946 the Communists used this stratagem to gain time to complete their preparations for a final military showdown with the Government.

The Chinese and American peoples both believe in good faith and righteousness and both are peace-loving. Far-sighted people in both countries felt greatly perplexed in the face of this situation of neither war nor peace, of fighting and peace talks going on at the same time. By spreading malicious propaganda and false information, international Communists did their best to sabotage Sino-American cooperation. They used all sorts of tricks to isolate the Chinese Government. Finally the Chinese Government suffered from the cumulative effect of the Chinese Communists' sustained campaign of slander and malicious rumors which they started at the end of World War II.

The well-organized and well-planned propaganda offensives of the Communists abroad also bore fruit. Moscow's major overseas intrigue, the one against China, which was aimed at exclusively dominating the Chinese mainland, was almost a complete success.

But have the Russian Communists really solved the problem of the Chinese mainland? No. We do not have to mention the heroic resistance of our people from Sikang and Tibet in the west to the Yalu river in the east which has been going on incessantly against the Communist occupation. It is enough just to look at the determined fight which Chinese armed forces and civilians are pressing onward on what is a part of China's own territory under their own Government's leadership. We dare say that the Russian Communists' dream of turning the Chinese mainland into a new colony will remain a dream and will before long be dashed to pieces under the counterblow of the people of the Republic of China.

PART
TWO

The Successes and Failures of the World's Struggle Against Communism

THE STEADY PROGRESS OF THE COMMUNIST PLAN OF AGGRESSION AND THE FREE WORLD'S MISTAKES

The Reason Behind Napoleon's Victories in Europe During the French Revolution

In his various chapters analyzing the relationship between war and policies, Clausewitz advanced the view that wars of each era have their own characteristics and theories. From his study of political developments after the French Revolution, he found a new trend in war. He said:

The tremendous effects of the French Revolution abroad were evidently brought about much less through new methods and views introduced by the French in the conduct of war than through the change in statecraft and civil administration, in the character of government, in the condition of the people, and so forth. That other governments took a mistaken view of all these things, that they endeavored, with their ordinary means, to hold their own against forces of a novel kind and overwhelmnig strength—all that was a blunder of policy. . . .

We may, therefore, say that the twenty years' victory of the Revolution are chiefly to be ascribed to the faulty policy of the governments by which it was opposed. . . .

It is true that war itself has undergone important alterations both in its nature and forms . . . they arose from an altered policy which proceeded from the French Revolution . . . and which had called forth . . . other means and other forces by which it became possible to conduct war with a degree of energy that could not have been thought of before. Also the actual changes in the art of war are a consequence of alterations in policy, and, far from being an argument for the possible

197

separation of the two, they are, on the contrary, very strong evidence of the intimacy of their connection.*

This is to say that in the Napoleonic era which followed her Revolution, France tended toward unlimited war in her external wars and showed such ruthlessness and resoluteness as she had never exhibited before. The countries which opposed her failed through using antiquated tactics of limited war. Whether warfare can develop in the direction of the unlimited war, however, depends on policy. That is why Clausewitz said war is like a fearsome battle-sword, but in the hands of politicians, it becomes nothing more than a rapier. The mistake of the European powers was in opposing Napoleon's unlimited war with old-fashioned limited war. This was what made his success possible.

The Origin of the Russian Communists' Reactionary Character

I must point out that there was a crosscurrent in the French Revolution. This was none other than Communism flying the banner of Socialism. In 1848, when democratic revolutions were at high tide all over Europe, Karl Marx organized the Communist First International and issued the "Communist Party Manifesto," preaching class struggle and advocating "a union of the world's proletariat." Although the international Communists demonstrated their reactionary strength in their repeated attempts to stir up class struggle during the French Revolution, they accomplished nothing. In 1917 the Russian Communists seized power in their own country following a *coup d'état* in the course of a democratic revolution. They created a so-called dictatorship of the proletariat. This was how this antidemocratic crosscurrent first came about, and later became such a serious threat to human freedom and to world peace and security.

* Karl von Clausewitz, *On War* (Modern Library edition, p. 600-601).

Socialism is humanitarianism itself. A true socialist society is one of mutual help, kindness and happiness, on the basis of justice and righteousness. As a corollary, the state where Socialism prevails should be independent, free and peaceful, and certainly not one that is despotic, dictatorial, brutal and aggressive. Yet Marx described his theories as "scientific Socialism," and branded Socialism of the humanitarians as "abstract Socialism." Later, in the hands of the Soviet government as set up by the Russian Communists, the so-called Socialist Communism internally came to be merged with the historic traditions of Czarist totalitarianism, and externally it became an ideological instrument of Pan-Slav aggression. Waliezewski said: "The Russia of Peter the Great is a factory and a camp. He made his Russians a nation of officials, of laborers and of soldiers."* In commenting on Pan-Slavism, Engels said:

In the works of several Slavic dilettantes in the field of history there arose an absurd antihistorical current, the aim of which was to subordinate the civilized West to the barbarian East, the city to the village, trade, industry and education to the primitive agriculture of Slavic serfs. But behind this comical theory there stood the terrible reality of the Russian Empire—of that Empire which by every movement manifested a pretension to consider whole Europe the property of the Slavic tribe and, in particular, of its only energetic part—Russia.**

Soviet Russia after 1917 was a modern war machine built on the backs of serfs and slave labor. Engels' remark is a most apt description of Soviet Imperialism of today. It is also a most appropriate interpretation of the reactionary nature of Communism as it stands today.

Following the establishment of the Soviet regime in Russia, and especially after the merging of Communism with Pan-Slavism, the Russian Communists have taken advantage of all wars, no matter whether they were imperialist wars of ag-

* Waliezewski, *Peter the Great.*
** Felix Gross, *European Ideologies,* p. 808.

gression or national wars against the old colonialism. In fact they were the authors of some of the wars and had directed their fifth columnists in the countries concerned "to transform wars into revolutions" and "to transform democratic revolutions into class wars" for the purpose of seizing political power. The Russian Communists gloated over their success in Russia toward the end of World War I and in conquering China at the end of World War II. Their present scheme is to overthrow Western capitalism and to dominate the world during World War III.

We know that the Soviet bloc is controlling at most only one-third of the world's population, and the overwhelming majority of these are opposed to Communist dictatorship and tyranny. Although Soviet Russia now controls the Eurasian heartland, she is still inferior to the democratic nations on the sea and in the air, and the latter are still in possession of superior forces. Why has Russia been able steadily to unfold her plans of aggression during the thirty years since the establishment of the Soviet regime? Why has she been able to maintain initiative and achieve her objective in every incident and in every struggle against any area in the free world? My answer is that every Soviet advance has been made possible by the mistakes of her opponents.

CHAPTER TWO

CHINA'S STRUGGLE AGAINST COMMUNISM: GAINS AND LOSSES

*China's National Revolution and Counterrevolution—
The Importance of the Spirit of the Age*

China turned a new page in her history at the end of the Sino-Japanese War. With the abolition of all unequal treaties, China's days as a subcolony were over and once again the nation was independent and free.

Yet, in less than four years' time, the Government's military campaign against the Communist rebels collapsed and the Chinese mainland passed behind the Iron Curtain to become Asia's first new colony in a new dark age of slavery. China's disaster, historically unparalleled in its tragedy, is something which people both at home and abroad have found difficult to comprehend. In my opinion, before we can trace this disaster to its source we have to understand the background of China's National Revolution and also the spirit of the age it represents.

The world currents stirred up by the American and French revolutions caused great reverberations in China's political, social, economic and cultural life, and brought forth various reactions. Most of the Chinese people at the time adopted a negative attitude and tried to stop these currents instead of trying to meet them in a positive manner. Dr. Sun was the only one who faced the new situation in a creative spirit and took definite steps to propagate a national revolution based on the Three People's Principles. From his study of the precedents set by the American and French revolutions, he worked out the directives for China's National Revolution, which were as follows:

The racial revolution, political revolution and social revolution were to be completed all at once. The Republic of China was to be built up as a modern nation with a government of the people, by the people, for the people, in accordance with the Three People's Principles. This revolutionary enterprise was to be pushed to its conclusion without any midway interruptions.

The National Revolution was to be made a common enterprise of the people as a whole, and the entire people's strength was to be employed to achieve freedom and equality for the country.

Class struggle was to be opposed and only peaceful methods were to be used in solving problems of the people's livelihood; and a spirit of cooperation and mutual assistance, as typified in the equalization of the right of landownership and the regulation of private capital, was to be followed in economic reconstruction in order to forestall any class struggle.

Destruction caused by revolution was to be followed by construction of a revolutionary character in which local self-government was to be the basis of a democratic constitutional rule in the country.

The American and French revolutions marked the beginning of a new era. Europe and Asia entered upon it one after another. The world currents of this new era have been characterized by democracy in the West and nationalism in the East. To be more specific, the spirit of the age has found expression in political democracy and academic freedom in the West and national independence and political emancipation in the East. Consequently, the reawakening of the people and the revolutionary risings in the East were predestined to be opposed to old colonialism of the West.

In propagating a national revolution in accordance with

the Three People's Principles, Dr. Sun showed unusual fore-
sight and high ideals. From his basic directives as enumerated
above, it is clear that the Three People's Principles constitute
an ideological system, represent a merger of the nationalist
spirit of the East with democracy, freedom and scientific
spirit of the West. The Three People's Principles, therefore,
are the concrete manifestation of the epochal spirit of China's
National Revolution. This being the case, it was only natural
that China should want to remove the bondage and oppression that had been imposed on her by Western colonialism
and to build up China as an independent, free and modern
country. In the meantime, once her sovereignty had been
restored, China was to open her resources and market to the
Western nations on a cooperative and equal basis in order to
eliminate the cause of international war and class struggle. It
was this spirit which made our National Revolution the mainstream of a new force released by Asia's oppressed peoples.
Dr. Sun said: "This force is made of morals and truth." To
the East this mainstream was the forerunner of national independence and freedom, while to the West it was the key to
world peace and stability.

However, when we were still battling the old counterrevolutionary forces, namely, the remnants of the mon-
archial system, at the front, new counterrevolutionary forces
in the form of the Chinese Communist Party operating as a
branch of the Communist International began their intrigues
of infiltration and subversion in our very midst. Meanwhile,
when we were clashing with the old guards of colonialism,
apostles of new colonialism were subjecting us to vicious
though indirect aggression.

The history of China's relations with the Russian Communists during the last three decades has been a record of
conflict between our forces of revolution and their forces of
counterrevolution, each trying to overwhelm the other in
order to ensure its own survival. This historical record alone

is enough to show that new colonialism and the new forces of counterrevolution have constituted a greater threat to us in our efforts to achieve freedom and equality for our country. The form of struggle used by new colonialism and the new forces of counterrevolution, namely, "Peaceful Coexistence," carries with it a greater menace and threatens to bring on a greater calamity than that ever posed by armed aggression of the old colonialists as typified in their gunboat policy.

As already indicated, China after 1924 was in an unenviable position in that she had to fight both new and old colonialisms as well as new and old reactionary forces. Because old colonialism and old reactionary forces both tried to stop our National Revolution, we had to launch the Northward Expedition and to fight against Japanese aggression. Because new colonialism and new reactionary forces both tried to sabotage our National Revolution, we had to put down Communist insurrections between our wars against the northern war lords and the Japanese aggressors. Let us analyze this crosscurrent caused by the new reactionary force which has risen in the course of our National Revolution.

In the two main currents of the times, namely, democracy in the West and nationalism in the East, the Russian Communists' totalitarianism and international Communism obviously constitute a reactionary force. The Russian Communists' attempt to apply the formula of the Russian Revolution to China has increased the reactionary nature of the Chinese Communists. The formula they gave as explained earlier was the three-fold program of joining in China's anti-imperialist National Revolution, dividing Kuomintang and then turning the democratic struggle into a class war by means of an agrarian revolution. The plans was as follows:

a. During the first stage of the agrarian revolution the farmers were to be pitted against the landlords.

b. During the second stage the poor farmers were to be pitted against the rich farmers.

c. During the final stage the poor farmers were to be used as a tool in setting up a Soviet regime.

The Russian Communists, as part of their strategy for world conquest, sought to use the forces of nationalism and the vast population in the East against the West's old colonialism and, at the same time, to undermine the nationalist spirit in the course of the Eastern people's national struggle and to use agrarian revolution as a means to the creation of Soviet satellites in the East.

When Lenin stressed, in 1922, that "China's revolutionary movement has already become part of a struggle for world revolution,"* and when Zinoviev declared that "the East with its 900,000,000 people is waking up,"** they saw in China's revolution a major instrument for world revolution. That was why Communism constituted the only antirevolutionary crosscurrent in China's National Revolution.

A Study of the Campaigns in China's National Revolution

In the course of our National Revolution, we succeeded three times in overcoming this crosscurrent which was opposed to historical progress and against the spirit of the age. Today, for the fourth time, we are engaged in a continuous struggle against the same crosscurrent. Let us summarize the successes and failures in our Northward Expedition, the Sino-Japanese War and the punitive campaign against the Communists from the standpoint of military thought.

Why did the Russian Communists find it necessary to hinder our Northward Expedition before it began and try to sabotage it after it had started? I have already narrated the actual happenings earlier in the book. For our present purpose I want to re-examine the military operational ideas and strategic principles of the expedition.

* Lenin, *Collected Works*, vol. 27, p. 293.
** Zinoviev's speech at Communist International's executive committee meeting on February 20, 1926.

At the beginning of the Northward Expedition, either in financial resources, in military strength or in armaments, we were not even one-tenth as strong as the northern war lords. Yet in three years' time we succeeded in defeating them and in unifying the country. The basic reason was that the expedition was a revolutionary war, and as such, it was fought fully in the spirit of a people's war. At the time China was undergoing a period of social changes and national awakening. The northern war lords, from both the social and political viewpoints, were at odds with the people's thinking and the needs of the times. Therefore, although they were much stronger and had the support of old colonialism, they were still no match for the National Revolutionary Forces, and went down in defeat.

It was our intention to achieve national unification by both military and political means after our troops reached the Yangtze Valley; and then, as soon as the regional occupation by the war lords was terminated, quickly to turn the forces of destruction into constructive channels. Externally our policy was to seek the abolition of unequal treaties through negotiations, and internally to lay the foundation for unification through social as well as economic reconstruction to improve the people's livelihood. Therefore, reconstruction began immediately after the Northward Expedition ended. During the years from 1929 to 1937, despite Communist destruction and Japanese aggression, China managed to set up a new record in political, economic, financial and educational developments.

At the time the Russian Communists were trying to take advantage of China's national struggle against imperialism to extend their scheme of aggression. As our purpose was to achieve freedom and equality for China, we were constantly on guard lest we fall into a trap of new colonialism while trying to free ourselves from the shackles of the old. The Russian Communists' plot was to seize political power when

Kuomintang was still confined to Canton, and then to launch the Northward Expedition in the name of Kuomintang with a view to converting China into Soviet Russia's first satellite in Asia. It was necessary, therefore, for us to launch the expedition for unification and independence.

Prior to the expedition we put down a revolt aboard the *Chungshan* gunboat, purged the Party of Communist elements to forestall a class war and foiled their conspiracy to provoke armed clashes with the foreign powers in Nanking, Shanghai and Hankow. These were the crucial points in our Northward Expedition.

From 1930 to 1934 the Chinese Government launched five drives against the Chinese Communist forces. As I have already described them earlier in the book I shall only point out now that our military operational ideas in these drives were those of a people's war, and that this was best demonstrated in the fifth drive, which was a success.

During this period the Chinese Communist forces made hit-and-run attacks in seven provinces,* laid out eight Soviet areas for guerrilla warfare and adopted the policy of "surrounding the cities with villages." Their basic operational principle was "to prolong the war for strategic reasons, to seek quick decisions in single engagements as a matter of tactics, to use the troops to arouse the masses in time of peace and to concentrate superior forces to envelop and annihilate the enemy troops in time of war." Their line of action was a combination of Russia's armed uprising and guerrilla warfare on the one hand, and the mobile tactics of the old Chinese brigands on the other. The only innovation introduced by the Chinese Communists was in using the two methods of warfare together in an "absolute war."

The Chinese Government was caught between the Japanese forces and the Chinese Communists. Its troops were put in a

---

* Hunan, Kiangsi, Chekiang, Fukien, Hupeh, Honan and Anhwei.

passive position, and that was why the first four drives against the Communists, which lasted for three years, all failed.

In October 1933 plans were formulated for a fifth drive in which the Government would devote 30 per cent of its efforts to military affairs and 70 per cent to political affairs. In this drive the Government troops followed the principle of "strategic offensive and tactical defensive," and consolidated each position before moving on to the next. They built roads all the way to the front. They divided the area into so many zones, and proceeded to clean them up one by one. They also used the tactics of converging on enemy positions as a countermeasure against the enemy's "human sea" and guerrilla tactics.

In the meantime, all able-bodied adults in the provinces concerned, irrespective of their occupations, joined *Pao Chia** organizations and took part either in actual fighting against the Communists or in security work in the rear. The Government also instituted tight economic and communication blockades against the Communists to cut off their sources of intelligence, to prevent their infiltration and to stop them from obtaining supplies.

Owing to coordination in the political, social, economic and other fields, the Government was able to use its military equipment to the greatest effect. The Communists' attempts to destroy the Government troops' lines of communication and their tactics of "isolating a point" and of seeking "a swift decision," were all set at naught. There was nothing the Chinese Communists could do to keep the Government troops from carrying out their operations according to plan. As a result of the fifth drive the Communists' lairs, large and small, in seven provinces in the Yangtze Valley were cleaned up, their Soviet regime was detroyed, making it possible for the Government to pursue its policy of "effecting internal pacification before resisting external aggression."

* A system of mutual assistance and security.

The force generated in China's National Revolution and its position in our military thinking were beyond the comprehension of the old colonialists. This was evident in the Japanese militarists' failure to understand our National Revolution which led to their ultimate defeat.

The Japanese militarists regarded our Northward Expedition from 1926 to 1928 as just another civil war such as northern war lords used to fight among themselves. They refused to believe that the National Government would be able to unify the country. Consequently, when our Revolutionary Forces entered Shantung in the Yellow River Valley, they sent troops to Tsingtao and Tsinan ostensibly to protect Japanese nationals there but actually to provoke a clash and to block further advance northward by our troops. The Japanese militarists would not have even dreamed that our National Revolutionary forces would succeed in unifying the entire country, including Manchuria, the same year.

Following the Japanese attack on Mukden the Chinese Government, in view of the Communist uprisings and the need of reconstruction, had to exercise the greatest self-restraint. I published a booklet in 1934 entitled *Friend or Foe?* in the hope that the Japanese militarists would wake up to the real danger in the Far Eastern situation. In November 1935, in my report on foreign affairs to the Fifth National Congress of Kuomintang, I summed up China's policy toward Japan in the following words: "Not to forsake peace until it is completely hopeless to have peace; nor to talk lightly of sacrifices until sacrifices are necessary as a last resort." I had still hoped that the Japanese militarists would abandon their military aggression against China.

After the Marco Polo Bridge Incident, which occurred on July 7, 1937, I made the following announcement at a conference at Kuling: "When the limit of our forbearance is reached, we shall have to risk the very life of our people for the sake of national survival. In that eventuality, no midway compromise will be possible, for compromise will mean surrender and our end as an independent nation. Once this limit is reached we shall have no choice but to be prepared to sacrifice everything and fight to the bitter end. Our only hope to win the final victory lies in our determination to sacrifice."

The Japanese militarists, however, still failed to understand the real nature of our War of Resistance. Claiming that they could conquer China in three weeks' time by fielding only three divisions of troops in a lightning war, they plunged headlong into war without giving heed to the consequences.

On December 17, 1937, following the withdrawal of Chinese forces from the national capital at Nanking, I said to my people: "The center of final victory in China's protracted war against Japan is not in Nanking or in any of the big cities in the country, but in the villages and in the stout hearts of China's teeming millions. So long as our people realize that there is no escaping the enemy's aggression, and so long as fathers instruct their sons and elder brothers encourage their younger brothers all to feel enmity toward the enemy and to fight every inch of the way, there will rise throughout the country enough fortresses, both visible and invisible, to destroy all the enemy troops. Therefore, our people should not be too mindful of momentary gains or losses, but, instead, should fully understand the meaning of our protracted war and have a firm faith in our final victory."

I should point out that this determination to keep on fighting to the bitter end and this faith in the final victory symbolize the spirit of the Three People's Principles and are characteristic of a people's war in our National Revolution. To put it more specifically, we accepted the idea of an unlimited war and resolutely decided on a policy of prolonged resistance to counter the enemy's attempts to seek a quick decision with a strategy of attrition, and to counter the enemy's "feed war with war" operational ideas with the scorched earth policy. I also announced my directive of "trading space for time, and accumulating small victories to become big victories," to oppose the Japanese militarists' new war of aggression which they launched for the establishment of the "Greater East Asia New Order." Finally, we were to use the vast inaccessible area west of the Peiping-Hankow and Canton-Hankow railways as the base from which to move from the defensive to the offensive in a final battle with the enemy.

Our decision for this campaign was in conformity with Clausewitz' principle that national policy should determine military strategy. Compared with Japan, China was a weak nation in economic resources, industrial development, science, technology, armed forces and weapons. Therefore, following the Mukden Incident, we had to endure humiliations and to negotiate with Japan. During the six years which followed we did not speak lightly of armed resistance. But once hostilities broke out we had no hesitation in adopting the scorched earth policy, "falling back into the interior," and pitting the new spirit of the Three People's Principles and the new methods of warfare developed in the course of our National Revolution in an absolute war against the Japanese militarists. We held fast to this strategic principle throughout our eight years of war and, despite countless intrigues of Soviet Russia and the insurrection of the Chinese Communists, we achieved common victory with the Allies in World War II.

During the Sino-Japanese War the crosscurrent of Communism was held down by the spirit of nationalism, and also by the strict precautions of the Government, with the result that the Chinese Communists' plot to turn a national war into a class war and an external war into an internal war was foiled. Yet, after the war, Soviet Russia and the Chinese Communists succeeded in carrying out their plans of aggression and we met with tragic reverses in our military campaign against the Communist insurrection. Why?

I propose now to analyze the defects in our organization and in our technique as well as mistakes in our policy and in our strategy that were responsible for our defeat.

First of all I must point out that China depended more on spiritual strength than on material strength in her war with Japan. It was this force of national spirit which enabled China to keep on fighting without falter for fourteen years (1931-1945).

The Chinese Government decided, at the outbreak of major hostilities in 1937, that it would be a prolonged war and also foresaw that Soviet Russia would take advantage of China's exhaustion at the end of the war to perpetrate her scheme of external aggression and internal subversion against China. For this reason, we formulated the Program of War of Resistance and National Reconstruction in 1938 to strengthen our spiritual mobilization during the war, to carry on national reconstruction and simultaneously to pave the ground for building up China into a modern and strong country with a rising standard of living. Of course, both the Russian and the Chinese Communists also saw this point. That was why, during the war, they coordinated their moves with the Japanese militarists against the Government troops.

When the war ended the Communists resorted to armed insurrection. They did everything to nullify all reconstruction projects, to hinder the Government's program of demobilization, to disrupt the nation's economic life and to upset its social order. They spread national defeatism at a time when the people were weary after the long war. Finally the general public became so confused and bewildered that all that they asked was peace at any cost, however transient it might turn out to be. This was the basic reason for the tragic reverses which China suffered in her war against Communism.

Organizational and Technical Defects in Our Struggle Against Communism

The first defect in our fight against Communism was that our organization was not strict enough and our vigilance not heightened enough.

It has been the Chinese people's philosophy of life "to conceal others' evils but to extol their virtues," and "not to bear grudges because of past injustices." Kuomintang was built on the basis of China's traditional ethics and national consciousness. This was how we felt toward Chinese Communists both after we took them into our Party in 1924 and after we allowed them to make common cause with the rest of the nation against Japan in 1937. This was also our attitude toward Soviet Russia after we resumed diplomatic relations with her in 1933.

In our dealings with the Chinese Communists we have always set a great store by ethical considerations, good faith and righteousness. It was our belief that every Chinese cannot help feeling loyal to his own country first. That was why we had sincerely hoped to move forward together with the Communists on the road of democracy to complete our task of national reconstruction.

What we did not realize was that Communists are Communists, first, last and always. They were traitorous and treacherous all the time. Everywhere they went they set traps for others. Any weak spot in our organization or a loophole in our precautionary measures would give them a chance to start trouble. In our war against Communism we made the mistake of judging the Communists by the same yardstick of national consciousness and democratic and ethical concepts.

For instance, we should have regarded the Communist Party as an illegal body and isolated it so that it could not operate openly. After our Party purge of 1927 we broke off diplomatic relations with Soviet Russia. Throughout the years, the Government steadily refused to accord the Communists a legal status. This was a fundamental way of preventing them from inciting the masses through propaganda. In 1937, however, we made the mistake of acceding to their request for cease-fire and surrender, and of lifting in part the previous ban on their freedoms of propaganda and organization. This

political and social loophole gave the Communists an opportunity for infiltration, concealment and expansion.

Both in 1924 and 1936 our Party was in a serious predicament on account of vacillations and internal dissensions. Our
greatest mistake lay in the fact that we were not rigid enough
in our organization and not heightened enough in our vigilance. Contradictions in our policy furnished the Communists
with a schism which they exploited to their advantage.

Then, we should have prevented the Communists from
effecting political and social changes. Over a period of thirty
years the Communists made common cause with the National
Revolution only to sabotage it, and joined the Northward
Expedition only to disrupt it. The tactic they used was "to
convert a democratic revolution into a social revolution," and
"to convert a foreign war into a civil war." We not only saw
this tactic in operation but actually experienced it. Of course,
we understood it for what it was and took precautions against
it.

The people in general, even including some members of our
Party and those who had fought Communism for a long time,
failed to understand the Communist tactics and, as a result,
let up in their vigilance. In some extreme cases they even
echoed what others were saying, branding our anti-Communist organizations and propaganda as undemocratic, cen-
suring our anti-Communist measures and laws and orders as
opposed to freedom. On the contrary, they came to mistake
the Communists' "New Democracy" for genuine democratic
ideas, their "United Front" for a democratic movement and
their "Coalition Government" as democracy itself. Little did
they know that all these were but the application in China of
the methods by which Moscow had conquered the Eastern
European countries. According to Moscow's formula, what
the Chinese Communists called "New Democracy," "United
Front" and "Coalition Government" were but combat slogans which the Chinese Communists had devised in ac-

cordance with their dialectic law of negation for subversive purposes.

Once the Communists seized political power they changed the country qualitatively first into a "people's democratic dictatorship" and then into a "socialist state," which, in fact, is nothing but a Soviet satellite. Their final aim was to push the Chinese mainland into Soviet Russia's Red orbit. This is plain enough today, but, at the time, most people were ignorant of the real nature of Communism, and their lack of vigilance enabled the Communists to perpetrate their intrigues and inflict on the Chinese mainland this unprecedented catastrophe. This was the greatest defect in our struggle against Communism.

Secondly, we lacked initiative in propaganda and substance in ideology.

Whenever the Chinese Communists met with reverses in the field, international Communists came to their rescue by spreading propaganda aimed at confusing the general public as well as people in the Government. This happened at the time of our Party purge in 1927, our successful military campaign against the Communist rebels in 1935 and again at the end of the war in 1945.

By comparison, our propaganda lacked initiative and was not militant enough in ideology to counter this international political and psychological offensive, nor was it strong enough to arouse indignation at home and a sense of righteousness abroad. In consequence, our Government was beset with difficulties both internally and internationally. Although several times we fought, we vacillated and did not press on all the way through.

The first point which the Communists used in their propaganda was "Opposition to Communism is Fascism." After World War I there were two crosscurrents. These were Communism in Soviet Russia, and Fascism in Germany, Italy and Japan. Both were antidemocratic totalitarianisms, and as such both were enemies of democracy. After the seventh congress of the Communist International in 1935 Communists in various countries were directed to form "United Fronts" with Socialists, and even with democratic parties, to oppose Fascism. Through the propaganda and rabble-rousing of Communists and their fellow travelers, the democratic nations developed a fear of Fascism. In the meantime there had come into circulation a "pseudo logic" which said "Opposition to Communism is Fascism." This finally forced us to hold peace talks and political consultations with the Chinese Communists. Our failure in propaganda was a major defect in our struggle against Communism.

Whenever the Chinese Communists were faced with defeat and destruction, they also paraded the theory that "the Communist Party is destructible, but not Communism."

Both after our successful military drive against the Communists in 1935 and after victory in 1945 we failed to counter this Communist theory, which in the end gained considerable credence. This not only saved the Communists from destruction, but also shook the people's confidence in their ability to liquidate the Chinese Communists.

The Communists also contended that "the Communist problem cannot be solved by military means and, therefore, it must be settled by political means." This point was made much use of by international Communists and their Chinese puppets in their propaganda at the end of our war with Japan. They argued that military force could only annihilate the Communist forces, but not solve the problem of the Communist Party. They alleged that if the Government should try to settle the Communist troops by force of arms, it would cause national bankruptcy, wreak untold hardships on the people, enable Communism and Communist organizations to spread and that the Government would wind up as the real loser. So the people, both in China and abroad, came to think that "fighting the Communists is tantamount to manufacturing Communists," and they used this slogan to oppose the Government's policy of suppressing the Communist rebellion by force. Again, our propaganda failed to counter this political and psychological offensive. Thus the only way open to the Government was to hold peace talks and to convene the Political Consultative Conference.

In reality what Moscow has laid down, and what the Chinese Communists have been faithfully following as a creed, is that "a peculiarity with the Chinese Revolution is the use of revolutionary arms against counterrevolutionary arms." This is to say that the Chinese Communists, in their struggle for power, must use force against the Government. The Chinese Communists feared that the moment they gave up their arms they would forfeit their very existence. In order to solve the Communist problem and to liquidate the Communist troops, therefore, it was essential for us to use both military and political strength to defeat their armed forces and also their political organization.

At the end of the Sino-Japanese War the contention that "the Communist problem can only be solved by political means and, therefore, it must not be settled by military means" led the people to the erroneous belief that a political solution was the only way out for the Government. This shook even the confidence of people in the Government's ability to suppress the Communists by force. Finally the Government had to yield and to agree to hold political consultation and peace talks with the Communists. This created a state of affairs when there was neither war nor peace, and when there were both fighting and peace talks.

Moreover, we failed to fortify our will against Communism and also failed to take drastic actions. Soviet Russia and its tool of aggression, the international Communists, always aim at either domination or destruction. The fate they have in store for the masses is either enslavement or oppression. All such things as united front, neutralism, peace talks, political consultation and even terms and agreements written in black and white are merely forms of struggle which they happen to use at the time. For the final showdown they will invariably resort to violence. They are ruthless in actions and treacherous in methods. If you do not destroy them, they will eventually destroy you. In our efforts to solve the Communist problem and to liquidate the Communist armed forces, often because of domestic and foreign obstacles, we were not sufficiently thorough in our actions. Thus we met with defeat.

First, we made the mistake of countering the Communists' unlimited war with limited war. The successful conclusion of the Government's fifth military drive against the Communists in 1935 was made possible by combining all our political, economic, social and military strength. In 1947 the situation was vastly different. By then the Communists had infiltrated the Government and defeatism was prevalent throughout the country. There were impediments to mobilization, chaos in schools, social instability, inflation and other financial difficulties. To make matters worse the Government was subjected to hostile international propaganda and the pressure of intrigues. The morale of both the armed forces and the civilian population was at a low ebb. Only the armed forces fought, and even they felt the effect of defeatism. In waging limited war against the Communists' total war, the Government was predestined to failure.

Secondly, we underestimated the Communists' capacity and capability for brutality and violence. China is a big country and has had a long history and a superior culture. Its people are traditionally peace-loving and have the highest respect for good faith and righteousness. Under Dr. Sun's guidance, the people have developed a strong faith in the Three People's Principles, and supported the cause of the National Revolution. Despite vicissitudes and setbacks, Dr. Sun held tenaciously to the belief that our efforts in revolution and national reconstruction would result in success. I share the same belief.

As explained earlier, Soviet Russia's Communism is not suitable to our national spirit and culture. The reign of terror which the Chinese Communists perpetrated in class struggle was opposed to our ethical concepts. As early as 1923 Dr. Sun and Joffe affirmed in their joint declaration that Communism cannot be applied to China. After admitting the Chinese Communists into Kuomintang, Dr. Sun was struck by the underhand methods used by Chen Tu-hsiu, leader of the Chinese Communist Party, and others with dual-party memberships, but he still thought that they could not cause China any harm. Though I became anti-Communist as a result of my visit to Soviet Russia, I was overconfident too, and failed to settle the Communist problem in a fundamental manner.

I have shown that in the years between our Party purge in 1927 and our successful military drive in 1935, our policy toward the Communists remained one of suppression short of annihilation. Whenever the Communists' military force was crushed and their political organization smashed, we tried to appeal to their national consciousness in the hope that they would mend their ways and work for the country. That was why we did not pursue the Communist remnants in their flight to the Northwest, and, later, even acceded to their request for truce and surrender.

In 1936 there were less than 5,000 men in their army when the Communists were bottled up in northern Shensi. With the Japanese war of aggression drawing increasingly near, the Government did not harass them further, but instead agreed to discuss a political settlement with them. During the war the Government cordoned off the Communist area to prevent them from establishing a direct line of communication with Soviet Russia through the Northwest.

At the same time the Government held five series of discussions with the Chinese Communists, hoping against hope that the latter, no matter how treacherous they might have been, would eventually yield to the pressure of patriotism and public opinion.

When the war ended the country was in need of rehabilitation and reconstruction, and the people were all looking forward to demobilization. As the unequal treaties had already been abolished, the nation felt a new sense of independence. Any Chinese with a national consciousness would feel loyal to the country and refrain from engaging in any traitorous activities against the nation. Consequently, the Government decided upon a program of peaceful reconstruction and accepted American mediation in its negotiations with the Communists. Today, looking back at the situation, we realize we were overconfident and failed sufficiently to take into account the Communists' brutalities and violence imbedded in their class nature and international character. We erred in being too lenient with them. This gave them a chance to perpetrate their political intrigues which ended in bringing on this unprecedented calamity to our people.

Moreover, though we took precautions against the Chinese Communists, we neglected their front organizations. These appear in various forms to serve various purposes. Whenever the Communist Party is outlawed, and hence cannot openly engage in activities, it directs leftist elements and fellow travelers to carry on such activities on its behalf. Even when the Communist Party does have a legal status and can be active in the open, it uses the leftist elements in making flank or envelopment attacks.

One of the mistakes which we made in our struggle against Communism, and which becomes perfectly clear today, is that we were not as strict in our preventive measures against the Communist Party as against the Communist armed forces, and we did not pay as much attention to the leftists and neutralists in the Communist front as to the Communist Party itself. For that reason, although we defeated the Communist armed forces repeatedly in the field, we did not destroy the Communists' organization. In other words, we succeeded in annihilating the visible Communist Party, but failed to check-mate the activities of the invisible Communist front. In reality, so long as the leftist elements and the neutralist bodies could carry on with their activities, the Communists would be able to conceal themselves. It follows that so long as the front organizations could expand, the Communists would always have a base for their armed uprising. That was why the Com-munists and their armed forces, despite their repeated defeats at the hands of Government forces between 1927 and 1935, were able to stay alive and to stage a comeback at a later date.

Then, too, our people's morale, which reached its height during the Sino-Japanese War, suffered a setback because of Communist propaganda. This also affected our spiritual mobilization.

It should be remembered that China had lived under un-equal treaties for a century, and consequently most of the people needed to restore their sense of national self-respect and self-confidence. In our National Revolution to save the country, we made psychological reconstruction our first task. The New Life Movement, which was started after the Japanese attack on Mukden, was in reality an organized effort at reviving national self-confidence through changing the people's way of life. Then during the war we launched the Spiritual Mobilization Movement to stimulate the growth of national spirit in order to accelerate mobilization in other phases of our national life. Upon the abolition of unequal treaties at the end of the war, China's national equality and freedom were assured. We had a wonderful opportunity for reconstruction. At this juncture the Chinese Communists and their front organizations spread defeatism while international Communists launched a smearing campaign against our coun-try and our Government. All our efforts at psychological re-construction were thus nullified. Finally, the people lost their will to fight Communism, and the Government's policy of putting down the insurrection by force, backed by a partial mobilization, ended in failure.

Two other factors leading to the disaster on the mainland were diplomatic isolation and economic collapse caused by malignant inflation.

From behind the Iron Curtain Soviet Russia directs the international Communists in the various nations in collecting intelligence, inciting the masses, manipulating public opinion, creating pressure and subverting the policies of the governments concerned. Meanwhile the Chinese society is free and open, and our country is still new to institutionalized democracy. In dealing with Soviet Russia, we found ourselves in a disadvantageous position. In fact, even in coping with the problem posed by the Chinese Communists, we found it difficult to win international sympathy and help. In the end, we were completely isolated. Consider a few instances:

We tried to counter the Russian Communists' treachery with good faith and sincerity, and consequently were put on the defensive in our negotiations with Soviet Russia. During the thirty years under review China and Soviet Russia had concluded the Sino-Soviet Agreement of 1924, the Non-aggression Pact of 1937 and the Treaty of Friendship and Alliance of 1945. We voluntarily adhered to every one of these agreements both in letter and in spirit, and used them as the basis for our negotiations. To the Russian Communists these agreements were just so many pieces of paper which they could sign and tear up at will.

The most infamous example of Soviet Russia's bad faith was in her obstructing the Chinese Government troops from moving into Manchuria at the end of World War II to reestablish Chinese authority there in accordance with stipulations in the Sino-Soviet Treaty of Friendship and Alliance and in her turning the territory into a base for rearming the Chinese Communists and setting them against the Government.

In dealing with the problem on Manchuria our Government was bound by the Sino-Soviet Treaty and restricted by American mediation. This was our reward for meeting the Russian Communists' treachery with good faith and sincerity.

Again, we and our allies tried to counter the over-all intrigues of the Soviet bloc severally and without unity. Soviet Russia decided upon her postwar world policy in 1943 and picked China as the first target. If the free nations had coordinated their moves at the end of World War II, and had reached an understanding concerning Soviet Russia, our Government would have been able to keep the situation at home under control, check Communist expansion and safeguard national security as our contribution toward the maintenance of peace in Asia and in the world.

Of course, the men in the Kremlin knew this. That was why they ordered the international Communists to discredit our Government both in world public opinion and in diplomacy before they defeated our forces in the military field. To alienate Sino-American cooperation, Stalin tried neutralism tactics on our Government to ensure China's neutrality. At the same time, during the Marshall mission, he used the same tactic to make the United States adopt a neutral policy toward China. It was under this pressure that the United States evacuated her troops from China, and also ceased her financial and military assistance to my country. Pro-Communists in the United States used all the slanderous attacks suggested by Soviet Russia against our Government, and against me personally. This meant that the Chinese Government, besides facing the enemy's pressure at home, was subjected to international pressure as well. This caused China's isolation. The free world, including ourselves, brought on this defeat by meeting Soviet Russia's over-all intrigues with divided views and individual efforts.

On the eve of our victory my Government and my people were all optimistic about postwar reconstruction. No sooner

was the war over than plans were laid for military demobilization and civilian rehabilitation. The pressure of inflation at the
end of the long war was mounting daily. This was all the
more reason for the people's anxiousness for demobilization
and economic reconstruction. If this had been smoothly carried out the problem of malignant inflation could have been
solved. The Communists, however, did everything possible to
sabotage the Government's economic policies and made it
necessary for the Government to combat them in the economic field as well as in the military and political fields.

In defending itself against Communist economic warfare
the Government had to exert itself both in domestic affairs
and in foreign relations. Internally, the Government had difficulty in balancing its budget, the main reason being the ex-
cessively large military expenditure. In order to cut down
expenses for the armed forces it had to reduce the latter's size.
The Communists were fully aware of this point and did their
best to defeat the American mediation effort in order to prevent the Government from carrying out its plans for military
reorganization and demobilization. Meanwhile, for the sake
of restoring law and order disrupted by the Communists, the
Government had to mobilize again, this time to put down an
open rebellion.

Meanwhile, it was the Government's policy to welcome
foreign capital and technical cooperation on a basis of equality
and mutual benefit to develop our economy and build up our
industries for the purpose of raising the people's standard of
living. On the other hand, it was part of Moscow's plan of
aggression against China to isolate our Government and to
undermine our national economy and the Chinese people's
way of life. The Russian Communists were particularly determined to sabotage Sino-American economic cooperation
so as to facilitate their scheme against our Government and
our country. This economic war by the Russian Communists
was directed not only against China but against the United

States as well. On the one hand, they instigated the Chinese Communists to interfere with the Government's reconstruction plans by cutting communications and damaging factories and mines in various parts of the country. On the other, they ordered the American Communists and their fellow travelers to create sentiments, both in the press and in the diplomatic field, against the conclusion of a loan by the American Government to China, and also against investment in China by the American people.

The effectiveness of this economic war was proved by the sudden halt in the consummation of the US$500,000,000 credit loan which had already been agreed upon. This came at the time of the Political Consultative Conference and American mediation in the military field. It was the American Government's intention to bring pressure to bear on our Government to accept mediation for internal peace. It had apparently thought that this would help us in our postwar reconstruction. From the Chinese Communists' point of view, however, the successful conclusion of the loan would deal a mortal blow to their plot of armed rebellion and political subversion. Consequently they simply had to defeat it.

Meanwhile, as far as the Chinese people in general were concerned, they believed that whether China would have domestic peace or disturbances, economic prosperity or poverty depended on demobilization and reconstruction which, in turn, depended on whether the American Government could stop the Chinese Communists' intrigue against the Government. In other words, if the loan went through as agreed upon, it would be a demonstration of the American Government's determination and sincerity to help the Chinese Government in its effort to restore law and order in the country and to start peaceful reconstruction. This would be the only way to stop the rebellion of the Communists and to foil their subversive schemes.

Unfortunately, once the Chinese Communists made known

their opposition the United States postponed the execution of the loan agreement indefinitely. Thus, in a single stroke, the international Communists succeeded in undermining the foundation of Sino-American economic cooperation. The American Government's decision had a tremendous psychological effect on the Chinese people. As a result the people began to lose confidence in the chance of national reconstruction. For the same reason the Government's financial and economic measures failed to achieve their purpose, and its economic planning and implementation met with continuous setbacks. In improvising its actions the Government committed a number of mistakes. For instance, the first postwar Executive Yuan,* between September 1945 and February 1947, made use of our currency reform reserve fund in an attempt to cope with financial difficulties and disturbances in the monetary and credit field at the time. This made it impossible for the Government to lay down any concrete and effective policy in general or any long-term currency stabilization plan in particular. The second Executive Yuan issued U. S. dollar bonds in March 1947 but had to discontinue the issuance shortly afterward. The third Executive Yuan's currency reform plan whereby gold dollar certificates were issued in August 1948 resulted in further deterioration of our currency.

The Chinese Communists immediately seized upon this situation and through their malicious propaganda succeeded in confusing the people. To make things worse for the Government, the Communists manipulated the currency and price fluctuation in the various big cities. Soon inflation got out of control. This resulted in widespread demoralization among the civil servants as well as among the armed forces. It was no longer possible to maintain military discipline at the same high level as during the war years. This was one of the main causes for our defeat in fighting the Communists. Regardless of

---

* The first of five branches in the Chinese Government. It is roughly equivalent to the cabinet in the Western nations.

whether this was brought about by our own mistakes or by force of circumstances, it is imperative that we should restudy it analytically and draw lessons of vigilance from it.

Errors in Our Policy and Strategy Against Communism

Above we have noted the four major defects in organization and technique in our war against Communism. These, however, were all remediable. Even if they could not be completely rectified, so long as we remained determined, and so long as our strategy and policy were correct, I believe we still could have won.

Let us analyze the errors in policy and strategy which we have committed in combating Communism in the past.

What was our greatest error in policy in our struggle against Communism? Many thought that our first error was in accepting the terms of the Yalta Agreement and in concluding the Sino-Soviet Treaty of Friendship and Alliance because the secret terms at Yalta bartered away China's territorial sovereignty as a price for Soviet Russia's participation in the war against Japan. It was felt that by accepting these terms and signing the treaty we gave Soviet Russia a legal basis for her aggression in Manchuria and paved the way for the Chinese Communists to bring harm to the country.

We signed the Treaty of Friendship and Alliance with Soviet Russia, however, not because we recognized the Yalta Agreement or because we considered it binding on us. As the Republic of China did not attend the Yalta Conference, and as the United States did not consult us either before or during the Yalta Conference, we were not bound by its decisions. While it is true that we negotiated the treaty with Soviet Russia upon the advice of the United States, we did so after having given the matter our own consideration.

For half a century China, in her effort to win national independence and freedom and to help preserve world peace and security, had been faced with the dual threat of Japanese and

Russian aggression. After Japan's surrender in 1945 we needed from twenty to thirty years of peace for reconstruction and it was our hope to be able to find a way to live in peace with Soviet Russia. This was what prompted us to sign the Sino-Soviet Treaty of Friendship and Alliance.

We had considered duly the possibility that Soviet Russia, in view of her record of bad faith, might scuttle the treaty. What could we do in such an eventuality? I had this in mind when I told Kuomintang's Central Standing Committee at the time of the signing of the treaty: "Even if Soviet Russia should continue her policy of aggression against us, this treaty will serve as a yardstick with which the world can judge her actions, and also as a basis on which we can conduct our negotiations." What we did, therefore, cannot be put down *per se* as a great error in our policy.

It was generally thought that our second error was in accepting American mediation in our conflict with the Communists. Of course, the Chinese Communists had their own reasons for accepting it. Why did our Government accept American mediation and conclude the cease-fire agreement to bind its own hands and feet?

The international situation at the time was such that we would become more isolated if we did not sign the Sino-Soviet Treaty and did not accept American mediation. Although our Government was strong enough to dispose of the Chinese Communists, it alone did not have the necessary strength to oppose Soviet imperialism and stop Russian troops from entering Manchuria and from helping the Chinese Communists. The Government had to consider its moral and material resources. For the sake of domestic peace it was ready to do anything that was honorable. In dealing with friends it was utterly sincere. As long as we did our best and remained true to our moral standard, what we did can hardly be called a major error in our policy.

In the opinion of some people, our third error was in instituting constitutional government before we had put down the Communist insurrection. It was said that in the interest of effective prosecution of the war against the Communists the mind of the people should be concentrated and not distracted, and that elections, instead of promoting unity, would accentuate diversity and antagonism in the country. This would not only cause greater divergencies and contradictions between the various political parties but would also have an adverse effect on our party organization and discipline. The Communists, under the cloak of "democracy" and "freedom," took advantage of this situation to step up their infiltration and diverse activities and to spread defeatism. In the end the Government's military effort against the Communists failed.

It should be remembered, however, that the aim of our National Revolution was to build up China as a democratic nation. We had decided at the beginning of the war that the day of victory would also mark the commencement of constitutional government in China. Consequently, shortly after the war ended, our Government decided to convene the National Assembly for the purpose of initiating constitutional rule. I felt at the time that if we should really meet with defeat because of our decision to launch constitutional rule in the country, we should have no cause for regret or remorse. Subsequent events have proved that our efforts in this respect have been a success.

We firmly believe that only democracy and government by law can give us the necessary strength to defeat Communist totalitarianism, and only a democratic constitution can provide a sharp contrast to the reign of terror and brutality which the Chinese Communists have inflicted on the people. Therefore, we committed no serious error in launching constitutional rule before we had put down the Communist insurrection, despite the fact that this step did cause us certain disadvantages in our military effort against the Communists.

Since these three cannot be regarded as serious factors in

our military disaster, what then were our errors in point of policy and strategy? In my opinion, there were four of them.

The first one was the resumption of diplomatic relations with Soviet Russia.

After the Japanese attack on Mukden Moscow was anxious to stop the Japanese advance in the north and, therefore, hoped to resume diplomatic relations with China. The Chinese Government gave this matter its most careful consideration but it was not until December 1932 that an agreement was reached.

For five years (1933-1937), however, there was no progress whatsoever in Sino-Soviet relations. On the contrary, Soviet Russia tried hard to move closer to Japan. This was made abundantly clear in her sale of the Chinese Eastern Railway to the Japanese puppet state of "Manchukuo" despite the fact that it was in violation of China's sovereign rights in Manchuria.

In 1937 China and Soviet Russia concluded a Nonaggression Pact and a barter agreement. Soviet Russia drove hard bargains regarding Chinese exports, and the arms she supplied us were mostly not accompanied by enough spare parts and were not available when they were most needed. This flow of supplies stopped completely in 1941.

In April 1941 Soviet Russia and Japan concluded a Neutrality Pact which encouraged Japanese aggression against the Western powers. This was in violation of the Sino-Soviet Agreement of 1924 and the Sino-Soviet Nonaggression Pact of 1937.

It should be remembered that, once Sino-Soviet diplomatic relations were resumed in 1932, Soviet Russia set up diplomatic, consular and trade missions in China which were used to harbor espionage centers and organs for directing the activities of Chinese Communists against our country. The Russians used the highway in the Northwest to provide a link between Moscow and Yenan. In Shanghai the Soviet consulate not only became the liaison office between Chinese Communists and Japanese secret service organs, but also represented Moscow in giving encouragement and support to the Wang Ching-wei puppet regime. In Tihua the Soviet consulate served as the command post from which all incidents and strifes in Sinkiang province were manipulated.

Thus, it is clear that the resumption of diplomatic relations with Soviet Russia, instead of bringing us any help in the Sino-Japanese War, had actually caused us considerable harm. China lost more than she gained as a result. Our fourteen years of war with Japan (1931-1945) showed how deceptive was the view, widely held at the time, that China could resist Japan only by aligning herself with Soviet Russia. Our Government made an error in policy and in strategy when it resumed diplomatic relations with Soviet Russia.

The reorganization and integration of the Communist troops was also an important factor. In 1934, two years after China had resumed her diplomatic relations with Soviet Russia, the Government launched its final military drive against the Chinese Communists. It proceeded to seek a political settlement of the Communist problem. After the Sino-Japanese War began the Government took steps to integrate the Communist troops into its armed forces. While it is true that we decided upon this policy in the face of the Japanese militarists' threat of invasion, we also overconfidently believed that the Communists' demand for "united resistance to Japan" was an evidence of the rise of China's national spirit and consciousness above everything else. Unfortunately, this belief played into the hands of the Communists, who, as we have seen, took advantage of the war to attack Government troops, to expand their armed forces, to spread defeatism and to subvert the Government in coordination with the Japanese.

So our decision to take in the Communist troops and to permit the Communist Party to join the national war effort against Japan on an equal footing with other political parties was definitely harmful to the nation. It was an error both in policy and in strategy for the Government to negotiate with the Communists and to take their troops into the Government forces.

Furthermore, the Government also committed a great error in handling the Manchurian problem.

It may be said that it was China's resumption of diplomatic relations with Soviet Russian in 1932 which subsequently led to the latter's entry into the Pacific region. By 1945 and 1946 Soviet Russia's intrigues and bad faith regarding Manchuria became perfectly clear. At first we decided to stop trying to re-establish Chinese authority in the region, but later changed our mind. We continued discussions with her and went on with the take-over operations. This was where we made a serious error in policy and in strategy.

Manchuria is a part of China, its people are Chinese citizens and its resources are *absolutely essential to China's reconstruction*. Our stand on this matter remained firm. Our security in Manchuria, in other words, whether or not it fell into the hands of Russian Communists, was a matter of international concern. Since China alone could not solve the problem, and since it could not be solved by our negotiations with Soviet Russia, we should have called off the take-over operations altogether. Then we could have concentrated our armed forces in the Peiping-Tientsin area, held Shanhaikwan and used Chinchow as a forward base. In the meantime, we could have submitted the Manchurian problem to the United Nations for a decision and held Soviet Russia responsible for all consequences by appealing to world opinion. In this way our Government would have had the necessary military strength below the Great Wall to put down the Communist revolt, control all of North China and use the international deliberations to expose Soviet Russia's designs on Manchuria and her eastward advance to the Pacific.

Owing to domestic and foreign interferences we failed to

adhere to our earlier policy. Instead, we held direct negotiations with Soviet Russia. At the same time we made the mistake of committing the best Government troops to Manchuria only to bog down there. Finally Manchuria fell, and the Government had to evacuate North China as well. By that time the entire situation was out of control.

A fourth error in policy and strategy was in connection with the cease-fire agreement.

It may be remembered that the cease-fire agreement was signed in January, 1946. This was followed by the convening of the Political Consultative Conference. Both the Chinese Government and the United States correctly maintained that Manchuria must not be included among the topics for political consultation; Government troops, sent to Manchuria or moving from one place to another in the region to re-establish Chinese authority there, were not to be affected by the cease-fire agreement.

As the Government looked at it, troops sent to Manchuria to re-establish Chinese sovereignty there did not come under the cease-fire agreement especially since Moscow had admitted that there were no Chinese Communist troops there.

Also, the fact that the Government was carrying on negotiations with Soviet Russia for the re-establishment of Chinese sovereignty in Manchuria on the basis of the Sino-Soviet Treaty showed that this was an international and diplomatic problem and not an internal and political problem. For this reason it should not become a topic for political consultation.

Soviet Russia and her Chinese puppets, including the Democratic League, however, sought to turn the question of restoring China's sovereignty in Manchuria into a problem between the Government and the Chinese Communists, and hence a matter fit for military mediation. They even suggested that the United States and Soviet Russia should mediate jointly. The Communists tried to wring from the Government recognition of their illegal actions and of accomplished facts in

Manchuria. It was in support of Soviet Russia's intrigue there that the Chinese Communists launched all-out offensives in several North China provinces.* This compelled the Marshall mission's Subcommittee of Three to discuss with the Chinese Communists a formula for military mediation in Manchuria. Our Government, however, still refused to let the Manchurian problem be discussed in the Political Consultative Conference or in its General Committee.

The Chinese Communists' main conflict with the Government was actually over Manchuria. Our attitude was that the question of re-establishing Chinese authority in Manchuria could no longer be solved by China and Soviet Russia alone, and that despite Chinese Communist agitation to the contrary, it should not be considered a domestic political problem.

The Chinese Communists tried to use their insurrection south of the Great Wall to make the Government yield in Manchuria. If the Government had concentrated its military forces and taken action against the Communist troops for their violations of the cease-fire agreement of January 1946, even at the risk of provoking an all-out war, it could have won. As to the question of restoring Chinese sovereignty in Manchuria, the Government had earlier decided to submit it to the United Nations so that it would not be confused with military operations below the Great Wall. Unfortunately, we vacillated on this all-important problem and failed to stick to our earlier decision. This brought upon ourselves a catastrophic defeat in the field.

The Secret of the Chinese Communists' Success in China— Antiwar Movement and Decisive Battle by Force of Arms

While preparing their own armed forces to take the offensive in a decisive battle, the Communists, as a political tactic, often use antiwar slogans to stop enemy attacks. One of its forms is to spread defeatism in an antiwar movement.

* Jehol, Chahar, Hopei, Shantung and northern Kiangsu.

During 1914 and 1915 Lenin came up with the "turn the international war into a civil war" slogan. He said: "The defeat suffered by the Russian troops is likely to weaken the government and make it easy for those who are against the ruling class to start a civil war."* In 1917 he spread defeatism to overthrow the Provisional Government and to establish the Soviet regime. Similarly the fourth of the twenty-one conditions laid down by the Communist International in 1920, and which the national Communist parties outside Russia were required to fulfill, was that they must "carry out propaganda and seditious activities resolutely and systematically in the armed forces, and establish a Communist cell in every military unit in their respective countries." Since then the spread of defeatism has become an important political tactic of the Communist parties in all countries. There were many glaring cases concerning the Chinese Communists.

For instance, the first time the Chinese Communists spread defeatism to foment revolts was during January and February 1926, when Kissanka and the Chinese Communists advanced the view that the projected Northward Expedition would inevitably end in failure. Shortly afterward there was the abortive revolt aboard the *Chungshan* gunboat.

Again, during 1944 when the Japanese forces made their deepest penetration into China's Southwest in a large-scale offensive, the Chinese Communists did two things. First, they charged in their propaganda that the Government had already failed in its leadership at war and would eventually surrender. Secondly, they concentrated their troops in the hope of being able to break through the Government's blockade and establish a direct line of contact with Soviet Russia across the Northwest, and finally to subject the Government to a Communist-Japanese pincer attack.

After the war, when the Chinese Communists and their front organization, the Democratic League, carried on peace

* Lenin, *Collected Works*, vol. 8, p. 149.

talks with the Government, their troops attacked Government troops in many places. In the meantime they spread defeatism in areas behind the Government troops to make the people, including those in Government, believe that the military campaign against the Communists could not possibly succeed and that peace talks would be the only way out.

In 1926, after having nipped in the bud the revolt aboard the *Chungshan* gunboat, we launched the Northward Expedition and succeeded in unifying the country. Then in 1944 and 1945, despite mounting difficulties, our armed forces and people remained firm and fought on till victory was won. In both instances we nullified that Communist tactic of defeatism. But in 1948 and 1949 the Communists succeeded in undermining the morale of the Government troops and in subverting our Government itself by spreading defeatism on a nation-wide scale. After the Hsuchow-Pengpu Battle,* with the exception of the battles fought on Tengpu Island and Kinmen Island,** Government troops put up no determined fight, and, as a result, province after province on the mainland fell into Communist hands.

Whether it is Soviet Russia against the free world or the Communist Party against the government in a free nation, the Communists not only make preparations but are actually ready to use physical force at any time. For this reason Soviet Russia is in a state of perpetual mobilization. So are the Communists in any free nation. This was what Lenin meant when he said in 1921: "Until the final issue is decided between capitalism and socialism, the terrible state of war will continue."***

From our experience of the last thirty years we have learned that when the Communists resort to physical force, control over the outcome lies at least partly in our hands.

* Fought north of the Yangtze in the fall of 1945.
** Kinmen is better known as Quemoy.
*** Lenin, "New Economic Policy," *Selected Works*, vol. 9, p. 242.

Defeat becomes certain only when we begin to waver for fear of the Communist threat of war and agree to talk peace with them in the mistaken belief that this is the way to peace.

Between 1930 and 1934 the Chinese Communists had laid out eight guerrilla areas and extended their control over seven provinces. They had 500,000 men under arms. Yet, the Government succeeded in defeating them after five major military drives.

Again, when the war with Japan ended in 1945 the Communists were in occupation of only seventy counties, and even during the accepting of Japanese surrender, their control extended only over 200 counties. If they had resorted to violence against the Government they would have been crushed and defeated as they were in southern Kiangsi in 1934.

Now we know that, although the Chinese Communists used violence in the final stage, the factor which brought them victory was not military strength but the application of the dialectic laws of turning "quantitative changes to qualitative changes" and "gradual changes to sudden changes" in the decisive battle.

During their all-out rebellion they relied only 20 per cent on their military strength, but as much as 50 per cent on international propaganda and intelligence and 30 per cent on organizing the United Front, promoting neutralism and spreading defeatism. Their effective use of propaganda, espionage and the deceptive tactics of contact, infiltration, organization, etc., and the fact that they could prepare war under the cover of their "anti-civil war" slogan, accounted for the Government's loss of control over the nation-wide situation. Thus, the use of military force was but one of the numerous weapons used by the Chinese Communists in the final battle.

The Laying of a Foundation for Victory
in the Midst of Reverses

These, then, were the defects in organization and technique and errors in policy and strategy in our struggle against Communism in the past. In reviewing them today our purpose is to utilize these lessons in our revolutionary struggle against Communism and Soviet Russia in the future. We must point out, however, that during the thirty years in question, despite these defects and errors, we have remained firm in our basic policy against Communism, and we have never compromised in our fundamental principles.

During the Communists' three periods of "peaceful coexistence" with us, they recognized that Communism is incompatible with China's needs and her people's aspirations. As a result they tried to carry on class struggle in the name of our National Revolution, to hide a Soviet puppet regime behind Kuomintang, to substitute Communism for the Three People's Principles and to use Kuomintang as a vehicle for establishing in China a Sovietized "dictatorship of the proletariat,"—all for the purpose of turning an otherwise independent and free nation into a Soviet satellite. Nevertheless, in our efforts to save the country and to upbuild it as a modern, independent and free nation on the basis of the Three People's Principles, we have sought to ensure China's historical continuity and traditional culture. Though subjected to repeated attacks by the international and Chinese Communists, we did not fall for their political offensive and "peace" chicanery. Our resolute stand finally forced the Chinese Communists to come out into the open and call their satrapy a "People's Republic" and "dictatorship of the proletariat." What better proof than this that they are Soviet puppets and would not stop short of selling China's birthright?

Although we lost the China mainland at the end of our

"peaceful coexistence," our Government resolutely refused to accept Soviet mediation or to sign any agreement with their Chinese puppets. Furthermore, we rejected repeatedly the Chinese Communists' demand for the formation of a coalition government and refused to buy a temporary peace by yielding to their intimidation and enticements. Thus, we were able to preserve our status as an independent country and maintain our dignity as a free people. It is in this spirit that we are now carrying on our struggle to restore national sovereignty and territorial integrity.

In Dr. Sun's General Outline of National Reconstruction promulgated in 1924, it was stipulated that, once the nation is unified, local self-government is to be introduced throughout the country and delegates chosen at the county and city levels are to meet in a National Assembly to enact a constitution and initiate the country in constitutional government. Following the successful completion of the Northward Expedition our Government proceeded in accordance with this program. Although the convocation of the National Assembly had to be postponed several times because of the Sino-Japanese War, the Government gave the pledge that constitutional government would commence as soon as victory was won. At the end of the war the Chinese Communists and their front organization, namely, the Democratic League, did everything possible to sabotage the National Assembly. Their objective was to set up a coalition government and then use it to bring about a "people's government" in the form of "democratic dictatorship." This, however, did not deter the Government from its original course. The National Assembly was duly convened and a constitution adopted. This was followed by the holding of general elections and formation of a popularly elected government. Not even the subsequent Communist armed insurrection could have kept the Government from establishing constitutional democracy in China. The Chinese Government today, with its program of local self-government in Taiwan, provides a revealing contrast to the Communist totalitarian "democratic dictatorship" on the mainland. Herein lies the foundation for our eventual victory against Communism.

When the tide of war was turning against us in the winter of 1948, when we were being attacked both from within and from without and when we found ourselves utterly isolated, we decided to withdraw from the mainland and turn Taiwan into the base for national recovery. For the past several years on this bastion of freedom—on this strip of China's own territory—we have sought to rally Chinese both at home and overseas to continue our struggle not only for national recovery but also in the interest of collective security in the Pacific. We have already succeeded in upsetting the Russian scheme of destroying the Republic of China as a major step toward the domination of Europe and Asia.

Although we have suffered heavily because of our sincerity and good faith in the face of Communist falsehood and treachery, we have not lost heart. On the contrary, we are more convinced than ever that eventually truth will prevail and that right will triumph. Throughout our thirty years of dealings with the Russian Communists, while they have encroached upon our territory, impaired our sovereignty, set up a puppet regime and subverted our government in violation of all the treaties and agreements they have concluded with us, we on our part have unswervingly and faithfully fulfilled our obligations. We have not violated any stipulation in our treaties and agreements, and even when finally we had to accuse the Soviet Union of bad faith in the United Nations and to renounce the Sino-Soviet Treaty of Friendship and Alliance, we acted honorably. Throughout these years nothing that we did could be used by the Russians as an alibi to justify their aggression in China. Our strength stems from the fact that all our actions have been guided by legal and moral considerations, and that although temporarily cast down, we are not destroyed.

Despite our trials in "peaceful coexistence" with the Russian Communists, we have never stooped to neutralism. After the Mukden Incident of September 1931, Communist front organizations posing as neutrals started a movement which would have China align with Sovet Russia against Japan. Their purpose was to force our Government to follow the Moscow line. Unhesitatingly we decided to resist this pressure and to hold fast to an independent policy as would befit a sovereign state, a policy which would promote international cooperation and at the same time sustain us in our war of resistance against Japan. Another instance was in 1945, the year after victory, when our Government rejected Stalin's proposal that China should take a neutral stand in world affairs. Bent on upholding international righteousness and in preserving our national independence and freedom, we refused to embrace a neutral attitude. This has been and is the consistent spirit of our National Revolution.

We have taken a steady view that China's freedom and equality are the vanguard of the freedom and equality of all other Asian peoples. Herein lies the key to a lasting world peace. Consequently, in the war against the Russian and Chinese Communists, just as in the former war of resistance against Japan, we are fighting as much for justice and peace in all parts of the world as for China's own freedom and equality. Whether in peace or war, we have shouldered our own responsibility. True to the Chinese teaching "to do the utmost that is within oneself," we have not evaded sacrifices. However successful have Soviet Russia and its international fifth columns been in causing misunderstanding between us and our allies, objective facts have shown that despite setbacks and unfavorable international public opinion we have taken a stand against aggression and fought for international justice. Our forthright resistance against Communism and aggression and our undying faith in the rightness of our cause provide the best guarantee for final success.

Admittedly, many factors have contributed toward our defeat. The mortal blows to our anti-Communist struggle, however, did not come from administrative failures alone. As a matter of fact, similar political and social shortcomings, unavoidable after a long war, occurred in other countries, too. The mortal blows had come from serious defects in organization and technique and serious errors in policy and strategy, and, above all, from the weakening in our national spirit at the time when it was most needed.

This, however, does not mean that there is no need for further improvement. Today we must continue to study ways and means of strengthening our administration. We must seek wherein we need to introduce ideological, spiritual and psychological reforms. We must have a better understanding of the Communist menace and be more vigilant in our precautions. We must recapture the spirit of the National Revolution and reaffirm our faith in the Three People's Principles. Only thus can we regain our combat strength against Communism and Soviet Russia, recover our lost territory and help destroy world Communism.

CHAPTER THREE

PROBLEMS OF BASIC CONCEPT IN THE FREE WORLD'S WAR AGAINST COMMUNISM

The Objectives and Types of War

Let us first study the war objectives of the aggressors and of those opposed to aggression. According to Clausewitz, the scope and the size of effort in any war are determined by its objectives, or its political aims. Some wars are meant as a protest or as a demonstration to prod the enemy to negotiate. Others are for the purpose of occupying part of the enemy's territory and forcing him to accept certain terms of settlement. These are limited wars. Conversely, if the wars are fought for immense political aims, such as occupying the entire territory of the enemy or forcing him to surrender unconditionally, then they assume the aspects of an absolute and unlimited war.

In World War II the political aim of the Axis powers was to divide the world among themselves. Hence, it was an absolute and unlimited war. The Allies, on their part, set the Axis powers' "unconditional surrender" as their objective, and therefore theirs was also a kind of unlimited war.

Although the democratic nations and Soviet Russia fought on the same side, they had different war objectives. What the late President Roosevelt had in mind was lasting peace for the world. The United Nations, both its organization and its Charter, was the concrete manifestation of his ideal. The Republic of China was in favor of this formula, and she was one of the nations that took part in drafting the United Nations Charter and also one of the United Nations' initial sponsors. Up to the present the Republic of China has remained faithful in her support of the world organization and the principles of its Charter.

Soviet Russia, however, had her own war objectives in the form of a realistic plan for unlimited war. In the West, she aimed at partitioning Germany and annexing countries in Eastern Europe; in the East, on the one hand she sought to destroy Japan so as to put herself in a position to start aggression in the Pacific, and on the other hand to annex the Chinese mainland so as to realize her ambition of outflanking Europe by way of Peiping and Calcutta. Both the Teheran and the Yalta conferences were diplomatic battlefields where the Allies fought out world strategies among themselves. Unfortunately, the Allies' ideas and ideals for the postwar world went down to defeat before Soviet Russia's plans of aggrandizement and aggression. In April and August 1945 respectively, Germany and Japan surrendered unconditionally. Most of the Allied nations thought that they had won World War II. Actually, the Allies had won only military victories, whereas their war objectives for a lasting peace had been sabotaged by Soviet Russia at Yalta with the result that their successes in the field really represented their political defeat. World War II, strictly speaking, ended without a real conclusion. Although the Allies succeeded in hastening Japan's surrender by means of atomic weapons, they failed to avert their political defeat as they could not do anything to thwart Soviet Russia's aggressive designs. This was how the crosscurrent, released by Soviet Russia during the war, has become an unlimited war against the free world ever since.

Both Nazism-Fascism and Bolshevism came into being after World War I. They have one thing in common in that both doctrines are totalitarian and aggressive. Hence both are inimical to democracy. The operational ideas of the Nazis-Fascists are to impose totalitarian regimes on their own people at home so that they could carry on total wars against foreign countries. Before they launched blitzkriegs against their enemy they carried out a war of nerves to put him in a state of psychological contradictions and policy vacillations. Then when the time of military attack came, they directed their fifth columns, already in the enemy country, to set up a Quisling-type puppet regime. They also poured out propaganda about the so-called New World Order which they proposed to set up. This was true of Hitler and Mussolini in Europe. It was also how Konoye and Tojo operated in Asia. Their strategy was similar to that of the Russian Communists except that the latter used different tactics. In the first place, Nazism assumed the form of a national struggle, while the Russian Communists used class struggle as their formula. Nazism played up the alleged superiority of the Master Race, and this was expressed in the oppression and conquest of other races, while the Pan-Slavism of the Russian Communists advertised the so-called dictatorship of the proletariat, and when translated into action this meant the use of the Communists in the various countries to help control the entire world.

Secondly, Nazism attacked directly by instigating anti-democratic movements in various countries in order to destroy their political structure, while the Russian Communists made use of "democracy and freedom" in the democratic nations to confuse and paralyze their governments.

Thirdly, Nazism used their own armed forces for direct invasion of an enemy country, while the Russian Communists did not use any of their own troops. Instead they directed their fifth columns to foment class war, or to stir up conflicts of interest among the democracies themselves, or to incite Oriental peoples to rise against Occidental powers in national wars. Despite the variations, the aim of the Russian Communists remained the same, that is, to have others fight for them.

In view of these characteristics in the Russian Communists' wars of aggression, if the democracies should try to use the same methods against the Communist bloc as they had previously used against the Axis powers, they will not be able to stop their aggression. Instead, it could lead to serious losses.

Like the Axis powers before them, the Russian Communists know of no limits to their aggression. But here is a difference. When the Axis powers used their own armed forces in direct warfare against unexpendable allies of the democracies, or attacked the territory of the democracies themselves, the democracies fought back, and Hitler had to fight on two fronts simultaneously. In the end he was defeated.

Today the Russian Communists will not make the same mistake. They will not invade any enemy country or any of the latter's allies with their own armed forces. Instead, they will employ indirect warfare. On the one hand, they will use tactics of political warfare and peace offensive to hypnotize an enemy country, and on the other, they will use neutralism to sabotage antiaggression alliances among the free nations. Meanwhile, they will direct their fifth columns, namely, local Communists, to create "peaceful transformation" in neutralist countries, enemy countries and the latter's allies. Unlike the Nazis, Russian Communists do not use their own troops for direct attacks against their enemy or the territory of any democratic nation. What they do is to isolate their enemy on the outside and to cause paralysis on the inside by peace offensives and the use of neutralism tactics. Finally, when they do use their armed forces in a surprise attack on a democratic nation, the latter will have already been defeated in the political and psychological fields. What happens then is no longer purely a military operation, and for this reason the situation can no longer be retrieved by any type of military weapon, however powerful it may be. Therefore, it would be just as futile for the democracies to wait for Russia's military attack and then retaliate as to wait for the Communist bloc to collapse by itself. Neither course will stop Soviet aggression or safeguard world peace and security.

That is why I propose to analyze the characteristics of the Communist bloc's unlimited war and the various measures which the democratic bloc should take to counter it.

A Contrast Between the Communist Bloc's War Objectives and the Democratic Bloc's Policy Toward Soviet Russia

What are Soviet Russia's objectives vis-à-vis the free world? Her military operational ideas and political aims will be taken up later. First let us analyze her actions of aggression and her objectives. These may be summed up as follows: To attain long-term national mobilization and armament by the institution of "dictatorship of the proletariat"; to establish a collective economy and a slave society and to destroy all forms of capitalism by Communism; to destroy nationalism and national cultures in various countries of the world by an international class struggle; to annihilate humanism and all religious beliefs and to restrict scholastic and religious freedoms by materialism; and finally, to destroy the political organization of all other countries and to replace it with the Soviet system for the purpose of world control.

In order to achieve their inordinate scheme of world conquest, the Russian Communists chose the absolute forms of unlimited war. In their war against the free world they are limited by neither time nor space. They can switch from one battlefield to another as well as from one form of warfare to another. They can carry out infiltration, propaganda, organization, political intrigue, subversion and even armed uprising against their enemy on the inside, in coordination with their frontal attacks—economic, diplomatic, cultural, political, and psychological—on the outside. Every one of their moves is for the purpose of the decisive battle, and every advance is to be evaluated for its effect on the final outcome. They keep on advancing toward the target, namely, the final battle, unceasingly and without limitations in full expectation of attaining the ultimate objective.

The struggle today between the free world and the Communist bloc is one between humanism and bestiality, between light and darkness and between truth and black magic. It is not a question of the life and death of any one country or any one people alone. So long as the Communist International and Communism exist, humanity will not only be unable to have peace and security, but will also face the constant danger of irrevocably losing freedom as well as a livelihood befitting human beings. From this we can see that the democratic bloc's responsibility toward humanity is unusually great, and yet its present objective with regard to the Soviet bloc is entirely out of step with this responsibility. What does this responsibility consist of?

It involves removal of the threat of aggression and of world war and the establishment of a lasting world peace; preservation of the free ways of life of mankind and ensuring of the peaceful development of their economic and social well-being; safeguarding of the independence of various countries in the world and balanced development of their national cultures; protection of the freedom of academic thoughts and religious beliefs; and finally, lifting of the Iron Curtain so as to remove the danger of Communist conquest of the world at its very source, and to turn the world into an international community of free nations on an equal footing one with another.

At present, however, the democratic bloc has set for itself only limited objectives and has adopted only limited plans in its struggle against aggression. All it asks is the maintenance of the *status quo* and the preservation of peace. Because of this policy, the democratic bloc, despite the fact that sometimes it can wrest local initiative, eventually finds itself in a passive position. As a result, though it may succeed in checkmating the Communist bloc's military advance in certain areas, it cannot take measures to prevent the latter's political aggression. Consider some of the basic concepts held by the democratic bloc and also some of the problems with which it is faced today.

The Outcome of the Contest Between Old and New Colonialisms

As pointed out in the foregoing, the ultimate aim of the Russian Communists' war against the free world is to destroy capitalism, nationalism and democracy, and to put human freedom in shackles. Yet, in the course of their unlimited war, they still capitalize on nationalism in the East for the purpose of political warfare. The Russian Communists said:

"We do not know and cannot know which spark—out of the innumerable sparks that are flying around in all countries . . . will kindle the conflagration . . . we must set to work to stir up all, even the oldest, mustiest and seemingly hopeless spheres.

"We must not renounce any drop which hollows out the stone."*

The nationalism aroused in the East by Europe's old colonialism is growing stronger daily and the vast population involved is considered by the Russian Communists as their "powerful and large reserve army." Therefore, the Russian Communists are utilizing it as a principal weapon in their assaults on old colonialism.

For thirty years the Russian Communists have made China the first target in their aggressive scheme against the world. Yet the old colonialists have failed to take notice of it. They did not realize that any fire of aggression, once lit on the Chinese mainland, will naturally spread to the Middle East, and the flames ignited by the Russian Communists in the

---

* Nathan Leites, *The Operational Code of the Politburo*, p. 11.

Middle East will eventually burn their way to the fountain-head of old colonialism. Why did they fail to be vigilant? The Russian Communists see some useful allies in several of the old colonialists' traditional ideas which they can use to good advantage in carrying out their political tactics in the East.

One is the idea of redividing the colonies. In the opinion of the Russian Communists the Western nations are way behind the times in deeming Soviet Russia's World Revolution as something similar to old colonialism both in nature and in scope. They think that if they cannot stop Soviet Russia from advancing eastward, there is no harm in reaching an understanding with her on the redivision of the land and resources of countries in the East.

They think that by a "feeding the wolf" policy, even if they could not satisfy Soviet Russia's appetite, they could at least slow down her advance in the Middle East and in Europe and thereby gain a temporary peace for the West. The Russian Communists' new colonialism is definitely nothing of this kind. We should understand that what the Russian Communists want is not to share the Western nations' colonies in Asia and Africa but to occupy Asia and Africa as a whole as well as the entire area of Europe.

Then, too, the Russian Communists consider "realism" on the part of the old colonialists as a weapon which they can use in their aggrandizement and aggression. A conspicuous instance is the recognition of accomplished facts even though this is incompatible with international righteousness. Since Soviet Russia knows no limits to her aggression, there will be no end to the accomplished facts which will require recognition.

Thus realism begets appeasement. When Soviet Russia instigated the Chinese Communists to seize China, the old colonialists thought they could slow down the advance of this new colonialism or at least avert the outbreak of a major war by appeasing her. Even after the fall of the China mainland, the old colonialists still entertained the illusion that the Chinese Communists might become practitioners of Titoism. Their slogan was: "Don't drive the Chinese Communists deeper into Soviet Russia's arms." This was the reason for their appeasement policy toward the Chinese Communists. Events have since proved that there is no possibility for the Chinese Communists to leave Soviet Russia's fold. Even Tito has not been able to leave Soviet Russia's fold. One must ask what has appeasement brought us?

It may be argued that in seeking the maintenance of *status quo* realism has not been entirely negative. It has a positive policy, too. It is the balance of power. In the eyes of the Russian Communists, however, this is but a historical relic of the 19th century, or at least something that dates back to the days before World War II. Moreover, the Russians believe this policy can help them extend their aggression over even wider areas sooner. Look at the Eurasian mainland today. Soviet Russia is steadily attaining absolute superiority there. The Western nations can hardly maintain a balance of power in this vast area. Even the United States is finding it difficult to pursue this policy. I feel that the West European nations are imagining that the current state of affairs between the United States and Soviet Russia will last indefinitely and thus give them an extended period of peace. What they have failed to appreciate is that the relative strength between the two countries is changing all the time. If the countries in Western Europe do not take a resolute stand against aggression but try to maintain a balance of power between the United States and Soviet Russia, it will encourage Soviet Russia and provide her with an excellent opportunity to use her neutralism tactics. If neutralism should grow further, a number of non-Communist countries in Asia will, one after another, follow the same path. This will enable Soviet Russia to seize upon the contradictions between the Eastern people's nationalism and Europe's old colonialism in extending the scope of their political aggression. Seen in this light, the indirect assistance given by the Western European countries to Soviet Russia further enhances her superior position in Asia for the eventual expulsion of all Western nations from this continent.

Then there is the "Europe First" theory. In the opinion of the Russian Communists this theory is proof of the soundness of Lenin's policy directive about detours. This theory has actually, though imperceptibly, improved Soviet Russia's chances of realizing their "Asia First" theory that much sooner. Soviet Russia's detours today are taking her to the Middle East by way of the Far East. Once she is entrenched in the Middle East, she will be on her last leg to Western Europe. The foregoing facts prove that the principal reason for the steady progress in Soviet Russia's new colonialism and her plans of aggression is to be found in ideological and policy mistakes committed by her opponents.

Nationalism of the East at the Crossroads—Differences in the Policies of the Communist Bloc and the Democratic Western Bloc Toward Peoples in the East

Today the nationalism of the East is at the crossroads. The harder the Soviet bloc presses its struggle against the democratic bloc, the more difficult becomes the position of nationalists of the East. Whether the latter will have any freedom of choice depends on the policy of the Western nations and on their methods of leadership.

Nationalism, of course, has physical attributes necessary for its existence, but its strength is greater than all its physical attributes put together. Nationalism is a kind of cultural consciousness which comprises national ideas as well as national sentiments. The essence of the spirit of nationalism is expressed in the way people treasure their own history, love their own culture, safeguard their own dignity and fight to retain the independence of their own country. The Western nations have been right in giving peoples in the East economic assistance, and, at the same time, expecting them to follow the path of democracy, because they are in need of both. If the Western nations, however, should disregard the Eastern peoples' nationalist feelings, or hurt their national pride, no amount of sincere friendship will be efficacious in promoting understanding and cooperation with them. That is why a number of underdeveloped nations in the East, because of their desire to secure independence and equality first, would rather endure a low standard of living than accept economic aid from the Western nations. In the meantime, the fact that the old Western colonialists, instead of forsaking their economic interests in the East, are trying to preserve them, tends to remind people in the former colonies of exploitation in the old days. Here lies the crux of the problem between the old colonialists of the West and the nationalists of the East.

The Russian Communists understand this problem thoroughly and, therefore, have taken the fullest advantage of this contradiction. It also explains why Soviet Russia, in her dealings with peoples in the East, has been following a different policy. She gives them what they want. She sugar coats her poisonous drug even though it is "heroin."

The Western nations regard poverty in the Eastern nations as a breeding ground for Communism and they use economic aid as the principal means of solving the problem of nationalism in the East. The Russian Communists on their part make indirect use of the Eastern peoples' nationalism and do not seek to promote the growth of Communism directly; they utilize the latter's nationalist ideas and sentiments and not just their low standard of living. Because of this, economic aid from the Western nations cannot stop the spread of Communism in the East.

This is especially true in the case of American economic aid to self-styled neutral countries. I can emphatically say that this kind of aid is tantamount to helping the spread of Communist influence and the anti-American movement in these countries. It should be noted that the amount of materials wasted in these aid programs is still small as compared with the effect it has had on the morale of those combating Communism. The neutralist nations actually depend on their fence-sitting to blackmail the United States for economic assistance. Therefore, whatever they receive becomes an encouragement for them to move closer toward Soviet Russia, and indirectly enhances the position of Communists in these countries.

Will these nations really throw themselves into Soviet Russia's arms and forsake the Western nations once the latter should cease such aid? In my opinion, the opportunistic politicians do not intend to do so because the neutralists need the West in order to increase their importance in the eyes of Soviet Russia, just as they need Soviet Russia in order to blackmail the West. It is my belief that once the United States ceases her aid to these neutralist nations the latter will either be abandoned by Soviet Russia or, after being subjected to Soviet insults and coercions, will hurry to the side of the Western nations. Even if they should side with Soviet Russia, it would only mean the addition of another contradiction in the Communist bloc, and will not increase the latter's strength to any appreciable extent.

In the second place, the Western nations' policy toward the Asian countries, including their demand that the latter effect political reforms and embrace democracy instead of Communism is correct and irreproachable. The Russian Communists in their policy toward the same countries hope to turn this movement of democratic political reforms into a class war. Thus the Western nations have inadvertently paved the way for the Russian Communists to employ their "peaceful transformation" tactic in the Eastern nations.

In the third place, the standard of living in the Eastern nations is lower than that in the West, but this does not necessarily mean a low cultural standard. Often, the Western nations have assumed a superiority complex just because of their higher standard of living. This has caused resentment among the Eastern peoples who have already felt the pressure of Western culture on their own national life. Usually two things happen when the Eastern nations are undergoing cultural reforms. One is the loss of national self-confidence following the decline of their own culture, and the other is bewilderment caused by the lack of time for a new culture to take shape. This creates a vacuum, making it possible for the Communists to use "independence" and "freedom" as a cover for their infiltration until they are strong enough to choke off the national spirit in these countries. That this holds a great danger for the future of the nations concerned should not be difficult to imagine.

In short, the growth of Communism in the East is not the natural result of the economic, political and cultural "backwardness" of the Eastern nations. Rather it is the outcome of the Russian Communists' deliberate efforts in infiltration, instigation, and their success in exploiting the contradictions between the nationalism of the East and the old colonialism of the West.

The Russian Communists have two policies toward nationalism.

It is the belief of people in the West that nationalism of the East is incompatible with Communism. People in the East, including myself, have likewise held the view that Communism cannot succeed in China. Yet Soviet Communism has actually witnessed a phenomenal growth in Asia, especially on the Chinese mainland. Why? We should consider Soviet Russia's policy toward nationalities both inside and outside the Iron Curtain, to see if it contains any secret formula. The best explanation is to be found in Lenin's two answers to the question of nationalism which he gave in 1913:

"To a struggle against national oppression," he announced, "we say absolutely yes. To a struggle for any national development, for a national culture in general, we say absolutely no."*

Today Soviet Russia is reaping benefits through adroitly applying the laws of dialectics to these two basically opposite answers.

She uses the first answer in dealing with the former colonies of the Western nations, and refrains from destroying the traditional culture of Eastern peoples outside the Iron Curtain to seek the direct expansion of Communism. Furthermore, lest the Eastern peoples discover the real aim of Communist aggression and see through their deceptive aid to national independence movements, she does her best to camouflage the true nature of Communism so that the Eastern peoples concerned will not be alarmed by the danger which Communism presents. Even when the local Communists arouse public wrath because of their destructive activities against the economic and cultural life of the nations concerned, Soviet Russia can always deny having any relationship with the indigenous Communists. This was one of the main reasons for the dissolution of the Cominform early in 1956. Therefore, in dealing with the Eastern nations Soviet Russia takes care not to belittle but to use their original cultures to oppose the West's old colonialism. In the meantime, she also cunningly abstains from directly exploiting the existing economic resources in the countries concerned and speaks of their low standard of living sympathetically in order to sustain them in their struggle against old colonialism.

If any nation, however, should fall behind the Iron Curtain, then Lenin's second answer comes into action until the nation in question becomes a slave to the Slavs in accordance with Moscow's policy on nationalities under the formula of "nationalist in form but Communist in substance."

The most pressing demands of Eastern nations still outside

* Julian Towster, *Political Power in the U.S.S.R.*

the Iron Curtain are: one, political independence; two, economic emancipation and freedom to maintain their way of life; and three, preservation of their own culture, a desire which has become all the stronger as a result of the impact of the Western culture.

After World War II the Western nations abandoned most of their colonial possessions in the East and permitted them to become independent nations. Of course, this represented a great step forward in their policy toward Asia. As pointed out before, however, they retain their old mentality. While recognizing the independence of their former colonies they still try to hold onto their special economic rights there and carelessly exhibit a superiority complex in cultural matters. This old mentality constitutes an obstacle in their policy in the East, and as a result, a fundamental solution of the contradiction between the Eastern and the Western nations has yet to be found. The Eastern nations do not feel the pains of their former oppression and exploitation any the less just because they have won political independence.

Utilizing this state of mind, Soviet Russia is employing with telling effect her United Front and neutralism tactics, leading the Eastern nations to mistake neutralism for independence. Some of these nations, in their struggle against the Western powers in the name of "anti-imperialism" and "anti-colonialism," do not hesitate to accept help from the Russian and Chinese Communists, and with their nationalistic feelings at a fever pitch, they fail to think of the consequences if they should one day be shut behind the Iron Curtain. In this connection, I wish to cite a prime pattern of Communist infiltration. In 1924 during our first period of "peaceful coexistence" with Soviet Russia when our revolutionary government in Canton was threatened by a revolt, we accepted Soviet Russia's proferred military aid, totalling some 3,000 tons of material. Again, between 1937 and 1941, as part of a barter agreement which followed the conclusion of the Sino-Soviet

Nonaggression Pact, China obtained 849 planes, plus some antiaircraft artillery and field guns from Soviet Russia. Little did we realize the fateful consequences of Soviet aid which eventually enabled the Communist fifth column to carry out its political infiltration and military insurrection both during the Northward Expedition and the Sino-Japanese War. I cannot, therefore, but view with grave concern the future of any countries accepting Communist aid, especially those in Southeast and South Asia, however hard pressed they may be for external assistance.

Today, Soviet Russia is offering both economic and military assistance to non-Communist countries in the Middle East and South Asia. Meanwhile, the Chinese Communists are paying generous lip service to the so-called "Five Principles of Peaceful Coexistence." Their so-called respect for each other's sovereignty and noninterference in each other's internal affairs served to cover up the real nature of Communist aggression. This has enabled the Russian Communists to carry out their political and economic infiltration and to impose a new colonialism on people in the vast area between the Mediterranean Sea and the Indian Ocean. Thus "peace" and "neutrality" slogans have become a gangplank on which nations which have only recently succeeded in freeing themselves from the lingering influence of old colonialism walk to the brink of the Communist Empire's Iron Curtain and eventually fall into the unfathomable sea of new colonialism without knowing what is happening.

I have traced the growth of Communism in China, described our own experience on the mainland and also drawn some conclusions from the Russian Communists' aggressive actions over a period of thirty years in the light of their dialectic laws of action. I am afraid that not all the Western nations yet comprehend these historical facts.

Who is the Eastern peoples' enemy? How can the Western nations and the Eastern peoples work together and help one

PROBLEMS OF BASIC CONCEPT

another in resisting their common enemy? These are questions we still must answer.

The Russian Communists today, through their strategy of detours, are turning their sword of aggression from the Chinese mainland to South Asia and the Middle East where the non-Communist countries have become the Communist bloc's object of their Cold War. The purpose of the Communist bloc is to pull nationalism in the Middle East to its side, to alter the relative strength between the aggressors and those opposed to aggression and to change the strategic situation both in Asia and in the Middle East in its own favor.

It is common knowledge that Soviet Russia is the Western nation's enemy in Asia and in the Middle East. This is because she uses nationalism of the East to attack the Western nations. In actuality, Soviet Russia is also the real enemy of the Eastern peoples themselves.

It is for the sake of expelling the Western influence from the Middle East that she has applied against the Eastern peoples her political tactic of "peaceful transformation" and her military tactic of disposing of the victims one at a time. This is part of her scheme of further extending her Iron Curtain and enslavement policy to Asia and the Middle East. Therefore, Soviet Russia is the common enemy of the Western nations and the Eastern peoples. The latter, however, have been made to fight each other by their common enemy through "peaceful coexistence" intrigues and neutralism tactics. Herein lies the danger in the Middle East, and it is also a basic problem in the free world's war against Communism, which should be solved first of all.

Consequently, we are of the opinion that the Western nations, in their dealings with the Eastern peoples, need to re-study their policy toward Asia as a whole.

As already mentioned, most of the Eastern peoples outside the Iron Curtain have gained their political independence since the end of World War II. What they are after now is economic emancipation and integrity of sovereignty. As to Eastern peoples already behind the Iron Curtain, their sole demand is the restoration of their national entities and deliverance from their present enslavement. This nationalist movement outside the Iron Curtain, and the anti-Communist revolutionary movement inside the Iron Curtain, constitute the greatest potential power in the free world's struggle against Communism and aggression, and it is also the crucial point in the spirit of the age in the East. It is not too late for the Western nations to help the Eastern peoples liberate those of their brothers already enslaved, and jointly to oppose the Russian Communists' new colonialism. Otherwise, no matter whether it is the economically exploited people in the old colonies or people enslaved by the totalitarian powers in the new colonies, and no matter whether it is imperialism, capitalism, democracy and liberalism, or free socialism, or national independence, they will all meet with a common fate at the hands of the Communists in their World Revolution and class dictatorship.

In view of such dire consequences, how can we help feeling disturbed and at the same time rising to meet the challenge with a new resolve? We must do away with the old ideas and old concepts that have come down from the days of old colonialism and selfish interests and replace them with new ideas of equality, independence, freedom and democracy, and with a new spirit of mutual help and cooperation, and a new solidarity against the common enemy. Only thus can we save mankind from an untold calamity. Only thus can we reestablish a world community of universal brotherhood and lasting peace. In the final analysis, it all depends on whether imperialism in the old colonies and capitalism in the democratic and free countries are determined to oppose Communism, and if so, what practical actions they are prepared to take for the purpose.

The Democratic Bloc's Military Thinking in the Eyes of the Communist Bloc

As already stated, the Russian Communists, in launching their unlimited war against the free world, are pinning their hopes of victory on mistakes of the democratic bloc. In the eyes of the Russian Communists, the democratic bloc's mistakes are rooted in the Western nations' old ideas of limited war, and these old ideas in turn have given rise to a number of erroneous conceptions.

First, there is the theory in military affairs that "weapons are all-powerful."

According to the Russian Communists' principles of military education, military organization and operational principles are the product of social and political factors, and the outcome of war is mostly decided by social, economic, political, academic and psychological conditions, and not decided purely and simply by military affairs, or by weapons. That is why Soviet Russia and the international Communists always precede their military attacks on an enemy country by infiltration in order to affect its public opinion, to assail the basis of its national policy and to strike at the morale of its troops, with the result that the latter cannot get the full use of such superior weapons as may be in their possession in a bid for victory. Thus, in the eyes of the Russian Communists, the "weapons are all-powerful" theory is actually the residue of the "military combat is all-decisive" theory, and is definitely unsuitable for countering the type of war involving indirect attack and strategy of detours as employed by the Russian Communists.

In view of the Western nations' preoccupation with armaments, the Russian Communists are not only unafraid of, but actually welcome the "hydrogen bombs are all-powerful" strategic concept, for any war, once lost in the social and political fields, cannot be retrieved in the military field.

Besides, even in military operations, exclusive reliance on one weapon such as the hydrogen bomb will not be enough to overcome one's enemy. Therefore, before the Russian Communists change their present inferiority in nuclear weapons to superiority, they will use political and psychological warfare to freeze the nuclear weapons in their enemy's possession, thus denying them a chance to use them. Even if the Western nations should make new discoveries in nuclear weapons, and even if their military techniques should further improve and remain ahead of the Russian Communists, they cannot stop the latter's aggression. This is because the devising of newer nuclear weapons to stop the enemy from using nuclear weapons is equivalent to freezing one's own nuclear weapons. Therefore, as far as the Russian Communists are concerned, the West's "hydrogen bombs are all-powerful" strategic concept suits their purpose of freezing their opponents' nuclear weapons, thereby gaining time needed to turn their present inferiority in armaments to one of equality.

Next, let us take up the question of disarmament and the antiwar movement.

When the Western nations began demobilization immediately after World War II, Stalin declared that the world could look forward to having thirty years of peace. He pointed to Soviet Russia's treaties of friendship and alliance with the Republic of China, Britain and France, each of which was for a period of twenty to thirty years, as a proof. Thus, while the Western nations accelerated in their demobilization, Soviet Russia had practically a free hand in carrying out her expansionist policy in the postwar period. Later, when Soviet Russia started the Korean War, the democracies had to declare the existence of a state of emergency and rearm in a hurry. After the cessation of hostilities was declared, Soviet Russia again carried on disarmament negotiations in the United Nations and at the same time instigated a disarmament movement within the Western nations.

It is not my intention to go into the details of the various disarmament proposals by the Western nations and Soviet Russia. What I shall do here is to deduce from our experience in discussing military reorganization with the Chinese Communists in 1946 the methods which the Russian Communists are prone to use in the disarmament negotiations. It will be remembered that the Chinese Communists demanded the convocation of the Political Consultative Conference and the formation of a coalition government in their negotiations with the Chinese Government. They also insisted on a veto power in the State Council. Similarly, what is there to prevent the Russian Communists from raising political problems at a future international disarmament conference as a prerequisite and, once it is granted, from asking for a veto power as their price for an agreement?

During the negotiations the Russian Communists will surely try to get the other nations to reduce their number of troops. As an inducement they may even agree to effect a parallel reduction. But after the other nations have carried out their part of the agreement, they may find that the Russians have not honored the agreement but have instead stepped up their own mobilization. Such was the sad experience of my government. It was agreed in 1946 that during the first period of military reorganization the Chinese Government was to reduce its number of divisions from 254 to ninety while the Chinese Communists were to reduce theirs to eighteen divisions. This was to be followed by the further reduction of the Government forces to fifty divisions and the Communist forces to ten divisions. The Government proceeded in all good faith with the reduction program. The Communists, on the contrary, expanded their armed forces. Today the Russian Communists are suggesting that both the United States and Russia reduce their armed forces to between 1,000,000 and 1,500,000 men. Should the United States agree to effect such a reduction, what guarantee is there that the Russians will do the same? And what about the troops in the Soviet satellites both in Europe and in Asia?

While negotiating for the withdrawal of troops from certain areas, the Russian Communists will ask that the other nations give up their present positions. When this is complied with, they will bring up a political issue to justify the non-withdrawal of their own troops and this usually takes the form of a demand that they be allowed to retain political power in the area to be so evacuated. I remember the Chinese Communists agreed in 1946 to evacuate the northern part of Kiangsu province but they insisted that the Government recognize Communist administration in the region. Today Soviet Russia is asking the United States to evacuate bases in the NATO countries before she will withdraw her armed forces from the Warsaw Pact nations. I predict that if the United States should actually give up its military bases in Europe, Soviet Russia will also go through the motion of withdrawing from Eastern Europe. But she will keep the Iron Curtain in Eastern Europe and maintain the puppet regimes in the satellites. She will take measures to ensure that after her armed forces are withdrawn from these countries she will be free to return and even increase her forces there at short notice. Therefore, even if the current disarmament talks should result in an agreement, one must ask: Will it help bring about world peace and security, or will it hasten the outbreak of a world war?

In the matter of international inspection, the Russian Communists naturally will participate in the inspection teams assigned to tour the Western nations and will have a chance to study military deployment there. Similar teams trying to enter the Iron Curtain, however, will be rejected on political grounds. During the Marshall mission to China truce teams sent out in 1946 received full cooperation in areas garrisoned by the Government troops, but those teams dispatched to Communist-controlled areas including Chihfeng in Jehol, points in Manchuria, Kalgan on the Great Wall and places in northern Kiangsu were either refused entry or expelled. Today the Communists are using the same trick against the United Nations' truce supervisory committee in Korea. I conjecture that the Western nations' plans of international inspection and "Open skies," even if they should be agreed upon, will not fare any better. For the Russians will use them to spy on military preparedness in the Western nations but at the same time make it impossible for international teams to inspect military conditions behind the Iron Curtain. It is not beyond the realm of possibility that the Russian Communists are using the disarmament talks to paralyze the democracies in their mobilization efforts while improving and concealing their own military expansion in preparation for their next military offensive. In the final analysis, therefore, disarmament talks are nothing but another manifestation of their "peaceful coexistence" political warfare.

As to the disarmament movement within the Western nations, the Western nations' strategic concept that "hydrogen bombs are all-powerful" lends itself to be used by the Russian Communists in propagating their antiwar movement. They play up the destructiveness of the hydrogen bombs to spread the idea that in any war fought with such weapons both the victor and the vanquished would meet with the same disaster.

At the same time they lead people in the Western nations to believe that further progress and advance in nuclear weapons will discourage Soviet Russia from risking a nuclear war and from challenging the Western nations, and that the world will henceforth have no more wars. They simply want people in the Western nations to think that if there is going to be no nuclear war, there is not going to be any kind of war at all.

As a result, in the democratic bloc there arise two movements: one is to disarm and the other is to avoid war by all means. The continued development of these two movements will create contradictions between military affairs and politics, and even between strategy and politics in the Western nations.

From a purely military point of view, it stands to reason that increase in firepower should result in reduced military personnel. Military preparedness and antiwar feelings, however, cannot exist side by side indefinitely, much less harmonize. The Russian Communists utilize this contradiction between military affairs and politics in the West to spread peace offensive and neutralism. Consequently, the Western nations, caught between the coordinated moves of peace campaigns at home and of neutralism in non-Communist nations in Asia, have failed to remain firm in their position or to take timely actions against the Communist bloc's indirect warfare and direct provocations. Most of the non-Communist countries, because of the existing policy of the Western nations and their antiwar sentiments, have been made to feel that they are alone and have no choice but to let the Russian Communists lead them by the nose to "peaceful coexistence."

The "weapons are all-powerful" theory as well as the "hydrogen bombs are all-powerful" theory, at a time when the two blocs are approaching parity in their nuclear weapons, have been instrumental in gaining for the Communist Empire time to propagate their "peaceful coexistence." It also marks a milestone in their progress toward winning the next war without military weapons. Time is obviously on the side of the Communist bloc.

Furthermore, there is the theory that firepower is more important than manpower in a nation's combat strength.

In days of great scientific development like these, further improvement in machines for industrial purposes automatically means more savings in labor. In the armed forces, the better the armaments, the fewer the personnel. In the battlefield, the greater the firepower, the greater one's ability to overcome the enemy. This is a sound theory.

Therefore, I think the democratic bloc's strategy in acquiring the latest nuclear weapons and the greatest firepower as part of its preparations to create a mobile world strategic force for the final decisive battle is also sound. The Western nations, because of their emphasis on humanitarianism and their high regard for human life, have sought to make up for their deficiency in manpower by firepower. As a countermeasure, the Communists, on account of their callousness to human life, have tried to waste their enemy's firepower by the "human sea" tactic.

Today the Communist bloc is in control of a vast population in Europe and Asia, and is, therefore, in a better position than ever before to use more devices to engage the enemy's firepower. Consequently, the Russian Communists believe that the Western nations' theory of attaching greater importance to firepower than to manpower is no match for their absolute superiority in manpower and space and their concept of unlimited war.

Being inferior to the Communist bloc in space and manpower, the Western bloc depends on the hydrogen bomb as the only weapon by which it hopes to defeat Soviet Russia in a short but decisive war. The Communist bloc, however, will certainly not want to wage such a decisive war. The Russian Communists will try to tip the balance of power in their favor before they engage their enemy in a decisive war. Besides, they can always hide behind their satellites and the old colonies, and have them fight the Western nations for them. By refusing to come out into the open to face their opponents in the battlefield, the Russian Communists hope to win without having to do any fighting themselves. Since they are now in a position of absolute superiority both in manpower and space on the Eurasian continent, the Western nations will find it difficult to bring to a decision any war fought on such a vast battlefield, especially if they should rely merely on their superior firepower. They will not be able to get the maximum use from the firepower at their command, even if they have a large stockpile of hydrogen bombs. After all, in the vast space represented by the great Eurasian continent, firepower cannot substitute for manpower in all military operations.

During the Korean War the United Nations forces were able to defeat the Chinese Communists' "human sea" tactic but one can be certain that the Communist bloc will not allow history to repeat itself in this respect. The Chinese Communists failed to stand up to the firepower of the allied forces in Korea for several reasons. First, they fought in a foreign country, where poor transportation facilities in the rear made it impossible for them to turn their "human sea" tactic to the fullest advantage in an unlimited war. Secondly, they did not possess adequate firepower, and especially lacked a powerful air force to support their land forces. These were the two basic reasons for the Chinese Communists' failure in Korea.

Henceforth, in any war against the free world, the Russian Communists will surely arm their unlimited manpower with great firepower. If the democratic bloc can grasp this point, it should be particularly vigilant to see how cunningly and wickedly the Communist bloc is making use of the vast population on the Eurasian continent and should strive hard to win them over to the antiaggression side, instead of permitting them to be turned into tools of aggression by the Russian and Chinese Communists. I hardly think that military experts in the democratic bloc will disregard the importance of this vast area with its teeming population and leave its political, economic, social and morale factors out of their over-all calculations and make the mistake of regarding war as purely and simply a military operation.

If both sides should reach parity in their nuclear weapons with neither daring to use hydrogen bombs, future wars may revert to the conventional type. Or, if no quick decision is in sight even after resort has been made to the hydrogen bombs, the war may become one of attrition. In either case, the man-power factor will increase in importance.

Moreover, in view of their ideas of unlimited war, the Russian Communists will surely use large parts of the Eurasian continent and the huge manpower under their control as a basic force in case of war, and then, in coordination with the unlimited time at their disposal, engage the democratic bloc in a prolonged war. That they will adopt this kind of war preparations once the hydrogen bombs and surprise attacks should fail to have their desired effect is something beyond any shadow of doubt. Therefore, the Western nations, in their struggle against Communism and aggression, must pay serious attention to the question of manpower, take steps to make up for their deficiency in this respect, so as to prevent the Russian Communists from using their numerical superiority in co-ordination with the time at their disposal to engage their opponents in an unlimited war of attrition without any fear of the consequences.

In the eyes of the Russian Communists the Western nations' traditional military concepts, instead of being any deterrent, will actually facilitate the realization of their over-all plan for World Revolution.

Furthermore, the conflict between the democratic bloc and the Communist bloc is not confined to the armaments race. There are contradictions in the whole sphere of human activities—social, political, economic, cultural and psychological—and these contradictions are going on incessantly. This is especially true in the East where nationalism and international Communism, freedom of religion and class struggle, anti-Communist sentiments in the new colonies and the demand of people in the old colonies for independence, the growth of neutralism outside the Iron Curtain and commotions created by the peace offensive, and the pressing needs of people inside the Iron Curtain for liberation—are all adding to the contradictions.

Amid these contradictions the Russian Communists and their international fifth columns are doing everything they can to gain time and strategic advantages. Unfortunately, the democratic bloc is showing signs of passiveness and hesitation, or procrastination and improvisation. The most its members do is to put up individual resistance. This only has the reverse effect of expediting the further development of the Communist bloc's plans for political and military aggression.

At a time like this the democratic bloc must evolve a positive policy against Communism and take the initiative to alter the world's strategic situation. More importantly, they must not let the Communist bloc retain superiority in manpower and space indefinitely. Only thus can world peace be reestablished and the purpose of preserving freedom for humanity be achieved as a final objective.

An Examination of the Democratic Bloc's Basic Policy Against Aggression

In examining our basic policy against aggression, we should first study not the Russian Communists' military operational methods but their policy toward the free world and their political warfare, which usually precedes the commencement of hostilities. In my opinion, their biggest political weapon is their basic tactic for World Revolution, namely, "peaceful coexistence." This should receive the democratic bloc's primary attention in discussing the Russian Communists' basic policy. Let us consider the various policies which the democratic bloc has already adopted in the past or may adopt in the future.

One is the policy of containment by bases. In his report to the 20th National Congress of the Russian Communist Party, Khrushchev attacked the Western nations' "position of strength policy." Since then the Russian Communists and their international fifth columns from the Atlantic to the Pacific have started anti-American movements, the principal objective being to force the United States to withdraw from her overseas bases. In the eyes of the Russian Communists the Western nations' "policy of containment by bases" is a product of the old idea of limited war. While it may prove efficacious for a while as a deterrent to Moscow's war of aggression, its inadequacy will become apparent the moment the aggressor follows a zigzag strategy. The Russian Communists and their international fifth columns have set no bounds in their political and psychological infiltration tactics. By the time those opposed to aggression take up their position around the aggressor to stop military invasion, the latter's political and psychological warfare will have already broken through the defense cordon to start provocation, division, vacillation and subversive activities among anti-Communist nations, between anti-Communist and non-Communist nations, and also inside these countries.

When their social, political and psychological warfare reaches a certain stage, the Russian Communists will suddenly change from political tactics to military tactics by using "peaceful coexistence" as a cover for their military operations. By that time it will become impossible for the policy of containment by bases to maintain the original line of defense and the shortcomings of the outmoded limited war ideas will be instantly exposed, and the enemy can stage a breakthrough at weak points. This will be the end of the containment policy. The best proof is in the Middle East and North Africa where the situation is already largely out of control.

Or take the reprisal and deterrent policies. The positive steps which the United States has taken in developing hydrogen bombs and intercontinental guided missiles and adoption of the flexible strategy of "massive reprisal" and "local wars" have forced the Russian Communists to abandon military adventure and expansion for the time being. During the three years since the end of the Indo-China War, the Russian Communists and their satellites have not dared to start any new military aggression. It can hardly be denied that the American policy of reprisal and deterrent has proved effective in the past and hence has been justifiable.

The Russian Communists, however, have in the past year used various other forms of expansion in Asia and in the Middle East. Since the winter of 1955, for instance, the Chinese Communists have launched both political and military aggression against Burma and started economic infiltration and political intimidation against Cambodia and Laos. Some of the countries concerned have for many years been opposed to Communism and friendly toward the Western nations. Now, in the face of threat and material inducement, they are showing signs of wavering and leaning to the Communist side. Can it be said that the deterrent policy has been effective here?

Even if it is conceded that what the Chinese Communists have done in Cambodia and Laos is political and economic expansion and, therefore, does not properly come within the scope of the deterrent policy, one still has to admit that the Chinese Communists' aggression against Burma is clearly a military action. Can it be gainsaid that this calls for deterrence? If the deterrent policy fails to deter the Communist bloc from military aggression, then what happens to the democratic bloc's prestige? Does it not add to its own difficulties? Besides, one must ask how it is going to make the Communist bloc alter its policy of aggression and its timetable. In the eyes of the Russian Communists the reprisal and deterrent theories both are relics of the outmoded ideas of a defensive war. Besides, the democratic bloc, in adhering to this policy, will have to continue the armament race in order to maintain its superiority over the enemy in order to retain its ability to retaliate and to deter. Once the enemy reaches parity with, or worse, attains superiority over, the democratic bloc in the armament race, then this policy will become untenable.

Nor is this all. Moscow, on the one hand, is freezing the democratic bloc's nuclear weapons and, on the other, is pressing on with its social and political warfare on the periphery of the democratic bloc for the purpose of altering the world's strategic situation and changing the relative strength between the aggressors and those opposed to aggression to help Soviet Russia's preparations for the final decisive war.

Meanwhile, they have been spreading defeatism and anti-war sentiments in the democratic nations to foster "peace at any cost" feelings. If this state of affairs continues, everything, be it political, economic, social, psychological, or military, in these countries, will come under the spell of defeatism. By the time Soviet Russia takes military action against them in the final war, they will have already been put in a passive position. It will then be too late to retrieve the losses in the political, social and psychological fields even if the Western nations should use nuclear weapons in retaliation.

Therefore, as far the Russian Communists are concerned, the reprisal and deterrent theories cannot stop them from seizing the initiative in a surprise attack in the last phase of such a war. It follows that the strategic ideas underlying the reprisal and deterrent theories, however much they may be strengthened by the possession of the most powerful new weapons, cannot have any spectacular effect or assure the Western nations of success in case of a major war.

There is also the "preventive war," or policy of punitive action. This implies that the Western nations launch a preventive war against Soviet Russia before the latter actually launches a military attack. Only totalitarian nations dare to adopt this kind of policy. The democratic nations will never approve of it. Therefore, we need not discuss it any further. I do wish to say again, however, that it has never been the Republic of China's wish that our Western allies should adopt such a policy and start a preventive war against Soviet territory itself. I shall take up this point at length later. All I wish to say here is that if the United States should initiate a war against Soviet Russia she would be provoking Soviet retaliation against her homeland. True, the United States is the leader in the free world's struggle against Communism and aggression and, therefore, has the responsibility that goes with her position. Yet it does not necessarily mean that she needs to be directly involved in war. I feel that the United States should of her own accord build herself up as the free world's arsenal against Communism instead of being a principal battle-field in an anti-Communist war and take positive steps to support anti-Communist countries both in Europe and in Asia, to coordinate and strengthen military preparations in both non-Communist and anti-Communist countries, so as to save her homeland from becoming a battlefield. For this rea-son I feel that the "preventive war" policy in not only con-trary to the historical traditions of the democratic nations but, as far as the free world's war against Communism is con-cerned, it is not necessary.

Let us now consider the policy of liberation. Anti-Com-munist nations in the East think that this is the logical policy for the free world to take vis-à-vis Communism. It is our considered view that this policy should comprise an over-all strategy and a coordinated operational plan. If the democratic bloc should fail to make liberation their basic policy against Communism and aggression, then all discussions about strategy and tactics are futile.

Where should we begin in this policy? This policy implies the support by the Western nations of Asian countries that have been forcibly divided by Soviet Russia's Communist aggression so that the forces of national revolution outside the Iron Curtain and of anti-Communist revolution inside the Iron Curtain will merge into one for the purpose of national reunification. It is our belief that without German unification there can be no European peace and security. As a corollary, it is also our belief that if China, Korea and Vietnam should remain part slave and part free there can be no peace and security in Asia.

But how should this policy be implemented? Admittedly there are certain misgivings abroad. Nevertheless, I would like to suggest some practical measures. First is the strategy of detours, and second is indirect warfare.

In their conquest of the Eurasian continent the Russian Communists used the strategy of detours from China mainland toward South Asia and the Middle East, and also from the Middle East toward Europe and Africa. Today, in their deep thrust into the Middle East and their threat to Western Europe, the China mainland has already become their rear. In these circumstances, in order to save the Middle East and to remove the threat to Western Europe, the soundest strategy will be to attack the aggressor's rear.

As I have pointed out, if the Western nations need to pick a battlefield, it should be neither in Europe nor in the Middle East, where they will necessarily have to engage Soviet Russia directly in hostilities. The best battlefield is in the Far East, where the war will be fought as a war of national revolution by the Eastern peoples against the new colonialism to gain independence and freedom for their countries. Such a war will win the sympathy and support of all Eastern nations. Above all, it will restore to the Western nations the prestige they have lost during the past decade. If this war of national revolution by the Eastern peoples could be positively prosecuted before Soviet Russia completes her preparations for a major war, it will be an indirect blow to her and will have the desired effect of removing the latent danger of a world war.

As a strategy this will be far better, both in nature and in effect, than waiting for the Russian Communists to strike the first blow in a direct surprise attack to set off a world war. Therefore, the strategy of indirect warfare against Communism is what the Western nations should adopt as the highest guiding principle in their policy of liberation.

However, in pointing out the democratic bloc's shortcomings in its military concepts and in its policies against Communism, it is not my purpose to say that the democratic bloc need not develop new weapons or further strengthen its military preparations; nor is it my purpose to say that the democratic bloc's strategy of deterrent and massive reprisal is unsound. Similarly, it is not my purpose to say that the democratic bloc should change its defensive strategy to offensive strategy and take positive steps to use force against the Soviet bloc. On the contrary, I feel that these policies and stratagems are not only necessary but also important in the world's struggle against Communism. Nevertheless, new military preparations and new weapons should be coordinated with various other new elements—political, economic, social, psychological and nationalist—so that they can, as part of an over-all political strategy, attain the maximum effect in a united action against Communism. Meanwhile, the form of struggle should be flexible and be decided in the light of Soviet Russia's policy, strategy and tactics, so as to ensure practicality and effectiveness.

In conclusion, the position occupied by weapons and military strength, and their usefulness in our struggle against Communism today, can be accurately assessed only in the context of social and political conditions. If the weapons and military actions should become isolated devices either for retaliatory purposes or as a deterrent, this will play right into the hands of the Soviet aggressors.

Furthermore, if the Western nations should try to use their position of strength to stop Communist war of aggression in the vast area in the East, Soviet Russia will surely condemn this as another manifestation of the gunboat policy or of old colonialism, in an attempt to arouse anti-Western feelings in Asia. If the Western nations should try to exert direct pressure on Soviet Russia, and back it up with military force, if necessary, Soviet Russia could play it up as "imperialist aggression," and rally her people in an "anti-imperialist" and "patriotic movement."

For these reasons, in their struggle against Communism, the democratic bloc must use indirect warfare in a strategy of detours, revive the free world's confidence in the outcome of its anti-Communist efforts, shatter the neutralists' illusion about peaceful coexistence and bring about coordination between military and political tactics and between the nationalist movements outside the Iron Curtain and the revolutionary movements inside the Iron Curtain all under one positive and unified strategy.

The aim should be for the free world to make the fullest use of both human and material resources so that it could achieve the two-fold purpose described earlier: passively, to stop and check the Russian Communists' ambition of world conquest, and positively, to remove the danger of world war and to ensure a lasting world peace. Otherwise, either the theory about military combat being all-powerful, or the notion about the hydrogen bomb being all-decisive, will merely provide the Russian Communists with further material in their political and psychological warfare. Likewise, the single form of struggle, as envisaged either in the containment policy, or in the reprisal policy, will only enable the Russian Communists to continue their political infiltration in anti-Communist countries and, in the meantime, to create opportunities for "peaceful transformation" in the neutralist countries.

PART
THREE

The Communists' Strategy for World Revolution

CHAPTER ONE

CHANGES IN THEIR STRATEGY AND MILITARY OPERATIONAL PATTERNS

As a result of our thirty years of struggle against Communism we have acquired an unusually clear understanding of how the changes in Moscow's strategy and military operational patterns for World Revolution have affected the situation in China. On the other hand, we can also see how changes in the China situation have had a decisive effect on Moscow's strategy and military operational patterns. An analysis will make this clear.

From Lenin to Stalin

After the October Revolution in 1917 Lenin thought that Russia's Soviet regime could not be consolidated until Socialist revolutions had succeeded in industrialized nations in Western Europe. Consequently, during 1918 and 1919, Lenin was several times tempted to give military support to Communists in Germany in their uprisings and to people in Hungary in their revolution, but he had no success. In 1920 he sent troops into Poland, but this venture ended in disastrous defeat. Then Lenin became more active in his Eastward policy, and Kuomintang was picked out to be the target of the subversive activities of his fifth column, the Chinese Communist Party.

After Lenin's death Stalin made two important changes in his operational patterns. Lenin's external policy was to use Soviet Russia's strength to support "revolutions" by Communist parties in various countries. Stalin reversed this policy by using "revolutions" by Communist parties in various countries to sustain the Soviet regime at home. For the sake of the Soviet regime, and sometimes merely for his own sake, Stalin did not hesitate to sacrifice the Communists in any foreign country. This constituted the first change.

The second change introduced by Stalin was that he placed greater emphasis on the East than Lenin did. After 1928 he launched a series of Five-Year Plans at home and started a peace offensive against the Western powers abroad. In China, however, he directed the Chinese Communists to follow a policy of sovietization and to try to overthrow the Government by armed insurrection. The formulation and growth of Soviet Russia's policy of holding firm in the West and moving forward in the East may be regarded as Stalin's handiwork, which saw considerable development in his lifetime.

Stalin's Repeated Changes

Under the direction of Lenin and Stalin the Communist International and the Russian Communists often analyzed the question of war at their meetings and adopted relevant resolutions. The program adopted at the Sixth Congress of the Communist International divided wars into three categories and laid down specific stipulations regarding the missions of the Communists in the various nations in these wars.

The first category comprises "wars of imperialist states among themselves," meaning wars among powers other than Soviet Russia. Soviet Russia should stay out of such wars, but, at the same time, Communists in the belligerent nations should launch antiwar movements and try to transform these wars into revolutions.

In the second category are "national revolutionary wars against imperialism" fought by Asian or other peoples in colonies or semi-colonies against European powers. Communists in these countries should support this kind of anti-imperialistic wars and try to transform them into class wars.

"Wars of capitalist counterrevolution against proletarian

revolution and countries of socialist reconstruction" constitute the third category. These are wars fought by foreign powers against Soviet Russia. Communists in the various countries should start antiwar movements in order to sabotage the mobilization and military operations of the countries concerned, and should go a step further by fomenting a pro-Soviet revolution.

To sum up, Stalin's policy toward international wars as shown in the Sixth Congress of the Communist International was that war provides the only path to world revolution and world dictatorship.

By 1935, although Soviet Russia's peace offensive against the Western powers had aggravated the contradictions between Britain and France on the one side, and Germany on the other, her policy of inciting armed revolt in China was a failure. At the Seventh Congress of the Communist International called by Stalin, the "United Front" strategy was decided upon. This was not a basic change of the operational ideas laid down by the six previous congresses, but merely to use "United Front" as the principal form of struggle of international Communists. The purpose of the "United Front" was not to promote world peace but to promote world war.

Lenin said. "The experience of the history of revolutions, of great conflicts, teaches that wars—series of wars—are inevitable."* This was also Stalin's view. He likewise believed that once war broke out Soviet Russia would be dragged into it, but he maintained that "Soviet Russia must be the last one to enter it." In 1939 he concluded a Nonaggression Pact with Germany, thereby precipitating the war in Europe. In 1941 he concluded a Neutrality Agreement with Japan, thereby encouraging Japan to advance southward. Taking advantage of developments during World War II, Stalin hoodwinked the democracies at the Teheran and Yalta conferences, extended his strategic intrigues into the postwar world and

* Lenin, *Collected Works*, vol. 26, p. 12.

created the existing threatening situations in East Europe and in East Asia.

From Malenkov to Khrushchev

After World War II Soviet Russia committed aggression in Europe and in Asia. In Europe she dominated the countries in Eastern Europe, partitioned East Germany; in the Far East snatched China's Outer Mongolia, Sinkiang and Manchuria, divided Korea, and also helped the Chinese Communists push the entire Chinese mainland behind the Iron Curtain. In order to resist the aggression of the Soviet bloc and to preserve world peace and security, free nations of the world evolved the North Atlantic Treaty, the Pacific collective security system and the Bagdad Pact, forming a united antiaggression front.

Under this tremendous pressure Moscow had to change its operational pattern again. As early as the 19th National Congress of the Russian Communist Party, held in October 1952, Stalin came out with the slogan of "peaceful coexistence." During the three years which ensued, although Stalin had died and power in Moscow had passed from Malenkov to Khrushchev, the peace movement and neutralism tactics went on just the same. In February 1956 Khrushchev submitted to the 20th National Congress of the Russian Communist Party a strategic plan of his own, complete with a different operation form.

In appearance, Khrushchev has modified Stalinism. Stalin believed that war was inevitable, and considered war as the highway to Communist domination of the world. On the contrary, Khrushchev maintained that war was not inevitable; he adopted "stop all wars" as his slogan. In substance, however, Khrushchev's "peaceful coexistence" campaign together with his "United Front" and neutralism tactics is a repetition of Stalin's "United Front" of 1935-1939. The antiaggression front formed by the free world is defensive in strategy. Although both Malenkov and Khrushchev used the same "peaceful coexistence" slogan, yet as an operational pattern there is a shift from strategic defense to strategic offense. In other words, in Malenkov's time Moscow's "peaceful coexistence" was still an attempt to prevent the signing of the Paris Agreement, established of the Pacific security system and development of joint defense in the Middle East. Khrushchev's "peaceful coexistence" is a strategic offensive against this antiaggression front with a view to its breakup or nullification.

A Turning Point for the Changes in Russian Communists' Military Operational Patterns

Between 1918 and 1920, when the international clique in the Russian Communist Party, headed by Lenin and Trotsky, was focussing its attention on the revolutions in Central Europe, Stalin published an article entitled "Don't Forget the East." Stalin pointed out that the imperialist chain forged by Europe to shackle the rest of the world could only be broken in the East.

After he came into power Stalin turned his sword of aggression toward China. This, of course, did not mean that the Russian Communists had forgotten about the West. In the Russian Communists' timetable for long-term aggression, China was their first target of "peaceful coexistence." By the time they think they have secured control over China's 450,000,000 people, and are in a position to create "big storms" in the midst of the 900,000,000 people in the East to influence Europe on the rebound, they will turn their sword of aggression toward the West.

From this we can see that changes in the Russian Communists' world strategy and their operational patterns came as a result of the changes in the China situation.

*Reasons for China's Failure to Defeat the Russian
Communists' "Peaceful Coexistence" Intrigue*

China was the first victim of Soviet Russia's aggression, and
also the first nation in the world to take up the fight against
Communism. There are at least two factors in the international
situation which account for China's failure to nullify the
Russian Communists' "peaceful coexistence" tactic and the
reverses China has suffered as a result.

First, we lacked experience at the time in fighting the Communists and the world did not have any precedent to offer us.
Every time we came into contact, or entered into negotiations,
with Soviet Russia or the Chinese Communists, and every
time we broke with them or fought them, we had to grope in
the dark and improvise our methods as we went along. Sometimes we fell into their traps unsuspectingly; sometimes we
did so with our eyes open. As a matter of fact, the anti-Communist struggle requires general mobilization and an all-out
war. Sometimes, even if we clearly uncovered Soviet Russia's
real intention, and even if our policy and methods had been
correct, we met nevertheless with reverses for want of our
people's support and of international understanding.

Then, the world had never had any experience with such
a grandiose Communist plot. Few, therefore, realized that
Soviet Russia could harbor so aggressive an ambition as to
wish to dominate the entire world. Moreover, still fewer had
the faintest idea that China's defeat in her anti-Communist
struggle could have such serious consequences for world
peace and the freedom of mankind. Therefore, after World
War II, although nations in the Pacific area were all faced
with the threat of Soviet Russia's aggression and hence ob-
jectively had interests in common, subjectively they did not
trust one another enough. They listened to the enemy's lies.
They were indifferent to us. As a result, there were conflicts
between the policies of foreign nations toward China on the

one hand and China's anti-Communist policy on the other. These conflicts gave the Russian Communists and the Chinese Communists opportunities to divide them and to defeat China first. This was the principal reason for China's past failure in her struggle against Communism.

Changes in the Relative Strength Between the West and Soviet Russia in Asia and Their Effects

As a direct result of China's failure in her anti-Communist struggle and the fall of the Chinese mainland, our country and our people have suffered immensely. At the same time the world at large has also felt the impact, the exact extent of which is as yet difficult to assess. Communism's evil spell is not yet over; in fact, it continues to grow as time goes on.

Because of the fall of the Chinese mainland, international Communism has made a spectacular advance, especially in Asia where the Communists have virtually gotten out of control. That is why today Khrushchev can boast that Communism has broken out of the confines of one country to become a world system.

Soviet's Russia's prestige and power have risen higher than ever before. Apart from the Communist countries themselves, even the non-Communist countries have come to feel for a few years already that they can coexist in peace with Soviet Russia by being pro-Russia and pro-Communist, and that Soviet Russia is sincere and reliable in its aid to nations in the East. It follows that what Soviet Russia calls her "large reserve army" in the East has become the vanguard in Asia's opposition to Western colonialism.

By contrast, the prestige and influence of the Western nations have declined in the eyes of Asians. This perpendicular drop was due to the disappearance of the Chinese mainland behind the Iron Curtain. The reverses suffered by this major Asian anti-Communist force under my government have caused a major change in the world situation. Not only was it a crucial point in the relative strength of Soviet Russia and the Western nations in the East, but also a turning point in world security and the future of mankind. The question now is: How can this situation be reversed to save mankind from an even greater calamity in the future?

Soviet Russia's Internal Contradictions and Weaknesses

Today the Russian Communists and the Chinese Communists are moving into South Asia and the Middle East. While making war preparations and keeping up the threat of war, they again resort to "peaceful coexistence" as a political tactic. Khrushchev has boasted to the free world of the tremendous size of the area and population under his control and bragged about the effect of his peaceful offensive and neutralism tactics. He said: "As a result, a vast Zone of Peace including peace-loving states, both socialist and nonsocialist, of Europe and Asia, has emerged in the world. This Zone embraces vast areas inhabited by nearly 1,500 million people, that is, the majority of the population of the world."* He thinks the time has finally arrived for him to give finishing touches to his "peaceful coexistence" strategy in preparation for Soviet Russia's final showdown with the free world.

However, I am convinced that by now the world has acquired enough experience and learned enough lessons from combating Communism to defeat its purpose. Even if the Russian Communists could get away with their "peaceful coexistence" and neutralism strategy temporarily, the free world, including the freedom-loving countries in Asia, would eventually work together to smash such international intrigues and treacherous political tactics once they should understand China's bitter experience. This could mark the beginning of the end for Soviet expansion and aggression.

Furthermore, by linking Khrushchev's "peaceful coex-

---

* Khrushchev's report to the 20th Congress of the Communist Party of the Soviet Union.

istence" and "stop all wars" slogans to his maneuvers in demoting Stalin and dissolving the Cominform, we can see that at the present stage the Russian Communists face several serious weaknesses both in their internal situation and in their international plans.

First, in the near future, at least in the next three to five years, and pending the completion of their sixth Five-Year Plan, the Russian Communists have not the capability to fight any world war because they have not yet completed military preparations for a decisive battle. That is why they played up the appeal to "stop all wars," and dissolved the Cominform. The attempt is clearly to lead the Western nations to believe that the Russians have abandoned aggression, and to make the countries in Asia and Africa fall for neutralism.

Secondly, they cannot pacify the Russian people's hatred of Stalin's tyranny, a hatred which has been accumulating over a period of more than twenty years. In Khrushchev's case, politically, there are insurmountable contradictions in the so-called collective leadership. He cannot effect unity at the top nor can he do as Stalin did to bring everything under his effective control. That accounts for his de-Stalinization effort to mollify the people's resentment and hatred. Similarly, that also accounts for his paying lip service to peace in order to reassure the people at home. In the event of a war the Soviet Government would be seriously threatened with internal revolts and it is altogether possible that the entire regime might collapse.

Thirdly, Soviet Russia can no longer keep her satellites under such effective control as in Stalin's time. There will be more revolts against Soviet repression and tyranny in the satellites from time to time. In East Germany, Poland, Czechoslovakia, Hungary, Bulgaria and in areas controlled by the Chinese Communists, numerous fissures have been revealed. This is also a reason why the Russian Communists have found it necessary to condemn Stalin and to dissolve the Cominform.

At the same time they have to appease Tito, and in deference to the latter's views to alter somewhat the methods of control over the satellites. If in these circumstances Khrushchev should start a war outside the Iron Curtain, he would run the danger of not only the satellites but also the people in Soviet Russia rising up to oppose Communism. By that time he might not find it possible to maintain the *status quo*.

From the foregoing three points one must conclude that at the present stage the Russian Communists are in no position to start a world war. In fact, they are not even in a position to take part in any localized external war that may lead to a world war. This is the real purpose of the Russian Communists' "stop all wars" and "peaceful coexistence" slogans.

The Crucial Point in Determining the Free World's Success or Failure—Two Factors Calling for Special Vigilance in Dealing with the Communist Bloc

Despite the existence of insurmountable contradictions within Soviet Russia and the Communist bloc, all anti-Communist people in the free world should remain vigilant.

Although internal splits and strifes among the international Communist parties will weaken their control inside the Iron Curtain and their struggle outside it, thereby necessitating changes in their methods of control and forms of struggle in order to extend the timetable for their projected conquest and domination of the world, they will definitely not bring about changes in their basic idea of class war or in the international nature of the national Communist parties, nor will they cause them to change their common objectives of world revolution or the destruction of capitalism.

In other words, despite their internal struggle for power, the international Communist parties will cooperate in their efforts to keep people in their own countries under control so as to destroy the "capitalist class" in what they consider enemy countries. Whatever internal conflicts of interests and contradictions may arise, the international Communist parties will take common action to intimidate and blackmail the free world and non-Communist countries. Even if the satellites should revolt against Moscow, a new directing center will surely emerge in the form of a Fourth International. It should be borne in mind that "the law of unity of contradictions," as laid down by materialistic dialectics, is the only basic ideology in Communist countries. The free world should never lose sight of the traditional capacity and immutable nature of the Communists to hoodwink logic and smother contradictions. Otherwise people outside the Iron Curtain will inevitably draw wrong conclusions about happenings inside it. If people in the free world should think that revolts in the satellites will bring human freedom and world peace and that internal strife within the Communist bloc will make the Russian Communists drop their aggressive designs, they will be absolutely mistaken. We should remember that in 1949, one year after Tito's break with Moscow, the Russian Communists seized the China mainland, which is many times larger than Yugoslavia both in area and population. This is tantamount to exchanging one Yugoslavia for several Yugoslavias. It is hoped that the free world will never forget its arithmetic.

The international Communist parties always seek to make use of their enemy and in the meantime take care not to be used by him. Whatever conflicts may happen inside the Communist parties themselves, and whatever difficulties they may meet with externally, any country or individual trying to make use of them will find themselves used in the end. We should heed what Stalin said in his *Leninism—Selected Writings*, which reads in part as follows:

In our work we cannot dance to anybody's tune. Still less can we allow ourselves to be guided in our work by what the members of the opposition say about us. We must pursue our own path, brushing aside both the fraudulent attempts of the opposition and the errors of certain of our Bolsheviks who have fallen victims to the provocation of the opposition.

Therefore, irrespective of how contradictions should develop or erupt from within the international Communist parties today, we should know that, after all, the Communists are Communists to the marrow of their bones. This is particularly true in the case of Communist leaders in various countries.

Regardless of who should come out on top in their internal struggle, it will merely mean a change of personnel without any change in their nature. Transfer of power from one man to another will not reduce the danger of their aggression against the free world, of world conquest or of the total enslavement of mankind. We should know that it is now eight years since Yugoslavia broke with Moscow. Yet the Yugoslavs have neither been released from Communist domination nor have they known any freedom. This is a most realistic lesson taught by contemporary history. As long as a Bolshevik regime exists in Russia and as long as Communist regimes exist in the satellites, their people will not have any more freedom than they have today. Furthermore, the Communist countries can never be independent from one another. The Russian Communists, moreover, can always use various dialectic methods to retain control over them in a different form.

If the free world should fail to take timely advantage of the Communists' internal split and strife to help anti-Communist people behind the Iron Curtain in their revolution against the Communist regime and merely wait for the Communist parties to collapse by themselves, it will be like climbing up a tree to fish in its foliage. In the end this will merely give the international Communist parties a chance to reorientate their United Front and neutralism tactics, and even to start a new antiwar movement as a weapon of war. The result will be the split of the democratic bloc, not the Communist one as many people in the free world fondly hope.

We should know that if Communism and its organization have a legal status in any country, then that country will not know security in its political, economic and social life. So long as there exists a single Communist country, the world will know no peace, and freedom will not be secure. Therefore, anti-Communist people in the free world will be making a great mistake if they adopt a wait-and-see policy and expect the Communist bloc to collapse by itself, and this mistake will have serious consequences for the future of mankind.

I maintain that the only way before the free world is to adopt a positive policy, aimed directly at taking advantage of the Russian Communists' internal crises and contradictions. The purpose of such a policy is to enable anti-Communist peoples on both sides of the Iron Curtain to merge into a single power to hasten the outbreak of anti-Communist revolution inside Soviet Russia, and to help her people achieve real liberation. This will not only deter Soviet Russia's challenge to the free world, but will also accelerate the collapse of the Communist bloc from within. Only then could we be assured of the end of Soviet Russia's scheme of world conquest, the elimination of the danger of another world war and the establishment of a lasting peace. The present is indeed a rare opportunity which should not be allowed to slip by lightly.

Anti-Communist people in the free world, in their study of the Russian Communists and their affairs, should analyze the categoric events including the "peaceful coexistence," the "anti-war movement," the demotion of Stalin, the dissolution of the Cominform, and the strikes and riots in the satellites, the various anti-Communist and anti-Russian incidents, the unrest inside Soviet Russia and the contradictions that have arisen during the four years since Stalin's death. When they do, they will see that all these are signs of immense internal and external stresses. Unless they had found it difficult to hold their regime together, the Russian Communists would not have resorted to the posthumous attack on Stalin and degraded themselves with apologies and asking for forgiveness.

If the anti-Communist peoples should be satisfied with

being on guard against another trick of the Russian Communists to deceive the world and fail to grasp the deeper meaning of the internal crisis inside the Iron Curtain, their lack of penetration will bring in its wake serious consequences. It will give the Russian Communists another chance to gather strength for their eventual attempt at conquering the world.

CHAPTER TWO

THE ORIGIN AND BASIC PRINCIPLES
OF THEIR MILITARY THOUGHT

I have already described the shift of the Russian Communists' strategic objective from China to Southeast Asia and
the Middle East and the deceptive change in their operational
patterns from the tactic of manufacturing war to one of "stop
all wars" and "peaceful coexistence." I have tried to prove
that in reality their numerous instances of aggression or peace
movements over the last thirty years constitute one single
continuous war.

For the sake of our national existence and the freedom of
our people, China has been continuously engaged in various
forms of struggle against them. Our long and painful experience has enabled us to have a good idea of every change in the
Russian Communists' tactical objective and operational pattern. We have already discussed the various tactics the Russian
Communists have used against China. Now let us trace their
military thought and pinpoint their basic principles of war
because they throw light on their peace offensive in diverse
forms.

In probing into the basis of the Russian Communists' fundamental military concepts, I take those of Marx and Lenin
toward war as a framework of reference for ascertaining their
principles of war as expressed in concrete forms. Secondly, I
propose to analyze their operational patterns and tactics in the
light of our own experience in fighting the Communist armies.
Thirdly, I shall make a historical study of the wars of the
Russian Communists, from 1918 to the end of World War II

in 1945, in order to discover their basic character. As to the five principles underlying Soviet Russia's "permanent factors in military operations" and the various published Soviet military manuals, they do not come within the scope of our present study. The military thinking of the Chinese Communists is merely the residual of the Russian Communists and hence does not merit separate study.

The first point we should take special note of is that the Russian Communists' military concept represents the confluence of the East and the West. The sources of their military philosophy are Clausewitz in the West and Sun Tze* in the East. As to the types of war, they learned from Napoleon in the West and Genghis Khan in the East. In their study of military affairs, they paid particular attention to the theories and principles which Sun Tze and Genghis Khan had propounded.

There were two principal sources to Lenin's military thinking. One was Marx and the other was Clausewitz. From Marx he learned the theory of class struggle and the method of analyzing social structure and political situation. From Clausewitz he pilfered the basic principles of war and the method of directing war. Lenin himself had said that he was no military man, and he had produced no systematic works on operational ideas. But throughout his life he paid a great deal of attention to military science and the art of war. He took copious notes between 1913 and 1915 when he read Clausewitz' treatise *On War*. Today we can have a fairly good idea of Lenin's as well as the Russian Communists' operational ideas by reading Clausewitz *On War* and especially by studying Lenin's notes and comments.

The Absoluteness of War

Clausewitz' treatise *On War* began with establishing once and for all the "concept of absolute war." As a means of forc-

* A Chinese strategist of great renown in the early days.

ing the enemy to yield to one's will, war in its very concept permits of no restrictions to be imposed on the development and employment of violence. War stops only at its extremity. This is the unlimitedness and absoluteness of war.

In Clausewitz' views, most of the wars fought in the past were limited wars, thus giving rise to some doubt regarding the degree of reality in the "absolute war" concept. It was in the French Revolution and in the Napoleonic Wars that he discovered the new operational trend toward "absoluteness."

What are the differences in this "absolute war" or "unlimited war," as compared with the limited wars of the past?

First, a limited war is the outcome of a single decisive battle or of several engagements. Victory in war, therefore, is the sum total of a single decisive battle or of several engagements.

Conversely, an unlimited war comprises continuous actions which form an indivisible whole. Though this whole contains numerous engagements, the latter do not possess any independent intrinsic value, and their value, therefore, must be assessed in terms of the war as a whole.

Secondly, in the "limited war" concept, war is looked upon as a commercial transaction and each participant, according to the amount of risk to be incurred or the profit to be expected, takes a share in the conflict by committing so many troops, and feels that he cannot lose more than the amount of his investment.

Conversely, an "unlimited war" is the concept of a final decisive battle. For the sake of the final victory, the size of the armed forces and their organization as well as political stratagems and diplomatic actions, all have one purpose only— to be thrown into the decisive battle just as we put all our capital into one enterprise, and each individual transaction has no significance except for the sake of the final settlement.

Thirdly, the objective of limited war is to impose on the enemy one's terms for concluding a treaty, or to carve off a part of the enemy's territory. In this kind of war one needs to calculate the amount of time required against the size of the territory coveted.

Conversely, the objective of an unlimited war is to impose one's will on the enemy. Unless the enemy is compelled to surrender unconditionally and to accept absolute control, then whether more or less time is consumed, or whether territory is gained or lost, has no value in itself.

During the French Revolution and the Napoleonic Wars, there was a crosscurrent as later represented by Communism and class war. It was this crosscurrent on which Marx and Engels built their Communist ideological structure. They went a step farther by applying "unlimited war" to class war, thereby giving rise to their fantastic ideals about World Revolution and world dictatorship of the proletariat. The Communist Party manifesto which Marx drafted for the Communist International Alliance was the starting point of international Communism and World Revolution.

From mob violence in the "Paris Commune" of 1871, Marx concluded that the next time the purpose would be not to transfer the bureaucratic-military machine from one hand to another, but to smash it. Engels in the introduction to his book on the French civil war was even more specific when he said: "Look at the Paris Commune! This was the dictatorship of the proletariat."

In March 1919 Lenin organized the Third International. Its creed was contained in Article One of the Communist International's Charter which reads as follows:

The Communist International—an alliance of international workers—is the organization of the Communist parties of all nations. It is the World Communist Party. The Communist International is the leader and organizer of the revolutionary movement by the world's proletariat, and the propagandist of the principles and objectives of Communism. It would strive to enlist the support of the working class and the multitude of poor peasants in the struggle for the world's dictatorship of the proletariat, for the world federation of Soviet republics, and for the

destruction of all classes and the materialization of Socialism—
the first step toward a Communist society.

In waging war in various countries, nations and regions of
the world, Soviet Russia and her instrument, the international
Communist parties, have set the world dictatorship of the
proletariat as their final objective, for the attainment of which
they have naturally adopted Clausewitz' "absolute war" as
opposed to an ordinary or a limited war.

Simultaneous Use of People's War and Class War

To put it more specifically, the tendency toward unlimited
war after the French Revolution and the Napoleonic War was
to make war an affair of the people. Clausewitz pointed out
that during the 18th century wars in Europe were merely
affairs between the governments concerned. At the time of
the French Revolution war suddenly became a common affair
of the French people numbering some thirty millions. Thus
war approached much nearer its absolute nature, and the
primitive violence of war, freed from all conventional restrictions, broke loose with all its force.

In his chapter, "Arming the Nation," Clausewitz set forth
his ideal of an unlimited war. He said that when invaded, a
nation should withdraw its troops from the border to the
interior, and use the regular forces to support its armed
population against the enemy. The deeper the enemy pene-
trates into the interior, the more scattered will be his military
strength. The flame of people's war, thus kindled, will soon
spread until the climax is reached in a decisive battle.

When a nation rises to fight again after defeat, people's war
is an especially suitable form to use in resisting aggression and
ensuring survival. Clausewitz' philosophy of war may be said
to have made its valuable contribution toward the cause of
national revolutionary wars against aggression.

The basis of Clausewitz' ideal unlimited war is "arming the
nation" for its "people's war." What Marx extracted from

the French Revolution was its method of class struggle. Writing about the "Paris Commune" of 1871, Marx pointed out that the future class wars will become large-scale, bloody military struggles of the masses. The fact that Marx played up "people's war" no doubt had a great deal of influence on Lenin's military thinking.

Lenin, on his part, reiterated exclusively the "unlimited war" tendency from the French Revolution as pointed out by Clausewitz. He said people in the French Revolution set up a completely new strategic structure, broke away from all the old laws and old habits of war, created a new revolutionary people's army to replace the old army and also used new tactics. Yet in the Russian Revolution he completely adopted Marx's line of action regarding class war and dictatorship of the proletariat in directing the activities of his party comrades. He believed that although the lessons of the French Revolution were accepted by the Russians in their revolution of 1905, the proletariat abandoned "people's" and patriotic illusions and concentrated its class forces in its class organizations— the Soviets of workers, peasants and soldiers. In the October Revolution of 1917 Lenin turned an external war into a class war to overthrow the provisional government and to seize power. Later on, in the Civil War, the Soviet Government more than ever applied Clausewitz' "people's war" tactics to class war.

Lenin, of course, not only did not discard Clausewitz' "people's war" concept but adopted it as the ideological basis for Soviet Russia's military policy. First of all, he decided to build up the army in the process of revolution. He told Russion Communist cadres: "Clench your teeth, don't brag, but prepare your forces."* He firmly maintained that the Soviet army should fight with modern equipment and modern tactics. Next, after Soviet Russia's defeat in the Polish War in 1920, Lenin decided that the principal function of the Red Army

* Lenin, *Selected Works*, vol. 7, p. 311.

was to defend Soviet Russia's own territory and it should never fight outside the country again. Hence, during World War II, the Soviet armed forces fought Germany as a people's total war under the banner of Patriotism.

Harmony Between Military Tactics and Political Tactics

In his work *On War*, Clausewitz said: "War is the continuation of policy," and "war is to use other means to carry on the policy in foreign affairs." In a footnote Lenin said. "War is not merely a political act but it is the final political means." He also said: "Politics is whole, war is partial." Lenin and the Russian Communists made further deductions from this concept. His military thinking—"war is the continuation of peace" and "peace is the other means to carry on the war"— is so significant that it calls for analysis.

Usually it is thought that the moment war breaks out political intercourse ceases. Clausewitz, however, was of the view that war is only a part of political and diplomatic intercourse, therefore, by no means an independent act by itself.

The foundation on which war rests, and the circumstances which determine its leading features, viz., the military strength of both belligerents, their allies, the characteristics of their people and their governments, etc., are facts of a political nature. Clausewitz maintained that in a war all military and political activities constitute an organic whole from which its components cannot be separated. This organic whole is under the direction of the state's policy. It is this concept which paves the way for the theory of total war.

Clausewitz also explained how, in the organic whole of war, psychological warfare and political warfare should be coordinated with military operations. He considered the destruction of the enemy's military forces, the annexation of his territory and the breakdown of his willpower as the three objects of war. In order to create defeatism in the enemy, military operations and the occupation of the enemy's territory all become a means of psychological warfare. Besides, to force the enemy to accept one's conditions by influencing his calculation with regard to his probability of success without having to destroy his combat ability is a much more effective way than destroying it.

Both Marx and Engels may be considered as the forerunners of the modern theory of total war. Their so-called dialectic interpretation of history is the analysis of various kinds of social and political forces from the standpoint of changes with a view to controlling their inner relationship. They did not study war as an isolated phenomenon. They believed that war must be conducted by various means in the fields of politics, economics and psychology, and that military action is the final means. Therefore, even before the first shot is fired, victory or defeat in war is already decided in the field of economic and psychological warfare.

Consequently, in the Russian Communists' military thinking both the employment of peace methods and the resort to force constitute war. The simultaneous or alternative use of various means constitutes total war.

Lenin said in 1920: "Our morality grew out of the class struggle. Communist morality is the morality which serves that struggle. This means one could use any method that serves the purpose of class struggle." Lenin pointed out clearly what these methods were. He said: "Bolshevism passed through fifteen years (1903-1917) of practical history which in wealth of experience has had no equal anywhere in the world. For no other country during these fifteen years had anything even approaching this revolutionary experience, this rapid and varied succession of different forms of the movement—legal and illegal, peaceful and stormy, secret and open, small circles and mass movements, parliamentary and terrorist . . .

"The dictatorship of the proletariat is a persistent fight—bloody and bloodless, violent and peaceful, military and economic, educational and administrative—against the forces and traditions of the old society."

Again, the program of the Communist International of 1928 expressly stipulated as follows:

"The dictatorship of the proletariat is a continuation of the class struggle under new conditions. The dictatorship of the proletariat is a stubborn fight—bloody and bloodless, violent and peaceful, military and economic, educational and administrative—against the forces and traditions of the old society."

Therefore, Soviet Russia and the international Communists not only change the forms of struggle from time to time, but often change from one form to a diametrically opposite one. This is what is meant by "transformation into opposites" in their "laws of dialectics."

Unity of Offense and Defense

Students of war often criticize Clausewitz for laying too much emphasis on defense. What they fail to see is that the dialectic unity of offense and defense is the one greatest feature in Clausewitz' *On War*. Clausewitz deemed it a "primeval sin" for one to go from offense to defense in any offensive war because the one who does it usually ends in defeat. To switch from defense to offense is a glorious thing to do in a defensive war, and the one who does it usually wins the victory. Therefore, an offensive war is the weaker form of making war while a defensive one is the stronger. Clausewitz believed that "to preserve is easier than to gain." "All the time which elapses unused falls into the scale in favor of the defender. The defender reaps where he has not sown." Therefore, while other military specialists insist that only offense could lead to victory, Clausewitz maintained that this was so because the key to victory came from its defensive nature. He pointed out that an offensive war, pure and simple, could easily lead to defeat. He took great pains to explain the tactics which the defender could use in case of an attack, such as by retreating into the interior, and, at the same time, launching a people's war against the invader.

Clausewitz was particularly penetrating in his analysis of the offensive war. He believed that "the ideation of war does not properly arise from the offensive war which has as its ultimate object not so much combat as the taking possession of something." He had a famous saying: "A conqueror is always a lover of peace." This is because the conqueror would like to make his entry into a country without bloodshed and unopposed. This saying had Lenin's heartiest endorsement.

Lenin evolved his world strategy concept by using this principle of the "dialectic unity of offense and defense" as a basis of the dialectic unity of class war and people's war. Since Lenin's time, the Russian Communists have often used internal class war in an enemy's country to defeat it. As to Soviet Russia's military policy at home, its principle is defensive offense. Lenin absolutely refused to take part in any external war. If his country should be subjected to hostile attack, making it necessary for it to take part in such a war, he would rather fall back into the interior to fight the enemy there because then he could rally the people by patriotic slogans to engage in a people's war for which the entire people would bear arms.

In his refutation of the controversy involving "leftist Communists," Lenin said: "If one is really thinking of defending one's country, carefully calculate the interrelation of forces. If one anticipates that his own forces will be inadequate, then effect withdrawals into the interior, for this is the most important method of defense. (If anyone should think that this has application as a formula only in a special situation, he should read about the lesson which one of the greatest theoreticians on war, namely, Clausewitz, has taught us on this subject.) Yet there are those among the leftist Socialists who do not understand the meaning of the interrelation of forces." What is particularly noteworthy about Lenin's remark was that "withdrawals into the interior" is not restricted in its application to any special situation. This is to say that he used this kind of defensive warfare as a general principle in directing wars of World Revolution.

Unity of Frontal Assault and Surprise Attack

For the war as a whole, the Russian Communists adopt the principle of unity of offense and defense; for actions in a decisive battle, their basic thinking is the unity of frontal assault and surprise attack.

In Clausewitz' view almost the only advantage offered by attack is surprise, and every unnecessary expenditure of time and every unnecessary detour is a waste of combat power. This unity of frontal assault and surprise attack is a basic principle in Clausewitz' military thinking, and this, too, was lifted by Marx and Engels. Discussing insurrection in his essay entitled "Germany—Revolution and Counterrevolution," Marx said:

"Insurrection is as much an art as war itself, and is subject to certain rules of proceeding, which, when neglected, will ruin the party neglecting them. Once the insurrectionary career is entered upon, act with the greatest determination and on the offensive. The defensive is the death of every armed uprising. Surprise your antagonists while their forces are scattering, prepare new successes, keep up the moral ascendancy which the first successful rising has given you, rally those vacillative elements to your side, force your enemies to a retreat before they can collect their strength against you."

Lenin quoted this passage on the eve of the October Revolution in 1917 and suggested an immediate armed uprising. In May 1923, speaking on the October Revolution and its significance, he quoted Napoleon in saying, "One must first start a serious engagement and then see what happens." From this, one can see how Lenin directed the Russian Communists to launch surprise attacks.

It was part of Czarist Russia's tradition of aggression to take the offensive against Russia's neighbors. During the reign of Catherine the Great Russian armies invaded the Crimea in 1767 and their fleet raided Greece in 1768. Three times Russia partitioned Poland—in 1772, 1793 and 1795—and carried out large-scale massacres of the Polish people. At the time of Nicholas I Russia invaded Turkey in 1828, the Dardanelles in 1853 and the Crimea in 1854. All these were concrete instances of Russia taking the initiative in aggression. While insisting on ensuring that the war as a whole be defensive, the Russian Communists have fully inherited these traditional ideas of initiative in tactical offense from Czarist Russia.

At the beginning of the founding of the Red Army, Soviet Russia laid special stress on attack in their military thinking to the exclusion of defense. It was not until 1942, at the time of her war with Germany, that she included defense as a form of military combat. To date the Russian Communists still adhere to the fundamental tenet that "victory is possible only by mounting a decisive attack in the principal direction." In addition to the "permanent factors in military operations," they have introduced "temporary factors," and surprise attack has become their major principle of war.

From the purely military standpoint tactical surprise is often used in modern warfare, but it is not so easy to effect a strategic surprise. Hence, the Russian Communists and the international Communists do not expect their opponents to be totally unprepared before they launch a surprise attack. Their hope is that, despite their opponent's preparations, they can still effect a strategic surprise.

Before launching an actual attack their favorite tactic is to camouflage their own methods and objective and, at the same time, to distract the enemy's attention. In this way they hope to attain a tactical surprise at points where the enemy is not vigilant or is otherwise unprepared; they hope to attain a strategic surprise even when the enemy is vigilant and prepared.

Interchangeability of War and Revolution

Marx, Engels and Lenin also learned something from Clausewitz' writings on the science of war and on military tactics. Whereas Clausewitz pointed out the ways of waging a people's war in the French Revolution, from the same revolution Marx and Engels learned how to wage a class war. War and revolution, however, are interrelated and also interchangeable. Following the French Revolution Napoleon successfully used France's army of 300,000, originally raised to fight a people's war, to wage foreign wars. This was how an internal revolution led to an external war, and to new directions and new methods of war. Conversely, during the First World War revolution broke out in Russia when the country was engaged in an external war, and this gave the Bolsheviks a chance to seize power. This was another instance of "war is the midwife of revolution." In short, under the actual conditions at the time, revolutions against tyranny or against feudalism were bound to happen in France and Russia. Whether it will be nationalism and democratic rule or Communist struggle by violence that will eventually triumph in the course of a revolution depends on changes in the relative strength of various social and political forces, and also on the organizations, policies, strategies and techniques of various political parties.

From Lenin onward, Russian Communist leaders have been especially aware of the interchangeability between war and revolution and have always made full use of it. The fundamental principle held by the Russian Communists is not only to expect but also to bring about wars between nations outside the Iron Curtain. No matter whether it is an imperialist war among the big powers or a people's war waged by a colony or a semi-colony against the ruling nation, it always means an opportunity for the Communists to seize power by turning an international war into a civil war. For this reason, Soviet Russia always directs local Communists to take part in all kinds of war anywhere outside the Soviet territory, and uniformly gives indirect aid and postive encouragement to the belligerents, so long as it does not mean the employment of the Red Army itself. As to actual hostilities, they try their best not to get involved.

In March 1918, when the Soviet Government signed the Treaty of Brest-Litovsk with Germany, Lenin said: "Passive resistance is a much more powerful weapon than an army that cannot fight." By 1920, after Russia's defeat in the Polish War, Lenin's policy toward the enemies of the Communist International was to have the proletariat in these countries rise in revolutions and not to attack them with Soviet armed forces. This does not mean that Soviet Russia is without any plans for offensive warfare. What it means is that before her own military preparations for the final decisive war are completed, *she will absolutely refuse to participate in any military adventure herself, but instead will attack her enemy in the political and psychological fields.*

The Zigzags of War

As pointed out earlier, the unlimited war of Soviet Russia and the Soviet bloc is the dialectic unity of offense and defense, of military operations and political offensive, of war and peace. It is also the dialectic unity of class war and people's war. Such a war naturally does not develop along a straight line but along a zigzag path. Lenin said: "If the enemy's action is not along a straight line but along a zigzag line, we must zigzag in order to overtake him."

The operational zigzags of the Russian Communists may be explained under the following three headings:

First, in fighting an enemy the Russian Communists always

assess the military situation before determining their own strategy and tactics. At the time of the "high tide of revolution" they take the offensive by either starting an armed uprising or seeking a military decision in the field. At the time of the "low ebb of revolution" they assume the defensive even to the point of falling back or surrender. They maintain that "revolution does not develop along a straight, continuous and upwardly aspiring line, but follows a zigzag path and the ebb and flow in the tide."

Secondly, the Russian Communists often use indirect warfare against an enemy. They seek to defeat the enemy in political, social, economic, cultural and psychological fields before engaging him in a final battle in the military field. For this reason, in Lenin's military thinking: "The best strategy is to delay the attack until the enemy's troops are demoralized, until his people are confused and until everything is ready for the decisive final battle." Thus the Russian Communists make alternate use of political and military devices, peace and combat, in their war which, as a result, develops along a zigzag path.

Thirdly, in point of geography Lenin's strategy of detours has developed a supreme prototype in the sense that Soviet Russia is to move from Asia to Europe in her plan of world conquest. Lenin said of that conquest: "The shortest route from Moscow to Paris is via Peiping and Calcutta." This strategy of detours is also responsible for the zigzags in the Russian Communists' wars.

From this it is clear that ever since the time of Lenin's dictatorship, although Moscow's operational patterns have undergone numerous changes, their wars have actually proceeded in a zigzag path in accordance with their strategy of detours.

Everything for the Decisive Battle

According to Clausewitz the final outcome of unlimited war is the destruction of the enemy's military forces, the occupation of the enemy's territory and the imposition of one's will upon the enemy. If the enemy is to be forced by military action to do one's will, he must be disarmed or be put in such a condition that he is threatened with the probability of such a danger. Therefore, to disarm the enemy is the object of military action. While there are various means to achieve the purpose of a decisive battle, the principal one is the military engagement. Consequently, in war every operation must be subject to the supreme law of seeking a military decision. The other bloodless way of seeking a military decision can in no way be considered as the natural means of preserving one's own forces. In fact, any attempt to avoid a sanguinary engagement in order to preserve one's own forces will have the effect of putting one's troops in a precarious position and even risking their utter ruin. It can be said that there is no substitute for violence as a means to a decision in war.

Marx was opposed to humanitarianism and peace. He maintained that blood must flow in wars before a new society could emerge. Lenin also felt that a correct program for Communism was "to arm the proletariat for the purpose of overcoming and destroying the propertied class." He believed that "not a single capitalist country can escape its fate at the hands of Soviet Russia." The Communist International at its Sixth Congress held in 1928 under Stalin's leadership adopted a program which clearly stipulated: "The seizure of political power by the proletariat does not mean the peaceful capture of ready-made bourgeois state machinery by means of a parliamentary majority. The seizure of power by the proletariat is the violent overthrow of the bourgeois power, the destruction of capitalist state apparatus and substituting it with new organs of the proletariat power." It is, therefore, obvious that the Russian Communists and their international Communist organizations have never admitted, not even in principle, that there are peaceful methods to take the place of "violence" and "decisive battle."

In launching an unlimited war against the free world, however, the Russian Communists do not intend to enter into a sanguinary decisive battle the moment hostilities break out. Nor is it their intention to substitute political and psychological warfare for the final decisive battle in the hope of winning the final victory. This is because in an unlimited war more time is taken up by a state of truce than by engagement, and military actions do not cease just because such a state of truce exists. The chief purpose of the Russian Communists' political and psychological tactics is to change the balance of power between themselves and their enemy, and to delay the decisive battle until the enemy's material and spiritual superiority have been turned into inferiority and their own material and spiritual inferiority turned into superiority. This is the crux of the Russian Communists' resort to "peaceful coexistence" as a tactic.

Consequently, before the Communists engage their enemy in any decisive battle, they employ various methods of "peaceful coexistence," and then particularly indulge in political and psychological warfare. Even after they have entered into the decisive stage they continue with their political and psychological warfare to change the balance of power between themselves and their enemy and to conceal the means they intend to use and also the ends they seek in the final decision.

Basic Principles in the Russian Communists' Military Thinking

At the time of founding the Red Army Trotsky laid down the following four cardinal points vis-à-vis its combat principles:

First, the basic trend of the state's internal policy (class character); second, the international orientation of workers' countries; third, the organic relationship of the Red Army with the state; and fourth, the strategy and tactical knowledge of the Red Army.

These four principles are much too abstract and are not in line with the existing military reality of Soviet Russia. Furthermore, they are not representative of the Russian Communists' military thinking of today.

In my opinion, if we make an analysis of the Russian Communists' new military thinking by keeping in mind its objectives as laid down in Lenin's dictum of "breaking away from the old rules and habits of military operations, creating a new revolutionary army to take the place of the old one and adopting new methods of warfare," and deducing therefrom what Lenin described as the new army and new methods of warfare, and finally ascertaining the existing actual military reality and trends, we should arrive at the following four principles:

First, a final decisive battle in an unlimited war which is at once an absolute war or a war of annihilation.

Second, a strategy of detours in a total war in which political and military forces are coordinated.

Third, a people's war by the "Revolutionary People's Army" which is of a class war character.

Fourth, a "World Revolution" as the ultimate objective.

CHAPTER THREE

THEIR FINAL CONCEPT OF "PEACEFUL COEXISTENCE"—THE COMBINED USE OF PEACE TACTICS AND WAR PREPARATIONS

Let us study Khrushchev's final concept of "peaceful coexistence" with the free world in the light of the Russian Communists' military thinking and of our experience. His concept is that Soviet Russia should continue to strengthen her peace offensive and neutralism tactics against the free world and, at the same time, spread the "antiwar movement" while positive preparations are being made behind the Iron Curtain for an all-out war. This is the combined use of peace tactics and preparations for war. In other words, he wants to destroy the world-wide anti-Communist front with his peace offensive before launching military surprise attacks against the capitalist countries in a decisive battle. In this way he hopes to realize his final concept of developing Communism into a global system and subjecting the world to Russian Communist domination. For this purpose he has laid down three plans, political, military and economic, all for war.

Plans for Political Warfare in Soviet Russia's Concept of "Peaceful Coexistence"

From the Soviet bloc's Cold War activities in various parts of the world, and also from the performances at the 20th National Congress of the Russian Communist Party in February 1956, we can see what are Soviet Russia's plans for political warfare in its concept of "peaceful coexistence" against the free world.

(a) Five Principles in the Communists' "Peaceful Coexistence" in Asia

The point of greatest emphasis in Soviet Russia's political warfare is Asia. This is not merely saying that the targets of its Cold War are the non-Communist countries from Southeast Asia to the Middle East. It also means that the way the Asian peoples turn will be a principal factor in determining changes in the relative strength of Soviet Russia and the Western nations, and that changes in Asia will be an important key to changes in the strategic situation of the world as a whole. Therefore, we should examine the political tactics of the Russian and Chinese Communists.

At the Bandung Conference in April 1955 Chou En-lai peddled his "Five Principles of Peaceful Coexistence" which are: 1) respect for each other's territorial integrity and sovereignty; 2) mutual nonaggression; 3) mutual noninterference in each other's internal affairs; 4) equality and reciprocal benefit; and 5) peaceful coexistence.

The Chinese Communists used the "Five Principles" to set in operation their political aggression in Southeast Asia and South Asia. They backed the Vietminhs in their military drive against South Vietnam. In the meantime they took advantage of international indifference to situations in Laos and Cambodia, two countries of pivotal importance in the Central-South Asian peninsula. They did this by neutralism tactics on the one hand, and on the other by directing local Communists to carry on infiltration and subversive activities in place of armed invasion to turn these two countries into satellites by the indirect method of "peaceful transformation." In South Asia the Chinese Communists have engineered revolts in Nepal, armed Afghanistan's troops to threaten both

India and Pakistan and established close relations with India and Ceylon to promote their own interests. The last-named two neutralist governments, judging by every one of their diplomatic moves on the international stage, are virtually Soviet satellites. In fact, they have been most active in pushing the sales of the Chinese Communists' "Five Principles of Peaceful Coexistence."

But were they not the same principles clearly stipulated in the Russian Communists' thirty years of peaceful coexistence with China beginning with their first declaration of friendship toward China in July 1918 through the Sino-Soviet Non-aggression Pact signed in August 1937, and the Sino-Soviet Treaty of Friendship and Alliance concluded in August 1945? Furthermore, did not Soviet Russia repeatedly declare to the world, and solemnly assure her American and British allies of, her good faith? Well, need we ask what has happened since?

In his report to the Russian Communist Party Congress in February 1956 Khrushchev put a Russian trademark on this product of the Chinese Communists and tried to sell it to the free world at large. Khrushchev said: "These Five Principles of Peaceful Coexistence provide the best form for relations between nations with differing social systems in the present-day circumstances. Why not make these principles the foundation of peaceful relations among all countries in all parts of the world? It would meet the vital interests and demands of the peoples if all countries subscribed to these Five Principles." From Khrushchev's talk, to anyone familiar with Soviet tactics, it is clear that the "Five Principles of Peaceful Coexistence" represent intrigues worked out by the Soviet bloc under the Russian Communists' direction, and certainly were not evolved by the Chinese Communists on their own initiative.

Furthermore, Khrushchev spoke of "countries" and "peoples" as different entities. Herein lies hidden much significance. He says to the free nations in Asia: "If your *countries* could accept the Chinese Communists' five principles of peace, that would meet the demands of the *people*." From this we know what he meant by "people." It conceals an important step in the Communists' political tactics of effecting "peaceful transformation."

If the free nations in Asia should believe the Chinese Communists' sugar-coated words about "mutual respect of each other's sovereignty," "mutual noninterference in each other's internal affairs," etc., and proceed to have "peaceful coexistence" with the Soviet bloc, they ought to remember that though, in form, the Chinese Communists' "Five Principles" are a pledge to the existing government in their "country," they are, in reality, an encouragement to local Communists, who are none other than the "people" Khrushchev has mentioned. Thus the "people" in their country, namely, Communists, could develop their strength with the indirect backing and assistance of the Russian Communists via the Chinese Communists, to engineer *coups d'état* for the purpose of seizing power.

This is to say that, in point of time, the full implementation of their "Five Principles" marks the conversion of a country into a Soviet satellite. This is the real meaning of these so-called principles. This has been the policy and form of action with Soviet Russia in its relations with China for thirty years. It is also the best explanation of the inseparable relationship between Soviet Russia and the Chinese Communists as well as the satellites in Eastern Europe.

In 1918 following their first declaration of friendship toward China in which they announced the abrogation of all special rights Czarist Russia had exacted from China, the Russian Communists carried on protracted negotiations with the Chinese Government in Peking. The fact that Soviet Russia showed no signs of actually giving up any special rights soon aroused suspicions of the Chinese people as to the sincerity of her offer. What they told Kuomintang, then still in Canton, was that the surrender of these rights would have to wait till Kuomintang had overthrown the northern war lords and unified the country. We have already shown that after our Government had unified the country Soviet Russia failed to keep her word especially regarding the Chinese Eastern Railway, which she refused to return to the Chinese Government on an agreed date. Later she sold the railway to the puppet regime of "Manchukuo" shortly after she had concluded a Nonaggression Pact with China. At the end of World War II Soviet Russia signed a Treaty of Friendship and Alliance with China. She tore it up and openly took aggressive actions against China in violation of the treaty. I feel that non-Communist nations in Asia will do well to intensify their vigilance, my hope being that they will not fall into the same trap as we did on the China mainland.

(b) Neutralism in the Middle East and Its Future

After the Chinese Communists had seized the Chinese mainland, the Russian Communists began a big detour from Asia to South Asia, the Middle East and Africa, and, at the same time, directed the Chinese Communists to move both eastward and southward in the Pacific. Using "anticolonialism" as their slogan, the Russian Communists have asked the Communists in various countries in South Asia, the Middle East and Africa to join forces with the local nationalists in a neutralist movement. They have cultivated Tito of Yugoslavia, Nehru of India and Nasser of Egypt as neutralists. In the future they will continue to aid the neutralist nations so that they will stay neutral, and play more important roles in the future.

As regards these neutralist nations themselves, they apparently have great confidence in their own political ability to outwit the Russian Communists, and hence are not afraid of their intrigues, threat of violence or outright aggression. They think they can keep on sitting on the fence, working for their own interests and indulging in the illusion of "neutrality and independence." Actually, the Russian Communists are making use of the neutralism tactics to promote conflict of interests between various nations in accordance with their law of dialectic contradictions so that they can manipulate and divide them. On the other hand, they develop, through contacts and offers of assistance, their infiltration and subversive schemes not only to isolate them but also to cause their automatic collapse. By that time the Russian Communists will go a step further and encourage these countries to form "United Front" and coalition governments with Communists in their midst. Eventually these countries will have no choice but to become Soviet satellites just like the Chinese Communists and the Eastern European nations. Little do they realize that the Russian Communists' neutralist tactic is a booby trap deliberately laid for their final "peaceful transformation" into satellites.

Besides its own smiling offensive and traveling diplomacy, Moscow needs to have agents to carry on its neutralism warfare indirectly. During the past years Tito of Yugoslavia has been an ideal agent in the Middle East and in Southeast Europe. But this move has failed. Now it is problematical whether Tito will ever return to the Russian Communists' fold again. Even if he does become a tool of the Russian Communists' neutralist tactics, he will not be as obedient as Mao Tse-tung. Titoism, like a two-edged sword, cuts both ways. Khrushchev and the Russian leaders will use Tito at a great risk. During the past year Khrushchev has used Tito because of the latter's slogan of "national independence" in the Communist bloc. It was for two purposes: to slow down the anti-Russian and antityranny revolutionary feelings in the various satellites, and to deceive the non-Communist countries, to befriend nationalists in the Middle East and to expel the Western influence from the Middle East. If Tito's "national independence" should be taken seriously at its face value, however, the satellites in Eastern Europe will all rise to oppose Soviet domination and to set up a Communist alliance of their own to take the place of Soviet leadership. The lifting of the Iron Curtain in Eastern Europe will mean a direct mortal threat to the security of Soviet Russia in Europe. Unless Khrushchev is sure of his ability to control Tito, he will not have dared to use him as an agent in the Middle East and in Southeast Europe. Otherwise, Tito could turn the "national independence" from a feint into a fact. That will not only mark the end of Khrushchev's personal power but will also doom the Russian Communists altogether. Henceforth Tito will also move to the brink of his own ruin. Tito may feel that he has won a big victory in his seven-year-long struggle against Soviet Russia. What he has failed to understand is that his victory has come from his complete break with the Russian Communists. If he should now return to the Russian Communists' arms and give them a chance to claim that "all Communists are of one family," the Russian Communists' infiltration into Tito's party and government will be more positive than into Nehru's and Nasser's administrations. Therefore, there are only two roads before Tito. The first is to break completely from the Russian Communists and join the antiaggression front in good faith. This road leads to a bright future. The second is to lean completely to the side of the Russian Communists and to accept Moscow's direction just as the Chinese Communists do, and serve once again as a tool of the Russian Communists to deceive the free world. In that case, his regime will be at the mercy of the Russian Communists, and the free world will never believe him again. This road will lead to his own doom. There is no third road before him.

(c) Russian Communists' "United Front" Toward Europe

As to countries in Northern Europe, especially Denmark and Iceland, the Russian Communists hope to be able to neutralize them. Their political warfare against countries in Western Europe and in the Middle East has a two-fold purpose:

First, they use the neutralists to promote "national independence" in order to stir up nationalist struggles against old colonialism in the Middle East and Africa and to force the Western European nations to withdraw from these two areas. Secondly, they direct the Communists in the various nations in Western Europe to form a "United Front" with the Socialist parties and to control their governments and policies by parliamentary maneuvers. Usually this begins with the neutralization of foreign policy and ends in delivering these countries to the Communist bloc through "peaceful transformation."

(d) Subversion and Isolation Tactics in America

Now let us see what are the roles that the Chinese Communists are playing in the political warfare waged by the Communist bloc in the Pacific region.

The Russian Communists have three routes from Moscow to Washington. The first one is via the Arctic Ocean. The second one is across the north Pacific via the Bering Straits. This is the route for a surprise attack in case Soviet Russia goes to war against North America. But she is most unlikely to use either of these except in the final decisive battle.

The third route is via the southwest Pacific. Here Soviet Russia will have to shatter the chain of island defenses in the western Pacific before she can enter the mid-Pacific, and similarly she will have to destroy the Southeast Asia Treaty Organization before she can enter the south Pacific in order to reach Central and South America. It is not my purpose to dwell on this point at any great length. What I propose to do is to point out Soviet Russia's line of political warfare. As it stands today, the plan is to use the puppet regime at Peiping as her agent in carrying on an indirect political offensive against North America from two directions.

First, in a frontal attack, the Chinese Communists are to hold direct peace negotiations with the United States. These negotiations can help the American Communists and their fellow travelers in their present movement "to change the United States' policy toward the Chinese Communists," and, at the same time, they can foster the growth of international appeasement and neutralism in South Asia and in the Middle East.

Secondly, in a flank attack, the Chinese Communists are to approach North America via Central and South America. This is really a point of emphasis in their political warfare against the Western Hemisphere. Vigilance is needed because the Chinese Communists have already begun their peace offensive and trade policy in Central and South America. Just as the Russian Communists are engaged in direct political infiltration in the Middle East and in Africa in order to outflank Europe, the Chinese Communists are carrying on political warfare against Central and South America in order to outflank the United States. Just as disturbances in the Middle East, fanned by the Russian Communists, can force the Western European nations to abandon Asia and fall back on Europe and Africa, and then force them to leave Africa to defend their homelands in utter isolation, the Chinese Communists' strategy in Central and South America is for a similar purpose. If they should fail to foment continuous anti-American movements in Central and South America, and cause them to spread far and wide, and if the security of the Western Hemisphere remains intact, they will not be able to force the United States to withdraw from Asia. Therefore, in the eyes of the Russian Communists, the road from Peiping through Southeast Asia, southwest Pacific, Australia, New Zealand, to Central and South America is, in point of political warfare, the shortest route from Moscow to Washington.

Consequently, Communist infiltration and subversion activities in Central and South America are not such as the Chinese Communists could carry on by themselves. In reality, Mao Tse-tung is merely an agent of the Russian Communists. Why should the Russian Communists use the Chinese Communists as vanguard in their political offensive in Central and South America? This is because people there are already on guard insofar as the Russian Communists' intrigues are concerned, so the Chinese Communists must act as an agent to provide a cover. It is in coordination with their own expansionist activities in Europe and Africa that they seek the growth of Communism in Central and South America. Furthermore, if countries in Central and South America should change their policy toward the Chinese Communists, this can be utilized by the American Communists to urge the United States to change its policy toward the Chinese Communists too. To put it bluntly, the Chinese Communists want the United States to withdraw from Asia and to fall back on America. What the Chinese Communists are doing today in Central and South America is to create a pressure to bring about this withdrawal. Whether Africa or America is to be communized first will depend on the spread of Communist political infiltration and armed insurrection in Africa and in Central and South America. This is their problem today.

Finally, the Russian Communists' efforts to sabotage and to destroy the North Atlantic Treaty Organization (NATO) and the collective security system in the Pacific are directed against two crucial points—West Germany in Europe, and Japan in East Asia. The two biggest accomplishments in the world's struggle against aggression since 1949 are West Germany's joining the North Atlantic Treaty Organization, and the conclusion of peace treaties between the Allies and Japan. Consequently, the Russian Communists are trying not only to obstruct and sabotage rearmament in these two countries but to neutralize them by intimidation and inducements.

(e) Milestones in the Russian Communists' Plan for World Domination

The Russian Communists' three roads from Moscow to Washington are also the roads leading from "peaceful coexistence" to the final decisive battle. If the democratic bloc should fail to stay alert and adopt effective countermeasures against the Russian Communists' strategy of detours and delays in launching the decisive battle, and against their political warfare during the period of "peaceful coexistence," it would be tantamount to permitting the world situation to change steadily in the direction desired by the Russian Communists and according to the timetable prepared by them. It would also be tantamount to permitting them to realize their final concept of world domination according to plan. At any rate, the Russian Communists, as a result of ten years of preparations in both Europe and Asia, have laid a solid foundation for their political warfare in the name of "peaceful coexistence." The first stage of their plan may be said to have been concluded. It only remains for them to coordinate their timetables for different parts of the world to ensure successful enforcement as far as this stage is concerned.

They are now in the second stage when they are building the groundwork in Africa and Central and South America. If they should be as successful as during the first stage, then at the end of the second ten years they will enter upon the third stage—the homestretch in their plan to conquer the world. It is my belief, however, that if the democratic bloc will only take advantage of the Russian Communists' internal crisis to remove the danger in the Middle East by way of the Far East, and to safeguard security in the Pacific region by starting from the East Asiatic mainland, then the comprehensive plan laid down by the Russian Communists could be smashed to pieces.

Plans for War Economy in Soviet Russia's
Concept of "Peaceful Coexistence"

(a) Four Characteristics in the Economic Planning of the
Russian Imperialists and Chinese Communists

That Moscow is making positive preparations for war cannot be made more evident than by the sixth Five-Year Plan
adopted by the Russian Communist Party at its 20th National
Congress, and by the first Five-Year Plan announced by the
Chinese Communists in 1955.

Although the Chinese Communists' plan was decided upon
before Soviet Russia's plan, it was revised accordingly immediately after the Russian plan had been formulated.

The best evidence of such a revision was in agricultural
cooperatives. Only in July 1955 did the Chinese Communists
decide on a program for the collectivization of agricultural
production. In January 1956, hardly half a year later, they
announced the "Outline for Nationwide Agricultural Development" which seeks "to complete the basic task of forming advanced-type agricultural cooperatives." The so-called
advanced-type cooperatives are nothing but Russian-style
collective farms.

Then in April 1956 Mikoyan went to Peiping. He made the
Chinese Communists sign on the dotted line, and under Soviet
Russia's control and with her help, the Chinese Communists
are to accelerate work on 156 kinds of industries and on the
construction of the Alma-Ata-Tihua-Lanchow Railway.
These are two instances of Chinese Communists shaping their
economic plans to dovetail into Soviet Russia's war plans.

A few of the characteristics in the coordination of plans for
war economy between the Russian and the Chinese Communists are noteworthy.

The first one is the development of Asia's heartland. Soviet
Russia is concentrating her effort on developing Siberia east
of the Urals. The Chinese Communists are increasing indus-

trial production in Manchuria to help industrial development in the northwest and the southwest. They are also moving industries from the southeast to the northwest where new industrial areas are being built. The plans of the Russian and the Chinese Communists, when viewed together, indicate that it is Moscow's hope to complete the establishment of war economy bases in Asia's heartland before 1960. After that it need not fear atomic attacks in a prolonged war against the democracies.

The second characteristic is the continued intensive development of munitions industries. By 1960 Soviet Russia is scheduled to produce two-thirds of America's 1955 steel output, to equal America's 1955 coal output and to catch up with America in power output. Only in petroleum will Soviet Russia still lag behind the United States. Of course, Soviet Russia expects that American-operated oilfields in the Middle East will sooner or later fall into her hands. As to the Chinese Communists, they are placing major emphasis on steel, power, machine-making, fuel, nonferrous metals, chemical and other basic industries to supplement Soviet Russia's war needs.

Geographically speaking, most of Soviet Russia's new heavy industries, new power plants and new railways are located in Siberia. For instance, the principal coal production centers will be developed in the Kuznetsk district, the Karaganda district and other regions to the east. As to petroleum, its principal production centers are the oilfields between the Ural and the Volga rivers. The principal hydraulic power stations are the ones at Plotsic on the Angara River and at Krasnoyarsk on the Yenisei River. These two hydraulic power plants, together with the thermal power stations at Kuzbass, Novosibirsk and Irkutsk, form a unified power network.

Soviet Russia's atomic energy industry is principally based in Siberia and China's northwest. Her present atomic power factories are located at Sludianka at the western end of Lake

Baikal. New atomic factories will be located in China's north-west close to the area served by the unified power network in Siberia.

The third characteristic is the accelerated development of strategic lines of transportation such as new railways and highways. In order to connect their war economy bases in Siberia with those in North China and Northwest China, Moscow has asked the Chinese Communist regime to speed up the construction of the Alma-Ata-Tihua-Lanchow railway and the Ulan-Ude-Urga-Tsining railway. The latter has already been opened to traffic, while the former will be completed in 1958. Meanwhile the Chinese Communists have constructed the Sikang-Tibet highway from Kangting in Sikang to Lhasa in Tibet, and the Chinghai-Tibet highway from Hokow in Kansu via Sining in Chinghai to Lhasa. They have also completed the Sining-Yushu highway which links the two trunk roads between Chinghai and Tibet.

By this network of railways and highways, Soviet Russia expects to have a strict control over Asia's heartland and extend her influence from Alma-Ata via Sinkiang right through the Chinese mainland to the harbors at Tsingtao, Haichow and Shanghai, on the western shore of the Pacific Ocean. Meanwhile she also expects to reach from Lake Baikal via Urga right through the Chinese mainland to the ports of Amoy, Canton and Yamchow, on the South China Sea. The Soviet aggressors believe that following the completion of their war preparations by 1958-1960, they will be in a position to sustain a world war. By that time they hope to consummate their final concept of World Revolution.

(b) Factors Determining the Success or Failure of the Russian Imperialists and the Chinese Communists in Their Economic Planning

Whether the Russian Imperialists and the Chinese Communists will be able to carry out their economic planning for war smoothly, whether they will be forced by difficulties to make revisions or whether their plans will end in failure, all depend on the following four factors.

First, exploitation of the farmers. From Soviet Russia's five Five-Year Plans in Stalin's time to its sixth Five-Year Plan under Khrushchev, the major emphasis has consistently been laid on heavy industries and collective farms. The basic policy in Soviet Russia's economic reconstruction is to build a foundation of heavy industry for war purposes on the blood and sweat of people in the rural areas. Under this policy the farmers, despite their year-long toil, have barely enough to keep body and soul together, as what they produced in the way of food and raw materials is practically all requisitioned to be used as rations among the government workers and the armed forces, the industrial establishments and people in the urban areas. Such products of light industries as the farmers receive in return are hardly adequate to maintain the minimum standard of living. The farmers are left with nothing for reinvestment in their farms. Because of this excessive exploitation the farmers have gradually lost interest in their work and their efficiency has gone down with a flop. This has resulted in reduced production and food shortage and even famines. In the end Soviet Russia's entire economic structure faces a basic crisis. There are only two remedies open to Soviet Russia. One is to squeeze more out of the satellites and the other is to increase the exploitation of farmers at home. But if this goes on much longer it will inevitably arouse the resentment of the farmers both in the satellites and in Soviet Russia itself and turn them against the Communist rulers. Unless drastic reforms are effected and the points of emphasis shifted, the Communists' economic plans for war will fail even with such modifications and improvisations as they may be able to effect.

Second, squeeze of the satellites. Under the numerous Five-Year Plans, Soviet Russia's economic structure may be likened to a suction pipe injected into the Russian farmers' blood stream or to a pressing machine mounted on the backs of people of the satellite countries. When the Russian Communists fail to get what they need through squeezing the satellites, they turn around to subject farmers at home to greater exploitation. This will surely lead to violence among the Russian farmers and national movements in the satellites. In due course these will merge into one powerful revolutionary movement against the Soviet regime from both without and within. Unless this revolutionary movement can be averted, it will cause the failure of the Russian Communists' economic planning for war.

Third, grabbing and pillaging of new colonies. When the Russian Communists find it no longer possible to squeeze more out of their own farmers and people in the satellites, they need to reach out for new colonies in order to continue their external expansion. In so doing, however, they run the risk of provoking a world war. If they should stop expansion for fear of starting a major conflict they still have to face the danger of internal revolts which are bound to break out because of frustration and despair. This is the third cause for the inevitable failure of their economic planning for war.

Fourth, trade with the free world. Though both the Russian and the Chinese Communists, in their economic planning for war, have tried to attain self-sufficiency, they are basically deficient in certain essential items. As they need these for both maintenance and development purposes, they have to obtain them through trade with areas outside the Iron Curtain. The Russians are in a position to control the economy of their satellites but they themselves still have to trade with the free world. In the Russians' military thinking, however, trade is not a peaceful transaction. Instead, it is the extension of war or merely another form of war. That this is so becomes all the more clear when the Russians, finding their military aggression blocked by antiaggression forces and being thus denied access to new colonies and their resources, have to turn around to obtain what is needed for the implementation of their economic planning for war through trade with the outside areas.

During the Chinese Communists' intervention in the Korean War, the United Nations passed a resolution banning the export of strategic goods to the Chinese mainland. This of course was a severe blow to the Chinese Communists in their war planning and their subsequent Five-Year Plan. That is why during the past three years they have continuously used trade as a bait or enlisted the services of neutralists to induce countries dreaming of making huge profits to ignore this embargo. If this resolution can be violated with impunity, it will enable the Chinese Communists to pull through their present difficulties.

In their trade war against the free world the Chinese Communists not only hope to overcome difficulties in their economic planning but also assist the Russian Communists and the satellites in their political offensive in the form of "peaceful coexistence." The purpose of this offensive is to expel the economic interests and influences of the Western nations from the vast "peace area" stretching from Southeast Asia all the way to North Africa. The free nations need to have a thorough understanding of this particular factor and to maintain a heightened vigilance regarding the combat character and political poison in this trade offensive and to take appropriate countermeasures. Meanwhile, they need to maintain the ban on strategic goods, which is hurting the Chinese Communists, and to ensure its continued adherence. In this way they can hasten the collapse of the Communist bloc's economic planning for war and increase the chance for peace and security in Asia and in other parts of the world.

The Military Operational Plans in Soviet Russia's Concept of "Peaceful Coexistence" and the General Situation

(a) Russian Imperialists' Final Base For Their Wars of World Revolution

We have seen that the emphasis of Soviet Russia's sixth Five-Year Plan is on *developing the Asian heartland.* To be more specific, it is Soviet Russia's plan to build up a base in the triangular region east of the Urals, west of Lake Baikal and north of the Pamirs plateau. This region will also be the last-ditch base from which she hopes to control the Eurasian land mass in her war with the Western nations. Meanwhile she will use the Petropavlovsk-Novosibirsk-Irkutsk railway as a trunk route, and the Alma-Ata-Tihua-Lanchow and Ulan-Ude-Urga-Tsining railways to control the whole of the Chinese mainland, all the way from Sinkiang to Mongolia and Tibet, from Mongolia to North China, from Northwest China to Southwest China, and from Southwest China to Southeast Asia. Thus this vast area in East Asia will be turned into a source of strategic materials and manpower. If Soviet Russia succeeds in consolidating this base and in completing her sixth Five-Year Plan, she will be able to command what Lenin used to call "the Western powers' store of inexhaustible manpower and natural resources in Asia." With them she can proceed to achieve world domination by World Revolution.

(b) Russian Imperialists' Three War Theaters in the Eastern Hemisphere

From this main base Soviet Russia plans to fight in three war theaters, that is, in Europe, in the Middle East and in the Far East.

First comes the European theater.

In the Western European countries are found a high degree of scientific knowledge, big industries, intricate communication networks and densely populated cities. Although none of them is economically self-sufficient or militarily strong enough for self-defense, together they still constitute a mighty force in the world's antiaggression movement. At present they are united in the North Atlantic Treaty Organization, which, however, has not stopped Soviet Russia from trying to exploit their conflicting economic interests as well as their internal social contradictions. Her aim is to create mutual distrust among them on the one hand, and to drive a wedge between them and the United States on the other. In other words, the forms of struggle which Moscow is using in Europe are designed to propagate "peaceful coexistence" and, by means of intimidation and inducements, to neutralize the Western European countries and isolate them from the United States.

Then there is the Middle Eastern theater.

This region stretches from Yugoslavia and Greece to Egypt and the Arab States and then to India. It is an important battlefield where Soviet Russia employs neutrality tactics in political warfare. The cultural characteristic of this region is Islamic. Geographically, the region is surrounded by the Mediterranean and the Black seas, the Persian Gulf and the mountain ranges and deserts northeast of the Indian Ocean. *Yet across this rugged and barren wilderness are located the principal oilfields of the world.*

Soviet Russia will not keep her hands off this vast region. In fact, she will not rest until she has it in her grasp, or unless she is halted. This is not only because the Middle East is a bridge linking the three continents of Europe, Asia and Africa. Nor is it merely because of its oilfields. The reason lies in its strategic importance.

If the Middle East remains a part of the antiaggression front when Soviet Russia fights her decisive battle against the Western countries, the Western countries can turn her left flank in the Middle East in case she advances westward toward Europe, or turn her right flank in case she advances eastward toward the Pacific. If the Western countries choose to start an offensive against Russia from the Middle East, they will be able to cut the line of communication between European Russia and Russia's heartland in Asia, and force her to fight on both the eastern and western fronts. This would put her in a serious predicament indeed.

To prepare herself for the final decisive battle, Soviet Russia must do her best to propagate such political tactics as "peaceful coexistence" and "neutralism" for the purpose of expelling the Western influence from the Middle East and to control the region completely before war breaks out.

The third theater is in the Far East.

As has been pointed out, the first target of Soviet aggression during the last thirty years has been China. Although the fall of the Chinese mainland has enabled Soviet Russia to control the Asian heartland and to move her forces of aggression to the western Pacific and to Southeast Asia, the Republic of China is pressing on with her struggle against Communism and Soviet Russia. In the meantime the resentment of people on the Chinese mainland against Communism is rising daily.

According to their program of aggression against China, the Russian Communists expect to finish off the Republic of China first, then proceed to control all the Oriental peoples, thereby paving the way for their conquest of the world. So far, however, they have not been able to realize their ambition in its entirety. At present not only has the Republic of China taken a firm stand at the forefront in Asia's struggle against Communists by fighting the Russian Communist aggression from bases on her own territory, but the Republic of Korea and the Republic of Vietnam are also vigorously fighting for their national independence and freedom.

The Far Eastern theater, however, is entirely different from the European theater in three respects:

If Soviet Russia decides to fight the Western powers in Europe, she will have to do her own fighting. This necessarily means a thermo-nuclear war. But in case of a war in the Far East, the Chinese Communist forces will do the fighting for her and Soviet Russia herself will not become a battlefield.

The Far Eastern theater also differs from the Middle Eastern theater. Either geographically or militarily, the Middle Eastern theater and the European theater are interrelated. Consequently, a war in the Middle East is perforce a war by the Western powers against Soviet Russia proper, and it will necessarily be an all-out war fought with thermo-nuclear weapons. On the other hand, a war in the Far East will take the form of a revolution for national liberation by the anti-Communist peoples in the East against the Russian puppets—the Chinese, Korean and Vietminh Communists. Such a war will not directly involve Soviet Russia proper.

In any war against Soviet Russia, whether it is fought in Europe or in the Middle East, the Western nations will be confronted with problems of nationalism. On the other hand, a war by the anti-Communist peoples in the East against the Communists will be one between the victims of aggression and the tools of Soviet aggression. It is a war against traitors to the Eastern nations. The collapse of the Chinese Communists —the principal traitors in the East—will spare other Asian peoples from the menace of aggression and help re-establish general security and a lasting peace in their midst.

From our thirty years of experience in fighting Communism, we know that the relations between the Russian and the Chinese Communists have been marked by two outstanding features:

Firstly, all tactics used by Communist parties in various countries, be they military or otherwise, are for the purpose of seizing or consolidating political power. In the last analysis the efforts of all Communist parties have but one objective, i.e., to safeguard their Communist fatherland and its Soviet regime even if this entails sacrificing themselves. This loyalty to Soviet Russia is the inherent duty of all Soviet satellites. This is especially true with the Chinese Communists. Therefore, we can predict that while the Chinese Communists can never extricate themselves from Moscow's control, the Russian Communists, on their part, will abandon them to preserve their own strength if and when the Chinese Communists should face defeat. There have been many such cases in the Russian Communists' dealings with the Chinese Communists over the last thirty years.

Secondly, the only thing which Soviet Russia and the Chinese Communists recognize is force. They will seize upon an opportunity to commit aggression when they are strong enough to do so, but will retreat and sue for peace when they are beaten back. As long as we, in the anti-Communist camp, remain firm, we can convince them that they cannot win in any future war. They will then retreat and give up their war of aggression. For this reason the antiaggression bloc's policy of force against the Communist bloc will *not* provoke an all-out war. *On the contrary, appeasement will only encourage the Soviet satellites to start aggressive wars on behalf of Soviet Russia.*

Today the Russian Communists boast that they have under their control 800,000,000 people in Europe and Asia, that they have built in the Asian heartland a base for all-out war and that they can win the final decisive battle in a thermonuclear war. All in all, however, the war will be decided by one fact, that is, what Lenin called "the overwhelming majority of the population in the East," the 450,000,000 Chinese people on the mainland constitute a main force in the Eastern peoples' struggle for independence and freedom. *Therefore, the success or failure of the Chinese Communists will have a decisive effect on the outcome of the Soviet bloc's aggression as a whole.*

If we look at the three theaters together, it becomes clear that Soviet Russia's base for her decisive battle against the

Western powers is on the Chinese mainland and in the heart-land in Asia. Today the Chinese Communists are guarding this base for their Russian masters. If the building of the base is allowed to go on uninterrupted and to become stronger, then Soviet Russia will be in an unassailable position in any all-out war in the future.

If nations in the antiaggression bloc should treat China, Korea and Vietnam as the vanguard in their struggle, and support them spiritually, morally, materially and economi-cally, so as to enable them to liberate their own countrymen from Russian enslavement and to strike at the Chinese Com-munists, this would not only pose an indirect threat to Russia's base and source of strategic materials, but also make possible a fundamental settlement. This would thwart Soviet Russia's ambition to advance westward and southward and deter her from starting a world war.

Herein lies the best way to deter Soviet Russia from starting World War III. Therefore, in order to avert such a war, we must first of all prevent Soviet Russia from completing the construction of her final base. Otherwise we are feeding a tiger which may turn around one day and devour us all.

(c) Four Forms in Soviet Russia's Military Operations

Now let us consider further whether the Eastern peoples, in their national wars against the Chinese Communists, will set off a world war and thereby involve the Western nations. First, we should study the various forms which the Russian Communists may take in using force against a free nation or a free area.

Their first form is to start a "civil war" in a free nation as a means to its conquest. This begins with the formation of a Communist party as a fifth column to carry out infiltration and subversion and ends with the resort to armed insurrection in a *coup d'état*. If the government of the nation in question should use force to suppress the rebels, the international Communists and their fellow travelers will immediately start a propaganda campaign alleging that "civil war" has broken out in the country. As a matter of fact, by its very nature this is Soviet Russia's war of aggression. It takes the form of a "civil war" because it is the Russian Communists' hope to conquer this particular country without using their own troops, thereby avoiding the risk of provoking a world war.

Another form is to engineer an international war in a free area so that the Russian Communists, posing as neutralists, can reap material benefits. This form has proved to be unusually effective in popular movements in the ex-colonies against the Western nations. The Russian Communists can be counted on to take advantage of national wars against Western colonialism—indirectly to assault the Western nations and directly to carry out their schemes of infiltration, manipulation and subversion. Their final aim is to seize political power in that country by turning its national war into a class war. This is how the Russian Communists push a country behind the Iron Curtain without touching off a world war.

Their third form is to dispatch regular Red Army units as "volunteers" into a free nation. The Chinese Communists, in sending their armed forces into Korea, have set a precedent for the use of "volunteers." Actually, the "volunteers" which the Chinese Communists used in their aggression in Korea were all part of their regular forces and they went into action under the direct command of the Chinese Communist Army. Chinese Communist forces in Korea were not subject to the command of North Korea's Communist forces; in fact, the Chinese Communists controlled the North Korean Communist forces. Furthermore Chinese Communist representatives participated in the truce negotiations and even signed the agreement. Thus the Chinese Communists admitted that the "volunteers" were under their direct command. Chinese Communist armed forces have since remained in occupation of North Korea following the conclusion of the truce agreement. All these prove that the so-called volunteers are really part of the Communist bloc's armed forces and that the use of "volunteers" is but another form of aggression and constitutes direct participation in war.

Their fourth form is the formal dispatch of regular troops for war on foreign soil. This is used only as a last resort because it contravenes the Russian Communists' highest principle in their strategy for World Revolution. In fact, it has no place in their traditional concept of war and for this reason its use is to be avoided by all means. For the Russian Communists directly to take part in external wars has two disadvantageous consequences: One, a direct war of aggression may lead to a world war. Two, such a war by their own theory may arouse the victimized people into a national war against them. I have repeatedly pointed out that before they complete their preparations for the final contest of force against the free world, the Russian Communists definitely will not dare to resort to direct invasion.

The foregoing analysis leads to the conclusion that if the free world seeks to stop Russian aggression and nip in the bud the danger of a world war, one effective way is to make it impossible for the Russian Communists to use indirect war through employing "volunteers" in what is actually direct war. The free world should regard any war, engineered or provoked by the Communists in any free nation, not as a "civil war" but as an international war. As a corollary, if Soviet Russia's armed forces should take part in external war outside the Iron Curtain, the free world should consider it to be what it is, even though Communist forces may pose as "volunteers." If the United Nations can hold fast to this principle, thereby making it useless for the Russian Communists to cover up their military aggression by camouflage and chicanery, it will go a long way toward preventing Soviet aggression and removing the danger of a world war.

(d) A Decisive Factor in Determining the Outcome of the Contest Between the Forces of Aggression and Forces Against Aggression—Revolutions by People Behind the Iron Curtain and the Independence Movements of People in Asia

To take a closer look at the problem, the war between the Soviet bloc and the democracies will not only be decided in the three war theaters, for there exists between the forces of aggression and the forces of freedom a determining factor, namely, the great anti-Communist revolutionary force repreresented by the masses behind the Iron Curtain, and the Asian peoples' struggle for independence and freedom. Whoever wins the confidence and support of these peoples will win in the end.

If the Western nations should carry the war to Soviet Russia's own soil from the European and Middle East theaters, Moscow will be able to rally the Russian people's nationalist feelings in a patriotic war just as she did during the German invasion in World War II. Moscow can also use the Asian peoples' anticolonial movement to harass them. Thus the strength of the revolutionary forces behind the Iron Curtain, and that of the Asian peoples, will be lost to the antiaggression cause and be used instead by the aggressor. This would surely lead to a world war, the outcome of which will be difficult to predict.

On the other hand, if the anti-Communist peoples in the East are given moral and material support by the world-wide antiaggression front, and launch coordinated counterattacks against Communist satellites in East Asia with the Chinese Communists on the mainland as their target, such a war in the Far Eastern theater will become a national war as well as a revolutionary war. As a national war, it will ignite a movement for national independence and freedom on the part of all Asian peoples; as a revolutionary war, it will inspire all anti-Communist people behind the Iron Curtain to rise and fight the Communists with us for their own liberation. Such a national anti-Communist revolution can succeed without the direct participation of the Western nations.

Once we grasp this point, we can see that, following the outbreak of the Korean War in 1950, the Western nations' appeasement of the Chinese Communists out of fear of Soviet Russia and their rejection of the Republic of China's offer to send an army to join the allied forces had the effect of emboldening the Chinese Communists in the latter part of the war to indulge in blackmail and other outrageous actions with impunity. People of the world only know that, after the Chinese Communists had entered into the Korean War, the United Nations forces, because of international political and diplomatic restrictions, could not cross the Yalu River and had to confine their operations to the Korean battlefield, and that, as a result, they could not fulfill their mission and left Korea divided despite the 130,000 casualties they had suffered. This was a most deplorable case in the history of world politics, and especially in the history of the United States. Even if the United Nations forces did pursue the Chinese Communist forces into Manchuria, however, the Chinese Communists could use their regular troops and their organized guerrillas in a people's war against such United Nations forces as had penetrated into the mainland. In that event the latter would have failed just the same, even without Soviet Russia's participation in the war.

If, in the Korean War, the Republic of China's troops had been used, the situation would have been totally different. After the Chinese Communist troops had crossed over into Korea, although they used the "human sea" tactics, they were no longer operating among their own people whom they had either deceived or intimidated into supporting them, and hence were not as effective as if they were fighting a people's war. If the Republic of China's armed forces had moved in, it would have had a great political and psychological effect on the Chinese Communist troops in action, and the latter could have been crushed in Korea. If the troops I offered could have pursued the enemy across the Yalu River into Manchuria, they would not only be fighting among their own people, but would have fostered an anti-Communist revolutionary movement on the Chinese mainland. Such a turn of events would have made it unnecessary for the Republic of China's forces to depend on the rear for military reinforcements and replenishments and would have turned a limited United Nations military action into a Chinese people's war.

I believe that the Western powers' objection to the dispatch of an expeditionary force to Korea by the Republic of China was the *greatest cause for the stalemate in the Korean War.*

I wish to say again that if the anti-Communist war in the Far East could be left to be started by the Far Eastern countries themselves, there would be no need for the Western nations to take any direct part in the fighting. In fact, their participation would harm themselves and hinder the anti-Communist war in the Far East. Meanwhile if Soviet Russia should send her regular troops to help the Chinese Communists against the anti-Communist peoples, she would find herself bogged down in the quagmire of Asia's national revolution. To people in Russia this would mean a chance to revolt against the Communist regime. Then Russia would be faced with the danger of "a foreign war being turned into a civil war." This would be against her traditional policy of World Revolution and also against the laws of dialectics. Moreover, this could touch off an all-out world war.

Before Soviet Russia completes her preparations for a general war, she will certainly not wish to participate directly in any national revolutionary war in the East. Otherwise, if she should take part in such a war, she could be held down and finally defeated in the Far Eastern battlefield even before the outbreak of the world war. For her own interest, she will not be directly involved in an anti-Communist war on the Chinese mainland. If she did, she would go down in defeat as Japan did in her war of aggression against China.

On the other hand, if the Western countries should participate in this war in East Asia with their regular troops, the Communist bloc would use the anticolonialism slogan and turn the Asian peoples' anti-Communist revolutionary war into an anti-Western national movement. This is why Western participation would hurt the cause of an anti-Communist war in East Asia. For this reason I do not think the Western nations should take part in our war to liberate our people on the Chinese mainland. *All we need from them is moral and material assistance and the supply of arms and technical aid.*

If the democratic bloc is afraid that a local war by the anti-Communist national revolutionary forces would touch off a world-wide thermo-nuclear war, and therefore seeks to avoid war at any cost, then the Communist infiltration and subversion will run its course and the Communists will have a free hand in conquering the free nations and extending their control. In that event, though it is possible to preserve peace temporarily, the free world will have only two courses before it. One is to wait for the enemy to strike first in a surprise attack of annihilation. The other is to accept the enemy's "peaceful coexistence" and to permit ourselves to be disposed of as the enemy may see fit. Therefore, if the democracies wish to prevent the outbreak of a world war, and to save mankind from a major calamity, the only way is to substitute a local war in East Asia for an all-out world war, and to fight a war with conventional weapons instead of a war of annihilation with thermo-nuclear weapons. Such a Far Eastern war of national revolution against Communism points a way to the defeat of the Soviet bloc and to the lifting of the Iron Curtain without a world war. It is also the free world's only way, apart from a world war using thermo-nuclear weapons, to foil the Russian Communists' ambition to dominate the world. This is also the only way to rebuild world peace and to safeguard human freedom.

Which of the two courses will the democracies elect to follow? The answer to this all-important question will determine whether the Russian Communists will succeed or fail in their scheme for world conquest.

CHAPTER FOUR

CONCLUSION

The Value of Neutralism to the Communists

In this book I have endeavored to present an objective account of China's as well as my personal experience with the Russian and Chinese Communists in the past thirty-odd years. I have sought to explain, as best I could, the circumstances in which my Party and the Chinese Government underwent not one, but three periods of "peaceful coexistence" with the Communists, in all of which certain overriding considerations of national or international importance at the time prevented the Government from adopting a stronger, perhaps I should have said a more ruthless, policy toward the Communists.

As I look back on those years of "peaceful coexistence," I become more convinced than ever before that neutralism is as dangerous as Communism itself. Therefore, even at the risk of repeating myself, I should stress again this question of neutralism. Neutralism is based on the assumption that a free democratic country can coexist with a Communist state in peace and prosperity. My experience with Communism has taught me that it is only when the Communists are in need of a respite in which to consolidate their gains or to prepare for their next move that they tolerate and would sometimes even encourage the existence of such a state of mind. This has been exemplified in the many instances that I have enumerated in the previous chapters.

Normally, neutralism has a natural appeal to those who lack confidence in their own ability to defend themselves and to others who seek to take advantage of the situation. But in recent years neutralism has flourished in two kinds of circumstances: one, where the opportunist has been encouraged by some initial gains from both the aggressors and the antiaggressors, or sees an occasion to realize such gains; the other, where the neutralist is motivated by a megalomaniac desire to see his own importance enhanced in the popular role of a world peacemaker. The reader will recall the part played by the Democratic League during the days of the Marshall mission. Many of its members were honest neutralists who, to my knowledge, had no membership in the Chinese Communist Party. In fact, the Chinese Communists took great care to ensure that members of the League should remain distinct from themselves as elements of a third party and, therefore, have more right to appeal to the public for the coalition which the Communists obviously wanted as a consummate step toward "peaceful coexistence."

In view of the above considerations, it is my opinion that any encouragement given to, or acquiescence in, neutralism is as disastrous and as potent as any direct assistance given to the perpetuation of Communism in any country. In the midst of a struggle between free and Communist ideologies, neutralism must be regarded always as a Communist front. As such it must be looked upon also as a Communist weapon of war.

Today when the strength of the free world and that of the Communist bloc seem to approach a state of balance, neutralism can be of the greatest harm to the cause of freedom.

Toward World Peace

In combating Communism it is a matter of primary importance that we examine carefully the Communist strategy of "protracted warfare," to which I have already made references. First of all, whereas ordinarily war is characterized by military action and a formal declaration, in the Communist concept war is a perpetual state. As far as Soviet Russia is concerned, it will only end when its scheme of world conquest is completed. In other words, the present protracted state of war will continue until its success is crowned with the disappearance of any vestige of democracy. Some people may still speculate as to when a war with Soviet Russia will break out. As a matter of fact, we are already in a state of war, a cold war it may be, but a war nonetheless. It is, therefore, incumbent upon us to consider every Communist move as of a definitive intent and for a calculated purpose. It means that when we come to judge or appraise facts and events concerning the Communists, it is impossible for us to be oversensitive in the usual sense of the word. The Communists themselves often use the phrase "heightened vigilance" to caution their own comrades against possible measures on the part of their opponents. For the same reason we cannot be too vigilant with regard to any Communist maneuver.

The only effective strategy against the Russian Communists' protracted warfare is one of total war. I strongly feel that this is what the free world needs to adopt. This positive total war strategy should be based on several principles:

First, the world-wide anti-Communist struggle should set as its over-all objective the safeguarding of human freedom, the liberation of the oppressed nations and peoples and the re-establishment of world peace and security.

Second, in this strategy, enlightened capitalism of the democratic countries, the independence movements of the Eastern peoples and the anti-Communist revolutionary movements behind the Iron Curtain should be coordinated. The combined strength of these three forces not only can stop Soviet Russia's long-term unlimited aggression against the free world but can also compel Soviet Russia to loosen its grip on the satellites and, at the same time, encourage the Russian people to rid themselves of the Soviet totalitarian regime which is based on violence.

Third, the free world should employ both military and political tactics, adopt multiple forms of struggle and free itself from such strategic concepts as would place exclusive emphasis on military combat or weapons. In fact, before any armed conflict takes place, the anti-Communist world should prepare to win ascendancy in the political, social and psychological fields. There is a possibility that Soviet Russia may be thus forced to abandon her attempt at armed aggression and her scheme of World Revolution.

Fourth, efforts should be made to maintain and strengthen the military power of all anti-Communist nations because, important as it is, psychological warfare cannot be a substitute for military action. The democratic nations, therefore, must not relax in their military preparations. Furthermore, they should build up the armed strength of anti-Communist peoples on the periphery of the Iron Curtain so that they, too, will be ready to accept the Communist challenge or to engage in a decisive war on the side of the democracies.

In Asia today the Communists are exploiting the legitimate aspirations of growing nationalism to arouse an anticolonialism movement against the Western nations. This brings up a vital problem. The lingering resentment against any form of Western influence in some of the new-born Asian countries has provided the Communists with an excellent opportunity for infiltration. I feel that the Western nations should guide these national aspirations into constructive and democratic channels and lead these peoples away from the traps of Russia's new colonialism so that they will realize that the Russian Communists are their only enemy, and that they should participate in the struggle against Communism.

The desire to live in peace is universal. With the potential destructiveness of thermo-nuclear weapons being what it is, no sensible statesman of any democratic nation can possibly want to lead his people to war again. Nevertheless, there is no denying the fact that since Soviet Russia and the Chinese

Communists occupied the Chinese mainland, the area of freedom in the world has been further reduced. If the Communist bloc should continue its aggression and if the free world should keep on retreating, and in the meantime hoping to avoid a world war without making any plans to fight one, if necessary, or to prevent one from breaking out, we are driven to ask: Are we, by avoiding such a war, to surrender our freedom to Communism?

I have advanced here certain ideas on how people in Asia may become strong enough to check Communism on the one hand and to continue to develop their democratic way of life on the other. Freedom, however, is indivisible. With such a large percentage of Asia's population already behind the Iron Curtain, one cannot possibly hope to defend freedom elsewhere in the world by leaving the enslaved peoples to their own fate.

It is my opinion that in avoiding any direct involvement in war the United States should not allow itself to be forced into a position where it has to use its homeland as a major battlefield. For the sake of the world-wide war against Communism as a whole, it should adopt the strategy of indirect warfare instead of being dragged into the whirlpool of war. Only thus can it control the anti-Communist war instead of being controlled by it. Also only thus can the main base for global war against Communism be secure. The United States should take upon itself the responsibility of serving as the free world's arsenal. Such responsibility as befalls it is incumbent upon any nation whose leadership is acknowledged by so many other countries. This is not to say that the United States should merely play the part of the manufacturer of arms and the provider of material aid to all countries seeking to retain or regain their freedom. She should also assume active leadership in the common war against Communism.

So long as the Russian Communists abstain from active war, it will not be advantageous to have the United States participate in direct warfare, nor will it be advantageous for the free nations to engage in war outside the Iron Curtain. In their struggle against Communism the free nations should mark certain areas on the periphery of the Iron Curtain as "points of emphasis." If the Communists should start aggression against any country, the free world should strike at previously selected areas instead of limiting its counterblows only to the area where Communist aggression has taken place. For it is most unlikely that the Communists will attack in areas where the democratic nations are militarily prepared or where there are systems of collective security in existence.

In Asia the United States should take into consideration the Russian Communists' final base in the heartland, coordinate the various Eastern peoples' plans for wars against the Communists and assume full leadership in directing the implementation of these plans. The highest guiding principles should be to bring about favorable strategic changes in the world and checkmate aggression by the Soviet bloc without plunging the world into a holocaust.

The Key to World Peace—A Free United China

It can be said that the greatest threat posed by international Communism lies in Asia, and this threat stems mainly from the Chinese Communists. The fall of the Chinese mainland was a tragedy to the world and its seriousness is only beginning to be recognized. Had my Government remained on the mainland, there would never have been such calamities as the Korean War and the Communist occupation of northern Korea and northern Indo-China. The place to begin combating Communism in Asia, therefore, is mainland China.

I personally cannot disclaim responsibility for the loss of the mainland. I have given in this book the circumstances in which our defeat was brought about to the disaster of the Chinese people. Lest I be accused of recriminations, let me say that I have never in the forty-odd years of my political life shirked any responsibility or blame that is justly mine. When the American Government published its White Paper on China in 1949, I was, at the time, not in office. Those in office wanted to publish a reply, also in the form of a White Paper, which would enumerate the mistakes made by the United States in China. I strongly opposed the idea. I told the then acting foreign minister, Dr. George Yeh, that if the Government should take such a step it would lose all its friends in the United States whose confidence in us would otherwise remain unimpaired in spite of the White Paper. Furthermore, it would cause irreparable damage to the traditional friendship which has been in existence between the Chinese and American peoples for the past century. In the end it would only help the Russian Communists in their intrigues to sow discord between China and the United States. During all these years I have not tried to answer the accusations contained in the White Paper against my Government and against me personally. I have written this book with much larger aims in view, as mentioned in the Introduction, because I have unswerving faith in the re-emergence of my country as a free united nation and in the eventful triumph of freedom over slavery throughout the world.

A STUDY OF THE COMMUNISTS' USE
OF DIALECTICS

After meeting with reverses in war, the Communists always turn around and ask for peaceful coexistence. Upon regaining strength, they break off negotiations and resort to insurrection again. While negotiating peace, they make secret plans for armed revolts. In their dialectics, this is what is meant by "unity in contradictions" and "shifts of things in opposition." Therefore, in combating the Communists, we must understand their military thinking and rhythm of actions before we can tell whether our own strategy and tactics have been correct. From our thirty years of experience in dealing with the Communists, we have learned that, first of all, we must study their actions on the basis of dialectics. We propose to share this experience with all the nations of the free world. It is for this reason that the following material is included as an appendix to this book.

Retreat, Defense, Attack

Every time Moscow has come out for "peaceful coexistence," people have invariably thought Soviet Russia was in retreat. But from the history of Russian and Chinese Communist aggression in China, we have learned that though sometimes they used "peaceful coexistence" to cover a retreat, at other times they used it as a means of defense, and at still other times, as a method of attack.

Retreat. The Communist International at its Seventh Congress (held in Moscow in August 1935) decided on the "United Front" strategy. Whereupon the Chinese Communists started their "People's Front" activities. After February 1936 the Chinese Communists, having been cornered in northern Shensi, knew they could not carry on much longer. In a circular telegram sent from Yenan, they asked for cessation of hostilities and peace talks with the Chinese Government. These talks led to the conclusion in

February 1937 of a four-point agreement. This was a clear case of the Chinese Communists using "peaceful coexistence" to cover a retreat.

Defense. The earliest instance of the Chinese Communists asking for "peaceful coexistence" and cooperation with Kuomintang and the Government for defensive purposes was after the suppression of the Canton revolt on March 20, 1926, when Borodin accepted Kuomintang's proposal regarding the reorganization of party affairs. The Chinese Communists sought to maintain contact with Kuomintang by a peace agreement so that they would have time to prepare for a coup during the Northward Expedition later on. This was an actual case of the use of "peaceful coexistence" by the Chinese Communists for the purpose of political defense.

During the war with Japan the Chinese Communists held five peace talks with the Chinese Government when they moved from the defensive to the offensive. The first three talks were still designed to cloak the growth of the Communist forces. The fourth and fifth talks were meant as a political offensive.

Attack. The most obvious instance of the Chinese Communists using "peaceful coexistence" as a means of attack was found in the peace talks at the end of the war with Japan, which constituted an active political offensive against the Chinese Government.

To judge the laws governing the actions of Soviet Russia and the international Communists, we must first understand that they defend or attack, retreat or advance in accordance with the dialectic laws of contradictions and qualitative changes. It is common sense that any army retreats in order to counterattack and defends in order to attack. But the Communists go further than this. They retreat *not for the sake of counterattack alone;* they defend *not for the sake of attack alone.* They make *simultaneous* use of retreat and defense in order to attain the maximum effect in splitting the enemy's strength and concentrating their own strength, and in undermining the enemy's will to fight while fortifying their own. When they retreat and assume the defensive, they try specially to subvert the enemy from within and alienate his allies by political and psychological infiltrations. When the right moment comes, they will deal the enemy the final blow. Only when we grasp this particular point can we understand why Soviet Russia and the international Communists make use of their "peaceful coexistence" slogan no matter whether they are in re-treat, on the defensive or going over to attack.

NEUTRALISM, UNITED FRONT AND ISOLATION TACTICS

In analyzing the methods of struggle used by the Russian and Chinese Communists in the name of "peaceful coexistence," a study of their tactics involving Neutralism, United Front and Isolation movements should be included.

Neutralism Tactics. Let us first examine the method which the Chinese Communists employ in the name of neutralism. Their initial demands on the neutralists are very simple. First, they do not ask the neutralists to help them; they simply ask them *not* to help the enemy. Secondly, they do not ask the neutralists to go along with them, but simply ask them to condemn the enemy. Thirdly, they want the neutralists to help neither side, but to oppose both sides. The Communist tactics begin with the neutral-ization of the person concerned and follow it up by encouraging him to criticize, oppose and ultimately abandon his government without his knowing it. Thus isolated, the neutralist will naturally have to follow the Chinese Communists when the latter have the upper hand in a fast-changing political situation. This is the way the Communists attain their objective through neutralism. The activities carried on by the "Anti-Japanese National Salvation Alliance" in September 1935 and thereafter constituted an ex-ample of the Chinese Communists' neutralism campaign against the Government. Toward the end of the Sino-Japanese war and during the postwar period, the Democratic League's operations provided another instance of neutralism in action. Still another example was the diplomatic efforts of the Chinese Communists at the time of the Marshall Mission. In all these instances, Chinese Communists employed the tactics of neutralism in two different ways which are worth analyzing. Before we do that, however, we should explain United Front and Isolation Tactics.

United Front. "United Front" is the principal form of offense of Moscow and the international Communists. In China the Com-munists used it many times against Kuomintang and the Chinese Government. The two outstanding cases were as follows: The first case happened after August 1922, when the Chinese Com-munists proposed to form a united front with Kuomintang to fight the war lords. In our party reorganization in 1924 the Chinese Communist Party cooperated with us in the name of the

United Front and arranged for their members to join Kuomintang. The second case happened after May 1936, when the
Chinese Communists asked to join us in fighting against Japanese
aggression. They even accepted the four principles outlined by
the Chinese Government and promised to abide by them, and to
take part in the war of resistance against Japan. The "united
front" as utilized by the Communists takes the form of an alliance with friends to oppose a common enemy. Actually, their
intention is to stab the friends in the back while fighting the
common enemy, thereby realizing their own aim of establishing
a Soviet regime. In 1920, when Russia's Social Democratic
Workers' Party and the Socialist Revolutionary Party were
negotiating on the question of cooperation, Lenin told his party
members: "Keep in mind that this is an unreliable friend, and
hence an enemy.* In 1924, speaking before the Fifth Congress
of the Communist International, Zinoviev said: "We do not have
to tell the Social Democrats that we do not want to form a united
front with other workers' parties for the reason that their leaders
are antirevolutionary. We would rather tell them that we are
willing to form a united front with them if their leaders should
accept these basic conditions (which everybody knows they
cannot accept)." This was also the attitude and practice with the
Chinese Communists on the two occasions when they formed a
"united front," and had "peaceful coexistence" with us. Later on,
when they realized that they could not subvert us, they broke
with us and started a war against us. This was the primary purpose of their "united front."

Isolation Tactics and Anti-Isolation Tactics. Before attacking
an enemy, he should be isolated. A military front should also be
isolated before attack. The way of isolating an enemy is to
alienate him from his allies and to cause his camp to disintegrate.
The way of isolating a front is to sever its two flanks and to cut
off its lines of communication with the rear. This is military common sense which any field commander must possess. But the
Communists apply this method of military operations to political
warfare. This results in their isolation tactics. In safeguarding
their own organization, the Communists take particular care not
to leave any door, or even a crevice open, which their enemy
can use for infiltration purposes. For the sake of avoiding their
own isolation, however, they are absolutely opposed to the so-

* Lenin's *Collected Works*, Russian edition, vol. 28, p. 143.

called "Closed Door Policy." Lenin said in 1902: "It is absolutely necessary first to demarcate oneself from all others and set the proletariat aside as a sole, unique, and exclusive group. Then we must declare that we want liberation for everybody, that we call on everybody, appeal to everybody."* This is the Communists' anti-isolation tactic, which combines fighting and making alignment. United Front is nothing but the manifestation of their anti-isolation tactics. The anti-isolation and isolation tactics were both constantly employed by the Chinese Communists. Here are a few concrete instances.

In October 1934 the Chinese Communists in Southern Kiangsi escaped in small numbers through Government encirclement. Afterwards, they worked through front organizations such as the "Anti-Japanese National Salvation Association" and others to organize a "people's front" in order to end their political isolation. But it was not until after May 1936 when the Chinese Communists in Northern Shensi offered to surrender to the Government and to take part in a war against Japanese aggression that their anti-isolation tactics began to take effect.

From January to May 1946 Stalin employed a combination of neutralism tactics and isolation tactics against the Chinese Government. He tried to alienate Sino-American friendship and cooperation in order to isolate China but without much success.

In 1945, after the termination of the war with Japan, the Chinese Communist Party working through its front organization, namely, the outwardly neutralist Democratic League, used the isolation tactics against the Chinese Government.

In January 1946, at the time of the Political Consultative Conference, the Communists tried to line up the various parties against the Government in the name of "democracy and freedom," and demanded the formation of a coalition government. This was foiled by the Government at the outset by its proposal to "broaden the basis of the Government" and "terminate political tutelage and launch constitutional rule." This move by the Government took effect and not only defeated the Communists' isolation tactics, but also won for the Government the support of various minority parties. Consequently, the Chinese Communists refused to attend the National Assembly, but resorted to all-out armed insurrection.

* *Collected Works*, Russian edition, vol. 6, p. 59.

Simultaneous Use of United Front, Neutralism and Isolation Tactics. In their two most glaring corruptions of "peaceful coexistence" with us, the Chinese Communists made simultaneous use of united front, neutralism and isolation tactics. As a result, "peaceful coexistence" and neutralism have produced different effects. After 1936 the Chinese Communists launched a campaign of strategic defense and tactical offense against the Government. To be more specific, their demand for "peaceful coexistence" at the time, in point of strategy, was a defense against the Government's sustained military pressure on the remnants of their armed forces. The so-called "cooperation for joint resistance against Japan" was nothing but a slogan for this strategic defense. On the other hand, the "people's front" they then organized was a kind of isolationist device used to support their neutralism tactics through the "Anti-Japanese National Salvation Association" in an attack on the Government. While asking for cooperation to resist Japan, the Chinese Communists insulted and abused the Government by branding it as "Fascist" and "not anti-Japanese." This campaign caused our country and our Government a considerable loss in prestige but opened up for the Communists vast possibilities for political expansion. So, in this particular instance, the Chinese Communists' "peaceful coexistence" was a strategic defense and a tactical offense. The peace talks held between the Chinese Communists and the National Government after the war, however, constituted the reverse: a strategic offense and tactical defense. In other words, they sought to shatter our strength by using "peaceful coexistence" as a strategic weapon to tie the hands of Government troops and at the same time to facilitate their own attacks. In point of tactics, however, they remained on the defensive and shaped their demands accordingly. They only talked of "peace." They said they wanted "democracy." They claimed that all they asked was that political parties should leave the armed forces and schools. They won the sympathy of the general public and the applause of opportunists and fence-sitters as part of their plan to isolate the Government. Therefore, the Communists' peace talks during this particular phase were a strategic offense and tactical defense.

That the Russian Communists have repeatedly directed their Chinese puppets to employ united front, neutralism and isolation tactics against China has been made clear in the foregoing. Now let us see what are the methods which they may use under the "peaceful coexistence" smokescreen to confuse world opinion and to weaken the anti-Communist front.

Use of These Tactics in the West. Since the establishment of the Bolshevik regime in 1917 Russian Communism has constituted a serious menace to capitalism in the Western nations. The Soviet form of government and the system of planned economy have had a disruptive effect on political democracy and free enterprise in other parts of the world. When Fascism appeared as part of an anti-Communist movement, the Russian Communists resorted to peace diplomacy and even joined the League of Nations. At the same time, by means of the united front and neutralism tactics they brought on a conflict between the democracies and the Axis powers. Thus totalitarian Soviet Russia practically overnight became not only just another "democracy" but the "most democratic country" in the world. It was this "most democratic country" which later took advantage of the democracies' preoccupation with the grim business of defeating the Axis powers to wheedle promises out of them at international conferences and to use these promises as grounds for aggression against China and for annexing countries in Eastern Europe.

Soviet aggression after World War II compelled the free nations to form an antiaggression front for self-defense. Whereupon the Russian Communists fell back on their political tricks again. Their first step was to use "peaceful coexistence" to deceive the democracies, to make them slow down their anti-Communist efforts and to undermine their opposition to Communism. In the meantime, they used neutralism tactics to stir up conflicts between the Eastern and Western nations so that the free world, beset with division and contradictions, will eventually find itself in chaos. Thus Soviet Russia, the aggressor, has come to pose as a "peace force" as well as a "spokesman for peace."

During the existing period of "peaceful coexistence" neutralism is the crucial point. Neutrality appears to endow an individual with "freedom" but actually it aims at confusing him, making it impossible for him to distinguish right and wrong and to discharge what is rightly his responsibility. As a corollary, neutrality appears to endow a country with "independence" but actually it aims at confusing it, making it impossible for it to distinguish friend and foe and eventually forcing it to back down from what is rightly its stand. The purpose of the Russian Communists' neutralism, therefore, is to befuddle politicians who move between nations in the free world so that they will not know what is right and what is wrong and who is a friend and who is a foe. Meanwhile, the Russian Communists will make use of the complicated situation to cause more contradictions, greater confusion and utter chaos so that they will have a chance to defeat anti-Communist countries one by one, and to bring about "peaceful transformation" in non-Communist countries.

In studying the Communists' united front, neutralism and isolation tactics, we can see how they apply the dialectic laws of contradictions and negation. Soviet Russia and the international Communists used the United Front to destroy their enemy by alienating the masses and by strengthening their own allies. They used neutralism to weaken their enemy's organization, as well as his prestige among the masses in preparation for their own offensive. In essence, the united front as employed by the Communists applies the law of contradictions for the purpose of offense, whereas their neutralism tactic applies the law of negation for the purpose of defense. As to isolation and anti-isolation tactics, they are also used for offense and defense purposes in their over-all strategy. In actual practice, the Communists always use the three tactics together, and in any one of the two forms, one being at once a strategic defense and tactical offense and the other strategic offense and tactical defense. From this analysis it will be seen that both "peaceful coexistence" and neutralism are used by the Communists as offensive weapons to achieve positive effects.

Tactics in Psychological Warfare

Clausewitz in his book *On War* said: "Physical force is the *means*; to impose our will upon the enemy is the *object*." The political tactic of Soviet Russia and the international Communists is to attack the enemy from within, and the principal target is his "will." In psychological warfare, contact always precedes infiltration, which in turn precedes propaganda. It is through propaganda that the Communists undermine the enemy's determination, make him change his policies and disintegrate his defense. Finally, after they have completed the preliminaries, they pick a time convenient to themselves for the *coup de grâce*. This operation takes various forms:

One Is Timing. The Communists have to make contact first before they can start to convert one to their point of view. One feature of the Communists' psychological warfare is the limitless amount of time they spend on the effort. If they do not succeed today, they will continue tomorrow. If they fail this week, they will try again next week, next month and even next year. There have been cases when the Communists made some fifty attempts to persuade a single person.

Another Is Space. If the Communists cannot establish a direct contact, or if one refuses to be persuaded, they have recourse to indirect methods. They will persuade those around him, such as his close relatives. They will use this tactic particularly if they seek to infiltrate policy-making organs or certain government departments in order to hinder anti-Communist policies and their implementation. In other words, they will make unlimited use of space to achieve their objective.

The Third Is Environment. In waging psychological warfare, the Communist tactics usually fall into three categories:

Their first weapon is *pressure*. In carrying out aggression against a free nation, Soviet Russia's fifth column needs to infiltrate the latter's government, steal its documents, and collect intelligence for Moscow's reference in deciding on its strategy and tactics. They must particularly incite the masses, manipulate public opinion and create a kind of pressure to coincide with that which Soviet Russia is exerting on the same nation, for its government to adopt a policy and strategy favorable to the aggressors.

Lenin said that the Bolsheviks should never assume that their enemies will make any concession of their own accord. In 1903 he said: "War at the congress, war up to a split—at any cost. Only thus will the opposition give in." The Bolsheviks believed that the only way to make the enemy yield is to bring all pressure to bear and to disregard all consequences, and that only concessions won in this manner are reliable.

In 1936, the year before the outbreak of the Sino-Japanese War, after the Communists had established contacts with us, discussions were initiated on how to reorganize and integrate the Communist troops and how to enable the Communists and other political parties to join in the national war effort against Japan under the Government's unified direction. Seizing upon this opportunity, the Communists took the lead to organize the "Anti-Japanese National Salvation Alliance," which established liaison with local armed forces in various provinces, incited students and masses in the cities, organized parades and demonstrations, thereby hoping to force the Government to yield to their pressure for a pro-

Russia and pro-Communist policy. The Sian Incident of December 1936 represented the greatest pressure which the Chinese Communists ever attempted to exert on the Government. They tried to force me into accepting their demands and signing certain fantastic documents which they had prepared.

Later, during the war years, although the Chinese Communists sent delegates to the People's Political Council, many times they tried to blackmail it by threatening to walk out or to boycott it. For instance, after the New Fourth Army Incident of 1940 and again during the negotiations in 1944, they tried to bring pressure to bear on the Government by making the People's Political Council censure the Government for its actions and by causing the general public to misunderstand the Government's policy. After the war and during the Marshall Mission Communist delegates again threatened the Government with a "total rupture" over the Kalgan Incident. They brought simultaneous pressure on General Marshall and on the Government to have their demands accepted.

Their second weapon is *terror and intimidation*. Lenin said in 1918: "Do people in the capitalist camp really believe that this unprecedented destructive revolution can proceed leisurely, quietly, and peacefully without any sufferings, without any pains, without any terror and without any brutality?"* This is to say, a Communist "revolution" cannot proceed leisurely, quietly, and peacefully, but must entail the use of terror and brutal methods. The Chinese Communists are true to type in this respect. In fact, they are even worse than the Russian Communists. The Chinese Communists use both deception and violence in controlling organizations and masses in their areas. Whenever they resort to violence, it invariably means the creation of a reign of terror and the perpetration of brutalities. They deliberately leave their own members as well as the masses in the dark as to who would be put to death next, nor would the victims know when, where and by what atrocious methods they are going to die. Besides, the Communists not only have the final say on one's life and liberty, threaten his property, enterprises, social positions and prestige, but also put his parents, husband or wife, children, and even his relatives, friends, and neighbors at their mercy. They make one worry over his life and liberty, and however strong might be his will power, the moment he hears the cries of his kin,

* *Collected Works*, Russian edition, vol. 27, p. 140.

sees them suffering, and comes to think of all the frightening consequences, he begins to vacillate, to weaken and finally to lose his will to fight.

In areas under their control, the Communists combine barbarous primitive methods with modern scientific devices in their chambers of torture with the result that the victims hover between life and death. The people in general become so terror-stricken that they are easily dominated. Since their early days of village uprisings in southern Kiangsi in 1927, the Communists have made continuous use of this method of torture and intimidation on an increasingly large scale.

Even in areas beyond their control, so long as they have secret organizations there, the Communists can exercise control over their members and influence the masses. Furthermore, through manipulation of personal relationships and through intimidation, they extend their sinister influence even to areas where their own organizations cannot exist or grow, by forming front organizations and espionage networks to spread terror and intimidate the masses, making it necessary for the latter to follow them.

For the purpose of making contacts, holding discussions and even conferences, the Communists not only create and shift targets to achieve their aim, they also try to create a favorable environment for peace talks, so as to make the Government and the general public waver in their determination against Communism and to cause confusion and eventually disintegration of the anti-Communist front. A conspicuous instance occurred at the end of the war when the Communists staged an armed revolt on the one hand and launched an "anti-civil war" movement on the other. At the same time, the international Communists conducted an extensive propaganda campaign to accuse the Chinese Government of fomenting "civil war" and creating a threat to world peace. In these circumstances, the Chinese Government had no choice but to accept American mediation and hold peace talks with the Communists.

In their psychological warfare, the Communists put the dialectic laws of negation and of qualitative changes into use. Their object is to shake the determination of people and to impose their will on them. To do so, they put on pressure, create a reign of terror, use various forms of intimidation, or manufacture an environment to make them waver and finally give up. In particular, they seek to create a neutral zone. On the surface everything is peaceful, quiet and contented. In reality they want people to abandon their original position, and to fall into Communist traps. Once the victims are in their hands, they will change them until they can lead them by the nose. From then on they will no longer constitute any problem.

TACTIC OF CONTRADICTIONS

The use of contradictions is a basic tactic with the Communists in the application of their materialistic dialectics. In order to weaken the enemy's will, change his policies, cause dissension, conflict and even war in his camp, the Communists often first create contradictions in his midst so as to pave the way for their infiltration and subversion tactics.

Creation of Contradictions. Lenin said in 1920: "It is possible to defeat a more powerful enemy only by exerting the utmost effort, and by being thorough, careful, attentive and skillful in taking advantage of various kinds of fissures, even the smallest ones, on the part of the enemy, of every conflict of interests among the bourgeoisie of various countries or in one country; by taking advantage of every opportunity, even the smallest one, of gaining an ally."*

Be it a country, nation or society, so long as it has any internal contradictions, the Communists will take advantage of them no matter what precautions have been taken to prevent infiltration; and in places where no fissures do exist, they can be counted on to create them to serve their purpose. In the end, the Communists will bring about some conflict in the enemy's midst and use this struggle to control both sides in the contest. This is the Communist way of "gaining allies."

To create class contradictions, the Communists always analyze a country's social structure before infiltrating it. They not only explore and exploit, but also create, professional, regional, and religious contradictions. Then in the midst of confusion, they win the masses over by disseminating propaganda about class struggle and establishing party cells among them.

After the establishment of the Chinese Communist Party in 1920 the Communists concentrated on labor movement among workers on the railways and in the big enterprises. As the class distinction in Chinese society was not well marked, and the number of factory workers in relation to the entire population was

* *Selected Works*, Russian edition, vol. 10, p. 112.

negligible, the Chinese Communists' chances of success in developing their organization through labor movements alone and then turning them into a political struggle were extremely slim. For this reason, the Communists decided to attach themselves to our National Revolutionary movement and to work through Kuomintang in order to organize the masses for their own purpose. After Kuomintang's purge of its Communist elements in 1927 all their schemes in the cities ended in failure.

It was in 1924 that the Chinese Communists began to organize farmers' movements in the rural districts. They did it through Kuomintang. But their object was to overthrow Kuomintang and to establish a Soviet regime through a "farmers' revolution." However, after the expulsion from Kuomintang in 1927, they could no longer incite revolts in the villages. The failure of Mao Tse-tung's "Autumn Crop Uprising" was a case in point. Thereafter, they had to resort to hit-and-run tactics, indulging in arson, murder, rape, kidnapping and other forms of violence against people in their areas.

In their infiltration and subversion activities in Asia, the Soviet imperialists and the international Communists exploit nationality problems more than they exploit social frictions.

After the reorganization of Kuomintang in 1924, we adopted a policy of alignment with Russia and of the admission of Chinese Communists into our party. We did so because of the belief that Soviet Russia was going to help us "achieve national unity and independence." But the assistance given by the Russian Communists was actually used to cover up their infiltration and subversive activities against us. The Chinese Communists plotted a *coup d'état* in Canton in March 1925. Had they succeeded at that time and had we failed to rid our party of the subversive Communist elements in April 1927, China would have become a proving ground of Communism thirty years ago. After 1936 the Chinese Communists found a second chance in our war of resistance (1937-1945) to expand their military strength. They tried to spread defeatism in the country in hope to be able to overthrow the Government and to reduce China to a Soviet satellite. This attempt was also unsuccessful.

The Chinese Communists have also tried to incite racial minorities to rebellion. In 1913 Lenin laid down the formula for the problem of racial minorities in Russia. It called for "self-determination for all racial groups" in Russia in order to disintegrate Russia's original national structure on the one hand, and, on the other, called for the "closest and fullest unity among the working classes in all racial groups" in Russia in order to establish a unified Bolshevik regime. This formula served in later years as the basis for the Chinese Communists' policy on racial minorities.

Our Government's policy on racial minorities is based on the Three People's Principles, which stand for the "equality of all racial groups in the country." This has been an integral part of Kuomintang's political program and has been embodied in the Constitution of the Republic of China. In their attempts to incite the racial minorities in the border regions and elsewhere in the country, the Chinese Communists accused the Government of having adopted a policy of "Pan Hanism" (meaning a policy putting the interests of the Han, the majority race, above those of other racial components in the country). They further used the name of "self-determination" to foment "autonomy movements" among the racial minorities. Once the Chinese Communists succeeded in gaining control, they separated these racial groups into "national autonomous regions" in order to divide them. They also fomented class struggle in these regions to wreck their internal unity. At the same time, they planted party cells among them in order to insure control.

After 1920 Soviet Russia repeatedly declared that she had discarded Czarist Russia's imperialist policy toward Outer Mongolia and that she recognized China's sovereignty in that territory. Actually, beginning in 1921, she proceeded to create a puppet satellite regime in Outer Mongolia.

Then toward the end of our war with Japan, Soviet troops invaded China's Jehol and Chahar provinces, where in league with the Chinese Communists Russia started a so-called "Inner Mongolia Autonomy" movement. But in reality Mongolian delegates from Jehol, Chahar and Suiyuan were present at China's National Assembly held in Nanking in November 1946 and took part in enacting a permanent constitution for the Republic of China. The chapter on "Border Regions" in the Constitution embodies the racial policy of the Three People's Principles and also fulfills the common aspirations and wishes of China's minority races.

Incidents on the Sinkiang border after 1943 and the Ili Revolt were all manufactured by the Soviet spies working from the

Soviet consulate-general in Tihua, to destroy China's territorial and administrative integrity, to detach Sinkiang from China's body politic, and to seize its rich natural resources.

The Chinese Communists have also tried to create contradictions in our National Revolutionary movement. In order to turn our National Revolution into a class struggle and to usurp political power, the Chinese Communists had to create contradictions and foment conflicts within Kuomintang.

As early as 1924 the Communists attacked the "rightists" in our party. The latter suffered, but at the same time the "leftists" also came under their control. Then, after 1945, the Communists, with a view to undermining our government and party, created such labels as "diehards" and "democratic factions" in describing certain groups. When they made the "diehards" the object of their struggle, the "democratic factions" also unwittingly came under their evil spell and were finally gobbled up by the Communist Party.

Creation of Targets. In their efforts to destroy a public body, or to infiltrate a government organ, the Communists first pick a target and then proceed to foment an internal conflict so that they can carry out infiltration and subversion. For instance, following Kuomintang's reorganization in 1924, the avowed objectives of the "United Front" of our party and the Chinese Communist Party was to overthrow the northern war lords. To facilitate their infiltration and subversion within our party to usurp leadership in China's National Revolution, the Communists started to create a new target in our party by dubbing some of our members as "rightists" or "bourgeoisie" and lining up the petty bourgeoisie among the "leftists" against them. In this way, the original target was soon lost sight of, and an internal strife within our party was soon in progress. The Communists would have taken over our party if we had not acted quickly enough to stop them.

Again, in 1926, the Chinese Communists in Wuhan at first aligned themselves with the "leftists," the so-called "petty bourgeoisie" against the Central Government in Nanking. As a result, there was a split between Kuomintang members in Nanking and Wuhan. Going a step further, they organized the so-called "revolutionary democratic dictatorship of the proletariat and the farmers" against the leftist "petty bourgeoisie." This caused another split and brought on the Wuhan tragedy.

Shifting of Targets. Soviet Russia and the international Communists not only manufacture targets to cause internal strife in the enemy camp, but also shift targets in their maneuver to push the anti-Communist forces into contact, and even cooperation, with them. This was how the Communists created their "united front." The best example occurred during 1934-1935 when Nazism raised its head in Europe, and when the Chinese Communists began their desperate flight to Yenan. The slogan which Moscow employed to cope with the threatening situation then was a "united front" against Fascism. As the Chinese Communists were not able to engage in any activities openly during this period, they worked through their front organizations, who brazenly posed as neutrals. In the name of a national movement to "Resist Japan and Save the Nation," they advocated "cooperation between Kuomintang and the Chinese Communists for joint resistance against Japan." This was a fine demonstration of the Communist tactics of shifting targets. At the time, the Government had scored a decisive success in its fifth military campaign against the Communists, and if the Government forces had been permitted to press the campaign to its logical conclusion, they could have wiped out the Communist remnants and destroyed their organization once and for all. The Communists, however, through their "Anti-Fascist Movement" abroad and their "stop internal fighting and resist Japan" movement at home, managed to shift our target from themselves to Japan. In the circumstances, our Government was compelled to settle the Communist problem by political means and to begin negotiations with the Communists.

Manufacturing of War. The most wicked device employed by Moscow and the international Communists was to manufacture and precipitate war, and then to take advantage of the situation to expand their own influence and turn free nations in Europe and Asia into satellites.

For instance, in August 1939 Stalin and Hitler concluded the Russo-German Mutual Assistance Pact, which precipitated the outbreak of World War II in Europe. Then in April 1941 Stalin and Matsuoka signed the Russo-Japanese Neutrality Pact, which made Japan move against Pearl Harbor, Manila and Singapore.

After 1935 Stalin pursued a double-faced policy. On the one hand, he used the "united front" to align Soviet Russia with Britain and France against Germany and Italy in the West and with China against Japan in the East. On the other hand, he moved closer and closer toward the Axis powers. Between 1939 and 1941 he pitted Germany against Britain and France in Europe and pitted Japan against Britain and the United States in the Pacific. He was thus able to make both Germany and Japan pull the chestnuts out of the fire for Soviet Russia.

The various types of Communist tactics described above were all based on their dialectic law of contradictions. They use it to change people's thinking, environment, policy, and target, and even so far as to make them fight Russia's enemy for them, so that they, the Russian Communists, can extend their tentacles of aggression over a wider area and make further progress in their plan to conquer the world.

CAMOUFLAGE, DECEPTION, SURPRISE ATTACK AND WAR OF PROPAGANDA

Camouflage and deception play an especially important part in the political maneuvers performed by Moscow and the international Communists. The principal aim of camouflage and deception is to add an element of surprise to their political and military operations. In political warfare we may say that every move of the Communists—be it a word or an action, a smile or a frown—contains camouflage and deception. They can turn emotions on or off at a moment's notice at any time anywhere. Their political tactics may well camouflage for their military operations. Likewise, their propaganda may well be unmitigated political deception. Communist propaganda is the direct opposite of their actions and intentions. Consequently, we need to examine the facts in their war of propaganda while we are on the subject of camouflage and deception.

Camouflage. The purpose of camouflage is to use other ideas and actions to conceal one's real ideas and actions. During the thirty years under review, the Russian Communists and the Chinese Communists, often resorted to camouflage in their political struggle and social movement to cover up the real aims and methods of Communism. Some of the more conspicuous and important instances were as follows:

First, the camouflage of ideas. On all three occasions when they practiced "peaceful coexistence" with Kuomintang and the Chinese Government, the Communists used the Three People's Principles as a cover for propaganda in Communism.

During the first period Li Ta-chao submitted a memorandum to Kuomintang at its First National Congress in January 1924 in which he declared that Communist elements were joining Kuomintang to fight for the Three People's Principles and the National Revolution under the guidance of Dr. Sun Yat-sen. Actually, however, the Chinese Communists merely used the Three People's Principles to propagate Marxism.

During the second period the Chinese Communists declared in their manifesto of September 22, 1937, that Dr. Sun's Three People's Principles were the answer to China's need and that they were willing to strive for their realization.

Then, in June 1940, Mao Tse-tung published his "New Democracy" in which he came up with the tortuous theory of "New Democracy and Communism as Two Stages in China's Revolution," claiming that "New Democracy" of the first stage was nothing but a new Three People's Principles. He used the Three People's Principles to conceal his real objective. During the third period (1945-1949) the Communists brought up the slogan of "coalition government" under the same kind of camouflage to carry out their political war against the Chinese Government and Kuomintang.

Second, camouflage under nationalism. In 1921 the Russian Communists created a China branch for their Communist International, namely, the Chinese Communist Party. The purpose was to use nationalism as a cloak to conceal the objectives and methods of international Communism.

For instance, in January 1923 Joffe announced the Russian offer to help China achieve unification and independence. During the five years which followed, the Chinese Communists attempted to use our National Revolution for the purpose of Sovietizing the country.

The year 1943 was a difficult year for China in her war with Japan. It was also a year of hope, because victory was in sight. In order to deprive China of the fruits of victory and sabotage China's post-war rehabilitation, Moscow dissolved the Communist International. This was to disguise the direct relationship between Soviet Russia and the Chinese Communists. At that time, the Chinese Communist Party had already carried out a "disciplinary movement" in their party. Their slogan was the "Chinanization of Marxism," to show that theirs was a Chinese political party and not a tool of Soviet Russia. Having put on this garb of nationalism, they launched their all-out political offensive against the Chinese Government and Kuomintang in preparation for their armed revolt.

Third, camouflage under democracy. The purpose of China's National Revolution is to secure freedom and equality for the country. The War of National Revolution was, in reality, a national war for independence and freedom. But the Communists sought to turn a national war into a class war in order to set up a "dictatorship of the proletariat." They found it necessary to hide under the cloak of democracy before they could "transform a democratic revolution into a social revolution" by means of political tactics. In other words, they intended to use the name of democracy to split our revolutionary camp first and to carry out their class struggle in order to overthrow the Government and establish a puppet or satellite regime. Consider a few concrete instances.

In 1927 the slogan used by the Chinese Communists in Wuhan was "democratic dictatorship of the workers, farmers and petty bourgeoisie." This was the forerunner of what the Communists called "New Democracy" in 1940 and thereafter.

In 1936 the Communists joined our anti-Japanese camp. At first, they used nationalism as a cover. Soon afterward, they turned the national war into a class war again and put on the garb of democracy. After the war, the Communists launched a sustained political offensive against the Government in the name of "democracy," "freedom" and "human rights."

Fourth, camouflage under land reform. Both during and after the war, the Chinese Communists enjoyed being described in glowing terms as "agrarian reformers." Actually, the Communists' "land reform" was a means of creating collective farms and preparing for military mobilization. The international Communists played up the Chinese Communists as "agrarian reformers" for the purpose of camouflaging their control of the farmers and their all-out mobilization against the Government.

Deception. The purpose of deception is to have the enemy misinterpret the aims and methods of one's own actions in order to make operations against him easier and more effective.

The Communists are most resentful and afraid of being taken in by their enemy's deception, and yet they themselves are inveterate users of deception. Intelligence or propaganda, peace talks or military operations, they all offer the Communists scope for deception. I shall take up Communist deception in propaganda presently, but first let me cite a few instances of their deception in other fields.

Deception in Intelligence. Communist parties in various countries are all Soviet Russia's spy organizations. The Chinese Communist Party is certainly no exception. It stole intelligence from our Government, and at the same time closed all avenues of intelligence to the Government. That was to be expected. But they went one step further by furnishing the Western nations with false intelligence about the Chinese Government in order to create wrong impressions of our country. This is their favorite deception in intelligence.

Deception in Simultaneous Use of Offense and Defense. To strike a defensive stance before attack is a deception often used by the Communists in their struggle for power. We know that the Communists invariably resort to offense in their military operations, but their usual practice is to cover up their attack with a defensive posture. This constitutes a mode of deception. During 1946 and 1947 the Communists used this tactic. They attacked Government troops and when the latter fought back they accused them of violating the cease-fire agreement.

Deception in Simultaneous Use of Peace and War. Another trick of the Communists is to alternate the threat of war with peace talks, thereby creating tension and relaxation in close succession. Sometimes, they make simultaneous use of both to create a situation in which fighting and peace talks go on side by side. This kind of deception strikes at the morale of Government troops at the front, obstructs war efforts in the rear, upsets the Government's decisions, and confuses the outside world regarding the real state of affairs. The best instance was found in the deception which the Chinese Communists perpetrated against the Government during 1946 and 1947 by negotiation and fighting the Government at the same time. In making simultaneous use of peace and war, the Communists practiced all forms of deception especially during these bogus peace talks. Every time they sat down at the conference table with the Government, they followed a set formula. While discussing military questions, they invariably raised political issues. While discussing political issues, they invariably advocated the holding of some kind of a conference. During such a conference, they always argued endlessly over procedure, either to delay the conference or to win some initial victory for the sake of prestige. Whenever their troops were not doing well in the field, they asked for peace talks in order to gain time needed for reorganization and replenishment. Even when their troops were winning or when there was a stalemate, they also asked for peace talks to cause disunity in the Government, and make their future military successes easier or more extensive. They signed truce agreements and peace terms, only to tear them up later on. When the peace talks broke down, they were quick to blame the Government. For these reasons, peace talks became a kind of camouflage tactics with the Communists as well as a form of deception.

Surprise Attack. Secrecy, mobility, camouflage and deception are all necessary conditions for surprise attack. They have all been favorite devices with the Chinese Communists, who make frequent use of the surprise attack in their political, propaganda and military operations. I shall take them up one by one as follows:

In their political attacks on the Government, the Chinese Communists often change from one formula to another to give the new assault an effect of surprise. For example, in the midst of a military campaign, they would suddenly propose peace negotiations. Again, in the midst of peace negotiations, they would launch a sudden attack in the field.

In their propaganda war, the Chinese Communists acted on the principle that the best defense is offense. They have been quite successful in this. When caught by their enemy on one point which they could not defend, the Communists would veer to launch a surprise attack on their enemy on another undefended point. In this way, they forced their enemy to drop his propaganda offensive on the first point and rush to the defense of the second. This has been a usual device with the Chinese Communists to turn an enemy's propaganda campaign from offensive to defensive.

In military operations, the Chinese Communists used to brag that "the Red Army resorts to surprise attacks as a rule." It was true. But their surprise attacks were effective only when Government troops entered areas where the Communists had organized the people and where Communist guerrillas could freely operate, making it necessary for Government troops to deploy forces to defend their rear. This often resulted in the Government troops being put on the defensive and gave the Communists a chance to concentrate their forces for lightning raids and surprise attacks. Conversely, if Government troops should consolidate their positions step by step, strengthen their defense and at the same time clean up the surrounding countryside, the Communists would find it difficult to find weak spots on the Government lines for successful raids and onslaughts. There would then be no chance for them to use their surprise tactics.

Both at the beginning of the Government's first major campaign in December 1930 and at the end of its fourth campaign in January 1933, the Communists resorted to guerrilla warfare to hold down Government troops at the front, or on the two flanks, and then concentrated their main forces against any weak points they could find. They detoured around strong Government units to launch surprise attacks on relatively weak spots either on the two flanks or in our rear. The Communists scored successes in this manner at the Battle of Lungkang in the first campaign, at the Battle of Futien in the second campaign, at the Battle of Liangtsun in the third campaign and at the Battle of Lichuan in the fourth campaign.

In the fifth campaign, however, Government troops adopted a strategical offense and a tactical defense. We consolidated one position before moving on to another. In due course, the Communist areas were steadily reduced in size, making it impossible for the Communists either to engage in guerrilla raids in small numbers or to launch a major surprise attack in large numbers. In the first four campaigns, the Communists waited until they had won the initial battle before redeploying their forces for the rest of the campaign. In the fifth campaign the Communists were defeated in the first battle at Lichuan, and after that they had to fight between the main Government forces and a network of forts and pillboxes. Throughout the campaign they could not wrest the initiative essential for victory. Finally they had to split into small groups and flee westward.

Propaganda War. Propaganda war involves the use of language, both written and spoken, or some other media to affect the enemy's attitude and feelings and to make him think and act accordingly. The object of war is to impose one's will on the enemy; the propaganda war is aimed directly at shaking, changing and subduing the enemy's will. Consequently, propaganda has been an important weapon of the Russian Communists to defeat their enemy by means short of war.

In order to make the enemy accept one's propaganda, one must disguise it so that he will not know it for what it is. Russian Communists do not recognize such a thing as "truth" in the world. Yet they always tried to persuade the masses to their way of thinking or to conquer their will in the name of "truth." Thus "truth" becomes a false color with which to cover up propaganda so that the masses will accept propaganda as truth. Therefore, in what the Russian Communists and their international "comrades" and fellow travelers have to say we cannot find any truth. We may add that the propaganda put out by the Communists in any country is nothing but lies and false accusations meant to deceive other people. A few types of Communist propaganda follow:

Chicanery. The Communists look upon their materialistic dialectics as an ideological weapon. They hope to defeat the ideology and faith of others with their materialistic conception of history. It is part of their dialectics to employ casuistry to make others believe that there is contradiction and conflict everywhere, and that the history of mankind is one of class struggle. This casuistry reached its climax during the Chinese Communists' "disciplinary movement" which sought to wipe out national consciousness and even humanitarian instinct and which maintained that society is built on class distinctions. Why did they do this? They were making preparations to turn China's national war against Japan into a class war, betray the Chinese nation and set up a puppet regime subservient to the Russian Communists. They launched the "disciplinary movement" because they had to deprive the Chinese people of their national consciousness and conception of a national state before they could achieve their own sinister purpose.

Rumor-Mongering. It is a common failing of many people to give credence to rumors. The Communists make use of this human weakness to spread rumors to magnify their strength, hurt the Government's prestige, manufacture social chaos, and affect the people's anti-Communist mentality. This is an important device in the Communists' propaganda war. For instance during the war with Japan, the Communists frequently spread rumors to the effect that the Government was secretly carrying on peace negotiations with the Japanese. They used these rumors as material in their international propaganda to make our allies think that there were people in the Chinese Government who would rather surrender and compromise with the Japanese so that they could start a "civil war" against the Communists.

Another instance was during the Government's campaign to put down the Communist insurrection in 1948 when the Communists and their front organizations spread rumors saying that the Government wanted to hold peace talks with them. The purpose was to create doubts and to arouse false hopes of peace. Once these rumors began to take effect and the people in general came to believe that the only way out was to hold peace talks, they followed it up by spreading another rumor saying: "Peace talks are possible only if President Chiang should agree to resign."

Lies. In order to be effective, propaganda for the masses has to be simple and repetitious. In their propaganda war, the Communists are fond of using "*non sequitur* logic" in coining simple phrases and repeating them over and over again for the deception of the masses. The slogan "Anti-Communism is Fascism," used by the Communists and their front organizations, was an example of this kind of "logic" in action. In reality, both Communism and Fascism are opposed to democracy. The objective of China's national revolution in accordance with the Three People's Principles is to build up China as a democratic nation. Therefore, we are opposed to both Communism and Fascism. In order to sabotage the Government's policy to suppress their insurrection, the Communists raised the slogan: "Anti-Communism is Fascism." This led many people to believe that the Communists were champions of democracy and freedom. Some even mistook the Communists for members of a democratic party, for agrarian reformers, and conversely branded the Government as a dictatorial and Fascist regime.

Intimidation. It is discussion and not propaganda when one expresses his views on a certain problem and offers two or more possible solutions. In propaganda for mass consumption, it is effective when only one solution is offered for each problem. The Communists may be said to have reached the zenith in their application of this principle. What is more, their propaganda usually carries intimidation. When they seek to impose their will on some one, they will attack him from all directions—innumerable publications carrying articles, innumerable organizations passing resolutions, innumerable groups holding discussions, innumerable people engaging in a whispering campaign, both at home and abroad, urging on him the same choice. On the surface it seems they are trying to persuade him; actually they are threatening him. They hold peace talks with him and at the same time they try to intimidate him.

One of the glaring instances of this kind of propaganda war by intimidation happened during 1925 and 1926 when Kuomintang was still based in Canton. At that time, nobody dared to utter a single word against Communism; and as a result, for lack of resistance, our party almost came under the complete domination of the Communists. Another instance occurred between 1946 and 1948, when no one in political circles or in the general public dared to speak against the peace talks promoted by the Communists, and as a corollary no one dared to suggest that the Government's campaign to suppress the Communist insurrection should be pushed to its logical conclusion through a general mobilization. These two instances are enough to show the social and political effect of the Communists' propaganda by intimidation.

Law of Contradictions and Law of Negation in Action. The Communists' camouflage, deception and propaganda war are practical manifestations of their dialectic laws of contradictions and of negation. For instance, their resort to political assault to disguise their military operations, their assumption of a defensive posture to cover their offensive action, their use of propaganda war containing nothing but casuistry and falsehood, and their combining enticements with intimidation, all these are based on the principle of "unity of contradictions." Again, for instance, their use of peace talks to negate or undermine their opponent's morale and their use of hostilities at the same time to negate the peace talks with their opponent, are based on the law of "negation of negations." In short, the Communists in their propaganda war stop at nothing wicked and mean to achieve their goal, i.e., in creating suspicion and disturbances. They are particularly adept in the fabrication of stories with no factual foundations, in misrepresentation such as "pointing at a deer and calling it horse," in distortion and in the forging of documentary proofs all of which they consider legitimate—even virtuous. Whenever it suits their purpose, they represent Satan as God or God as Satan. What the Communists say and what they do are entirely two different things. It is obvious that they had themselves robbed the people under their control of freedoms, and yet they asked the Government for all political freedoms. In areas under Communist control, there was nothing but darkness and regimentation, and yet in their external propaganda they boasted of political democracy and of a bright future for their slaves. In Communist terminology, "people" means the Communists themselves, "liberation" means enslavement, "peace" means another form of war and "coexistence" means exclusive Communist control. It follows that the smile they put on is another facet of their evil nature. The free world should be ready to expose and attack this kind of propaganda before anyone falls prey to it.

PEACE TALKS AND CEASE-FIRE AGREEMENT

In their "peaceful coexistence" campaign, the Communists have developed two methods of approach, which can easily lead the free world to think that the Communists are really seeking peace, or to consider their suggestions as genuine roads to peace.

Peace Talks. To ordinary people, peace talks represent a transitional path from war to peace. Whenever the Russian or Chinese Communists ask for "peace talks," people in the free world instantly take it to mean that they will not engage in any more war of aggression. But, to the Communists "peace talks" do not constitute a path to peace, but are just another form of war. They start peace talks not for the purpose of attaining the objective of peace, but for the purpose of attaining their objective of war. The peace talks which the Chinese Communists held with the Government were to serve the following purposes:

Peace talks could delay attacks by Government troops. For instance, the "cease-fire negotiations" asked by Chinese Communists on May 5, 1936, were for the purpose of delaying actions by Government troops.

Peace talks could cover up preparations for armed revolt. The first three peace talks with the Government between 1940 and 1944 served as smokescreens behind which the Communists planned their armed revolt.

Peace talks could enlarge the following for neutralism, and expand the reserve strength of the front organizations. Mao Tsetung's peace talks in Chungking in August 1945 were for this purpose.

Peace talks could undermine the morale of Government forces. Peace talks and military mediation after the end of war served this purpose.

Peace talks could create the impression of "two Chinas" in the free world.

Therefore, both the Russian and Chinese Communists love protracted negotiations. Lenin, writing to a "comrade" of his in 1916, said: "You write that you are sick and tired of correspondence and negotiations. I understand you completely, but you must be patient. Once you have gone into the business of negotiating, it is impossible to get nervous and fall into despair. That would not be proletarian." Lenin's remark has been a creed with the Bolsheviks in conducting negotiations with other parties. From this we can see that protracted negotiations carried on by the Russian and Chinese Communists represent a method of struggle with them.

Cease-Fire Agreement. "Respite tactics" are often resorted to by the Russian Communists. To secure a needed respite, they will not only negotiate with their enemy but will sign cease-fire agreements with him and, in fact, will even go as far as to conclude a peace treaty with him. After Soviet Russia signed the Brest-Litovsk Treaty with Germany on March 3, 1918, Lenin told his friends: "Unless I should be so compelled, I have no intention to carry out the undertakings in the treaty." He also said: "Is this treaty shameful? Every serious peasant and worker will say I am right, because they understand that peace is a means of gathering strength. History suggests that peace is a respite for another war. War is a method of obtaining a somewhat better or somewhat worse peace." This was the most obvious instance of the Russian Communists' "respite tactics" in action.

To the Communists, it is not simply a defensive tactic. They use peace talks and cessation of hostilities to reinforce and replenish their troops in preparation for the next attack; they use them also to start a political and propaganda campaign to sow suspicions between their enemy and his allies, to strike at his morale, and to shatter his internal solidarity. To the Communists, all these are positive functions of peace talks and cease-fire agreements.

The first time the Chinese Communists asked for cessation of hostilities was in 1936 when from Yenan they proposed a truce and the holding of peace talks with the Government. Their four pledges made in 1937 were in effect a cease-fire agreement which they themselves had signed.

The Chinese Communists' last truce with the Government was

signed on January 10, 1946. It was an agreement reached in the Committee of Three, composed of a Government delegate, a Communist delegate and General George C. Marshall, the U. S. mediator. During this phase of peace talks, the Chinese Communists accepted American mediation only to sabotage it, and concluded a truce only to repudiate it. This actual instance can best prove the fact that to the Chinese Communists the "respite tactics" is not simply one of defense but one of offense as well.

If we judge the Russian and Chinese Communists' proposals for peace talks and cease-fire in the light of the dialectic law of negation, we can immediately grasp their very essence. Why do the Russian and Chinese Communists always want to hold peace talks and sign a cease-fire agreement while at war but violate the cease-fire agreement and resume fighting after it has been signed? We must understand that in their ideology, peace talks and cessation of hostilities are the negation of war, and to sabotage the peace talks and violate the cease-fire agreement is the negation of this negation. When they cannot win by force, they stop fighting and hold peace talks instead, they may even sign a cease-fire agreement. When they succeed in splitting their enemy's camp, shattering his will to fight and destroying his morale, they will negate their peace talks and cease-fire agreements, for the purpose of waging, and winning, the final decisive battle.

Legal Status and Parliamentary Politics. There are two other weapons in the Communists' arsenal of "peaceful coexistence," which make the free world believe that they are not only fighting for peace but also fighting for democracy. One of them is legal status, and the other is parliamentary politics. In a free country, where they have been doing well enough in their political agitation, the Communists will seek to "shift from legal to illegal" activities and plot a revolt to seize power. If they have to retreat under government attacks, they will turn around and ask for peace, together with the demand that their party be accorded a legal status. Thus, legal status becomes a defensive weapon to them.

The Chinese Communist Party was outlawed after April 1927. Its armed bands took to the hills in Hunan, Kiangsi, Honan and Hupeh provinces to engage in hit-and-run uprisings. After October 1934 the Communists fled from southern Kiangsi to northern Shensi and in May 1936 they offered to surrender. During every peace talk that followed they invariably demanded a legal status for their party. The Chinese Government had insisted on two points, namely, reorganization and integration of the Communist troops into the National Army, and settlement of the Communist Party problem by political means. In practice, this meant that the Communists and other political parties could take part in the war of resistance on an equal footing, but the question of a legal status for their parties should wait till the time of constitutional rule when it could be solved according to the constitution.

Why is it that we did not accord the Communists a legal status? Because it is a favorite practice with the Communists to use such a status to develop their organization among the masses, to create conditions for armed revolt and to overthrow the Government by force when an opportunity should present itself. Therefore, the demand for a legal status is a kind of defensive weapon to them, which they are prepared to use in an offensive at any time. The only way to stop them from playing the trick of "shifting from legal to illegal activities" is to deny them a legal status.

Marxism is opposed to parliamentary politics. In his book, State and Revolution, Lenin laid down the dictum that "dictatorship of the proletariat" is the only form of government sought in a socialist revolution. To make it unmistakably clear, Lenin said: "The scientific concept of dictatorship means nothing else but power directly based on violence, unrestrained by any laws and absolutely unrestrained by any rules."* This kind of government by violence is naturally incompatible with any kind of parliamentary politics or any government by law.

However, it does not mean that the Communists will not take part in parliaments in free countries. Lenin admitted in 1920: "The Bolsheviks had taken part in reactionary parliaments. Experience has taught us that this kind of participation was not only beneficial but necessary in preparing for the Second Revolution [meaning the October Revolution]."** We must remember that Communist participation in parliaments has never been prompted by their approval of parliamentary politics as such, their motive always being to destroy it. Lenin made this point very clear when he said: "Our participation in parliaments not only caused the proletariat no harm, but made it easier for us to prove to the masses why this kind of parliament should be dissolved."

During the war with Japan, the Chinese Communists took part

* Lenin's Collected Works, Russian edition, vol. 25, p. 441.
** Lenin's Selected Works, Russian edition, vol. 10, p. 101-102.

in the People's Political Council. They did so not because they approved of parliamentary politics but because they wanted to use the People's Political Council as a propaganda forum and a political sounding board. In order to boycott resolutions unfavorable to them, they had never hesitated to resort to a threat of withdrawal or refusal to attend. It was a matter of tactics on their part to participate in a parliament in order to destroy it ultimately. On November 12, 1946, when the National Assembly was convened, both the Communists and a front organization of theirs, the Democratic League, refused to nominate delegates in an attempt to stop the National Assembly from being convened. They thought it would become a serious blow to the Government's prestige. They failed. Shortly thereafter, they openly resorted to armed rebellion.

The Chinese Communists demanded a legal status for their party in order to facilitate their preparations for rebellion. They participated in parliamentary activities in order to destroy parliamentary government. This kind of devious practice, when studied with reference to dialectics, is merely the application of their laws of contradictions and qualitative changes. According to the Communists, everything is the synthesis of contradictions, and when the contradictions develop to such an extent as to change quantity into quality, the thing itself is bound to turn into the opposite of its original quality. Therefore, whenever the Communists ask for a legal status for their party, they want it in order to facilitate their law-breaking plans and to turn their legal activities into an armed uprising to seize power which is of course illegal. When they take part in parliamentary activities, they do so with the full intention of destroying the parliament and turning the democracy into a dictatorship.

INDEX

This is a topical index of the relations between Soviet Russia and China from the time of the first Communist overtures to the Kuomintang in 1918 until the final collapse of negotiations between the Communists and the National Government after the Second World War.